Dordogne

The principal sights

< Lift flap for map

The troubadour Arnaut Daniel

Joy Law

Dordogne

PALLAS ATHENE

Château de Puyguilhem

Contents

Near Castelnaud

Acknowledgements

It is, as usual, difficult to acknowledge adequately all the help and encouragement I have been given in writing and revising this book by innumerable people in both England and France, but I owe a special debt of gratitude to the following, without whom I would not have been able to start, to continue or to finish: Christopher Sinclair-Stevenson, Hilary Rubinstein, and above all, Carol O'Brien, Mandy McMahon and Patricia Poisson. For their patience in answering my questions and for their tales of the past and practices of the present: M. and Mme Bouyssou; Mme Camy; M. Drouet; Mme Faure, departmental archives, Périgueux; Monsieur Faurel; Maître Gouyon; Mme Jardel; Mme Jayle; Mme Laurent; the staff of the Services Agronomiques des Tabacs, Sarlat; of the Chambre d'Agriculture de la Dordogne, Périgueux; and of the London Library; and for their support and practical help: Sue Browne; Professor Glyn Daniel; Joanne and Fred Dubery; Arlette Espinet; Alexander Fyjis-Walker; Ann Merryfield and Jenny Wilson.

And, as always, for so happily sharing our life in the Dordogne, my three children, Jennifer, Nicholas and Katie; their spouses and, nowadays, my grandchildren who have opened my eyes to new pleasures; and for having made it possible over so many years, my husband.

La Tourette 2000

Introduction

We first went on holiday to Dordogne, over forty years ago, because our interest had been aroused by an article by Cyril Connolly praising the region. He did not mislead us, and its physical aspect seemed so beautiful that we felt it would be an ideal place for future holidays, especially with young children who would learn not only country ways but French and French country ways. So, like many others, but, we like to flatter ourselves, a little earlier than most, we bought a house there.

Since then I have spent diaphanous autumns, crisp winters, pale shimmering springs and clear hot summers, enjoying the provincial calm and far from provincial cuisine, exploring golden châteaux and churches and reflecting on the life of the place which has become for me what it was for Henry Miller 'the nearest thing to Paradise this side of Greece'. I have sat peacefully on the shingle beach of the river watching the children swim and the anglers fish in the clean, fast-flowing water and marvelled at the green beauty of the landscape threaded by the silver ribbon which winds its way through the department to which it gives its name.

And I wondered how people in the past lived and moved and had their being in Périgord, for one cannot walk or drive five miles without being aware of what has gone into its making. I asked myself why the land is cultivated in small strips, who built and lived in the feudal ruins whose silhouettes stand stark on the skyline, what faith inspired the ravishing but now decaying churches, and what wealth engendered the prosperous bourgeois mansions.

So I set about discovering the answers to these questions and, having gone some way towards doing so, I thought I would set down for others the information that was not altogether easy to come by, so that they might share it and my love for a place that has given so much pleasure and whose hope for the future lies in an understanding of the past.

In the eighteen years since I wrote the first edition of this book, there have been many changes in the everyday life of the department. Dordogne has become one of the most frequently visited departments of France, by both the French and foreigners. Rising standards of wealth, and the visitors' expectation of more than the bare minimum in the way of amenities has brought about improvements in sanitation, a wider choice of local amusements, a proliferation of supermarkets and a rash of swimming pools. Not all of these are improvements in that what we think of as the tranquillity and charm of the country life in old provincial France are slowly being eroded.

One may regret the flight from the land but one can only sympathise with the

Opposite: Castelnaud

farmers, and their children, whose greater efficiency and feather-bedded subsidies by the common agriculture policy enabled them to enjoy a life of greater ease and considerably more comfort, though this too is changing once again.

It is good for the department that depopulation has been reversed to the point where there is now a net increase in the indigenous community and it is no good complaining about the loss of the old ways of life which we tend in any case to romanticise. The countryside remains beautiful and untouched by hideous industrial complexes (though some of the new housing estates leave a lot to be desired) and the *douceur de vie* is still a reality. For this relief, much thanks.

And a curious postscript. On my return from a day's work in the archives at Périgueux, I fell from the train in Sarlat station and broke my leg. It was far from a disaster for the surgical ward of the local hospital to which I was confined to a two-bedded room for a fortnight proved an invaluable source of information.

My vocabulary was enlarged – the overhead hoist is a *potence* (gibbet) – as was my grasp of current affairs, the student initiation rituals – *bizutage* – recently made illegal to little effect being much in the news at the beginning of the academic year.

It quickly emerged that the hospital, with 300 beds and built some twenty years ago in a leafy enclave outside the town, was a vibrant centre where patients and staff alike from a considerable catchment area felt part of a well defined community.

Close scrutiny of the nurses' names, embroidered on their tunic pockets, nearly always betrayed their home village of which they were proud and pleased to discuss. One girl, whose uncle owns the *cabanes* near St André d'Allas, rather disarmingly confirmed that they had indeed been restored for a film some years ago.

Fellow-sufferers, whether a 90-year-old who had lived hereabouts all her life, and having been born in Lille, found it very 'provincial'; a mere stripling of 78 who had been housekeeper for eighteen years at a nearby château; and even an 84-year-old Alsatian on holiday, all had pertinent observations which have helped my understanding – and appreciation – of the region. A happy accident indeed.

The River

This beautiful river, the Dordogne, is one of the longest in France; it travels 500 kilometres through widely differing landscapes on its journey from its source to the sea. The name probably comes from the Celtic *Durunna*, meaning rapid waters, rather than from the joining of two streams, the Dore and the Dogne. It rises 1886 metres high in the Massif Central, at the icy jagged peak of the Pic de Sancy, so brilliantly captured by Balzac in *Le Peau de Chagrin*. The hero of the novel, published in 1831, had fled to this countryside of beeches and firs and glorious alpine flowers:

> On the morrow of his arrival, he climbed the Pic de Sancy with some difficulty. Then he explored the higher valleys, the lofty nooks, the unknown lakes, and the peasants' huts in the rugged and wild district which is only now being discovered by the painters who are charmed with the refreshing landscapes contrasting so sharply with the asperity of the surrounding hills.
>
> Imagine an inverted cone of granite hollowed out on a vast scale, a sort of basin whose borders have been fractured by innumerable and eccentric twists and turns. Here lie level stretches without any vegetation on them, uniform and blueish, on which the rays of the sun glint as if in a mirror; over there are cliffs breached by fissures and gashed by ravines holding in suspense huge blocks of lava whose fall is slowly being prepared by rain and on the top of which stands an occasional stunted tree gnarled by the winds; then in certain angles you will see a dark and cool recess whence escape a cluster of chestnut trees as tall as cedars; or a cavern in the yellowish rock-face will disclose the entrance to the very heart of the mountain, encircled with brambles and flowers and decked with a little strip of greenery.
>
> At the bottom of this cup, perhaps the crater of an extinct volcano, was a pool of water as clear and bright as a diamond. This deep basin was fringed with granite boulders interspersed with willows, yellow flags, mountain-ash, and innumerable aromatic plants then in the heyday of their blossoming, in a setting as verdant and smooth as an

English bowling-green. The fine grass was watered by rivulets, which trickled down from the fissures in the cliffs, and enriched by the alluvial deposits of many a rainstorm. The pool was about three acres in expanse with irregular edges scalloped out like the hem of a dress. The mountains drew together at some points so that in places there was scarcely sufficient room for a cow to pass, but at a rough guess the meadow around the pool must have been from one to two acres in extent. All vegetation ceased at a certain altitude. High above, the crags took on the most fantastic shapes and were tinted with those vaporous mists which make most mountains resemble clouds floating in the sky. The contrast between the delicate valley and the bare, bleak ramparts above was notable; at any moment there might be a landslide among these strange rocky masses, one of which had been named le Capucin on account of its resemblance to a monk. The pointed peaks, the outrageous piling up of rocks, the airy caverns were lighted up one by one according to the position of the sun or the caprices of the atmosphere so that they were gold, or purple or bright rose-colour, or drab and grey. The heights presented a perpetual enchantment of changing hues as iridescent as the feathers on a pigeon's breast.

At sunrise or sunset, from between two masses of lava which looked as if they had been cloven in twain by an axe, a ray of light would penetrate into the circle of flowery growth and play upon the surface of the pool like a shaft of gold through the chink of a shutter in a Spanish room which had been carefully darkened for the customary siesta. At noon, the sun poured down on the ancient crater, warming the rocky sides, quickening with its heat and germinating seedlings, colouring the flowers, and ripening the fruits in this tiny forgotten corner of the earth.

This must surely be the end of the world.

From this end, then, the beginning.

The twin streams now united as the Dordogne trickle down into Le Mont Dore (1050 metres) in the Puy de Dôme, a skiing centre and a spa. There were baths and a temple here in the second century AD but it took until 1797 for it to be put on the map as a fashionable resort by Michel Bertrand, a medical inspector, who quickly saw its commercial possibilities. It soon attracted members of the *beau monde*. Chateaubriand's friend, Pauline, Comtesse de Beaumont, tried vainly to find a remedy for her consumption here in 1803 before going on to die in Rome later that year

The Pic de Sancy

and the Duchesse de Berry brought with her a great retinue in 1821. It also attracted the intellectuals: George Sand, Musset and Balzac were regular visitors. The splendiferous marble halls of the baths which delight today's visitors were not built until 1875 – a pity, because they need Balzac's luxuriant pen to do justice to them. It is a true mountain town, grey and glistening in sun and rain alike.

The river gathers a little momentum to run five kilometres north-west into La Bourboule (839 metres) in the heart of the extinct volcanic region of Auvergne. This leafy town has the slightly seedy appearance of all spas, as well as sporting a wedding-cake casino. The Dordogne runs straight through the middle of the main boulevard and is bordered on either side by wide streets lined with Edwardian hotels, one of which has the curious name of Balroy's. The curative powers of the waters have been known for a long time and, although in 1830 only 130 bathers visited La Bourboule, 150 years later, there were 26,000. Now during the season, from May to September, it is thronged with adults and children in search of a cure for their respiratory disorders, and in winter it is a flourishing centre for winter sports.

A still relatively childish stream runs north out of La Bourboule to start roaring and spluttering as it turns south into the Gorges d'Avèze, foaming white like the snow which lies on the surrounding hillsides throughout the winter. Then it pours past Singles and Confolent Port Dieu, into the lake of Bort. Towards the southern end of the lake, an artificial creation, stands the château of Val, accessible either by motor boat from Bort or by road. It was reconstructed in 1450 on the foundations of a twelfth-century fort and is a superb example of late medieval military architecture. Now, reminiscent of Chillon, it evokes more romantic fantasies. Val is today reflected in the calm waters of the lake, with sailing boats fluttering round it like moths, but once it stood on dry land, perched on a rocky spur, for the lake is in fact a reservoir for the first of the five great dams which over the past seventy years have been built to harness the river.

The somewhat grandiose project for linking the Dordogne by canal and the Chavanou and the Sioule to the Loire basin which had been discussed from the early days of the nineteenth century had made no progress, but the building of the bridge at Vernejoux between 1860 and 1880 (and that at St Projet lower down in 1847) greatly improved communications. It was not until immediately after the First World War that projects for damming the Dordogne were considered; serious work began in 1928 when the concession for the whole of the river from the Pont de Vernejoux (where the bridge had collapsed in 1918 and had had to be rebuilt) to Argentat was granted to a private company with access to guaranteed state loans. The first dam to be built was at Marèges (1932-35), followed by those at L'Aigle (1940-45), Bort (1942-52), Chastang (1949-51) and Le Sablier, at Argentat (1951-57). The workforce consisted largely of Spaniards who had fought on the losing side in the Civil War.

These five dams, like giant stepping stones, punctuate the 120-kilometre stretch of river from Bort to Argentat, using the drop of 450 metres in the water to produce 1610 million kwh a year. They are themselves marvels of engineering. Now that the scars made by their construction have been healed, they offer as good a reason for a

The dam at Bort les Orgues

visit as any cathedral or romanesque church. This stretch of water, once so violent and torrential as it poured through the gorges, has been put to the service of man and become a great deal safer than in the days when the *gabarriers* (the river boatmen) complained to the public authorities of its dangers. They would surely have approved of the pleasure boating now enjoyed on the lakes. 'Scenic' roads have been laid out with the taste and imagination so often displayed by the French and one is encouraged to make a *circuit des barrages* much as one is invited to do the *circuit des bastides*. To drive along this route is exhilarating even for those whose first interest is not engineering since the journey is through such grand countryside; and, even if they remain unconvinced that such concrete monuments to modern technology *méritent le détour*, such a journey will enable them to visit the small towns and villages high up on the plateau which they might not otherwise find an excuse to visit.

The first of these dams, a harmonious giant at Bort les Orgues, is enormous. Its base is 80 metres thick (L'Aigle is 'only' 47.5 metres), it is 120 metres high and it measures 390 metres along its crest; the lake itself is 17 kilometres long and contains 477 million cubic metres of water. The dam was extremely difficult to build; the preliminary work took three years and in 1948 it claimed the lives of twenty-three workmen. Every ten years this immense amount of water has been drained off so that the dam installations can be inspected and the river bed then looks like a curious lunar landscape. In May 1972 inquisitive tourists could have seen the unusual spectacle of Jacques Cousteau being lowered into the water in his diving bell to see if such a submarine inspection could replace the decennial drainage. But of course the dam still has to be drained for repairs to the structure to be carried out.

The town of Bort is busy and industrious, with the river rushing through heedless of the check it has received, and is a thriving tourist centre remarkable for its fortified romanesque church and its clinkstone columns – the *orgues* – which extend for three kilometres and rise to heights of nearly 100 metres. It was also the birthplace of Jean François Marmontel, the historiographer and friend of the Encyclopédistes.

From Bort the river runs, unaccompanied by roads, due west. A road travels to the north of it past the château of Peyrefitte and on to the Site du St Nazaire, to whom there is a fine statue and a good church at the nearby St Julien. Here the Diège joins the Dordogne and their confluence affords one of the most spectacular views of all France. The immense sweep of nature is almost frightening and one feels god-like in a primitive world before the creation of man. It is not surprising that the Saut d'Anglard, just above Marèges, has the reputation for being an extremely dangerous place.

But man cannot leave well alone, and the river is tamed yet again by the reservoir for the next dam, Marèges. The early work was undertaken by the Compagnie de Chemins de Fer de Paris-Orléans to supply electricity for their locomotives. Called after a nearby château, it too was difficult to build, partly because the river there was so wild and partly because dam-building techniques were then relatively primitive.

But it was obviously a great achievement, and a momentous occasion when, on 8 June 1936, it first went into service. One of the engineers who was responsible for its building was so moved that he uncharacteristically departed from official language in making his report:

> With the river foaming in full spate, the sluice gates of the temporary outflow were slammed shut and the current abruptly ceased. The roaring of the Dordogne was instantly superseded by complete silence. It was as though the river had disappeared. Below the dam men scurried about in puddles inspecting the slipway ensconced in the rock; above, the water noiselessly rose up the walls of its prison furtively seeking an escape.

After Marèges the river enters its own gorges, running and jumping, liberated, through the hills of Auvergne and the wild country down to the Pont de Vernejoux. Here the road that goes south of the river from Bort – crossing Champagne les Mines which shows no sign of its coal-mining past and is surrounded by belled Alpine cattle – joins the longer but more exciting northern road.

Beyond Vernejoux, the road, now on the north bank, comes back via Serandon with its simple twelfth-century church to the Belvédère de Gratte Bruyères just above its junction with the Sumène, where it affords a view of breathtaking beauty. It is difficult in summer to believe that nearby Charlane still reminds the locals of dire tales of shipwreck. The Route des Adjustants, parallel to the river, takes one through rocky and grandiose country, the verges mauve with heather in the autumn and the whole covered with trees so thick that the road cuts through like a swathe in a deep green pile carpet.

The road crosses the river by the bridge at St Projet and works its way back to the next dam, that of L'Aigle. Here securing its base created fewer problems for its constructors since the banks are of exceptionally hard crystalline rock, their granite walls falling sharply away from a peak 300 metres high, but the harshness of the terrain is softened by the ever-present chestnut trees.

Below L'Aigle the river runs west to Spontour and Valette, both *gabarre*-builders' villages, and thence the main road runs first along the river and then away from it, up to Le Poteau du Gay and St Merd de Lapleau. Until 1960 and the failure of a seven-year fight to keep it open, the *transcorrèzien* train from Tulle to Neuvic went close by. This small branch line was dearly loved by its passengers who viewed the driver of the locomotive, called rather endearingly *Libellule*, with particular affection. In winter he would tell the *patronne* of the café at Lapleau how many cups of coffee to have ready by giving the requisite number of toots on his steam hooter.

Back comes the road to the river (which from Spontour is only accessible to fishermen or walkers) in a series of hairpin bends to the Pont de Chambon, where it crosses the river to go back, on the south bank via St Privat and Servières les Châteaux, to the river at the Chastang dam. This is a magnificently impressive piece of engineering and is rather beautiful; it also has the highest output (520 million kwh per year) of all five dams. Both river and road from St Martin la Méanne now run together down past the château of Gibanel, where the Doustre flows into the Dordogne, to Le Sablier, a small ugly compensation dam built to complement the reservoir at Chastang, 10 kilometres above Argentat.

Argentat (188 metres) was and remains the first town of any size between Souillac and La Bourboule. It gave its name (Celtic for river-crossing) not only to the whole array of little boats which passed through it but also to their owners, and the basin at Libourne is still flanked by the Quai d'Argentat. Argentat, like Beaulieu, was a Protestant stronghold, and thrived on water-borne trade, its wine production and, after the discovery of coal there in 1775, a modest mining industry. It was a prosperous town, having had a ferry since its earliest days. In 1569 it took eight days for Coligny to cross the river, there being no bridge, with 5000-6000 horsemen and 3000 foot soldiers. Nearly 100 years later the Princesse de Condé took a whole day to get her household across. In 1824 the Comte de Noailles obtained a concession to transport coal from his nearby mines and the 'wire' bridge was completed in September 1829, though it was demolished to make way for a more substantial one in 1892. Today, with its wide quayside bordered by neat houses with pretty chestnut balconies and roofs whose grey schist tiles quarried from nearby Basteyroux glitter and sparkle, it is still a prosperous town and a good centre for excursions, including boat trips. One of its attractions is the *gabarre* under construction on one of the quays. Between 1850 and 1860 some 300 were built each year. A model of a *gabarre* in the Maison du Patrimoine gives a very clear idea of how the wood was

A small gabarre *under construction*

The tympanum at Beaulieu: Christ in Glory

18

transported downstream. It varied from pine to oak, beech, elm, chestnut and, from the banks, alder, poplar and willow.

The sombre tree-clad slopes that line the river banks hereabouts produced the wood from which the barrels for the wine coopers of Bordelais were made. The hinterland from Bort les Orgues to Argentat was studded with villages whose occupants owed their livelihood to the oak and the chestnut. The felled trees were carried to the river and its affluents, or sawn on the site, and both trunks and staves were sent floating down to Valette, Spontour, Naugenac, St Projet and Argentat where they were made into boats. Many of the boats built on this stretch of the river would not make the return journey, for no water traffic mounted the Dordogne above Souillac, and they would be broken up on arrival at Bergerac or Libourne to be sold for their wood. The boats, mostly made from oak, were of two main types, though all were flat-bottomed. Those destined for long service were variously known as *gabarres*, *coujadours*, *naus*, *chalands* and *guages* and could carry a cargo of up to 30 tons. They were 20 metres long by 4-5 metres wide. They trailed *courpets* of 15 metres in length to be used as towing barges on the journey back upstream. The flimsier vessels, destined to be broken up on arrival downstream, tended to be called *gabarrots* or *batelets*, though, confusingly, all constructed above Argentat were known as *argentats*. All required considerable skill to manoeuvre.

Between Bort and Argentat alone there were at least fifty treacherous passages to be circumnavigated and requests for cleaning up the banks, removing rocky protuberances or clearing islands away were constant. In 1597 and 1609 funds were voted for dealing with them but Henri IV's death prevented anything being done, and although Colbert sent Jean Truchet to see what improvements could be made he could find no solution. A society whose sole aim was to ameliorate these conditions was founded in 1706 but progress was slow. In 1785 it was reported that more than seventy people had been drowned in the previous ten years. Dangerous sites, marked by bankside crosses which served both as memorials to their victims and warnings to the living, were known in general as *malpas*, *tombans* and *despolhas* and some had vividly descriptive names such as the Trou du Loup or Saut du Diable. Suggestions for improvements, including the one for a canal, were made again under the First Empire but even in the 1830's and 1840's accidents continued to be reported with alarming frequency. Eventually the arrival of the railways removed the need for action since river traffic virtually ceased.

South of Argentat the river runs wider and a little more quietly, though still through wooded hills with sheep on the grass clearings and, in the summer, their fleeces hanging out to dry. Small villages, with greyish-yellow stone barns entered by high rectangular apertures, are scattered along the river banks, with fruit and vegetable gardens in profusion. In 25 kilometres, still in Corrèze, it reaches *Beaulieu*, the site of a religious community founded between 855 and 860 when Rudolph of Turenne, Archbishop of Bourges changed its name from Vellinus to Bellus Locus. Its name is as apt as its modern claim to be the Limousin riviera, for it is a charming, quiet town belonging more to the Midi than to its northern and eastern mountainous neighbours.

Little now remains at Beaulieu of the earlier Benedictine or later Cluniac abbatial foundations of the twelfth century except the chapter house and the church itself, which is spectacular. Built by masons who worked at Carennac, Collonges, Souillac and Moissac – they have left their 'marks' on the stone – it is, not surprisingly, similar in style to those other great churches. The whole complex was completed in 1140 but suffered disastrously in the Hundred Years War, the Wars of Religion and the Revolution. The church is a large, imposing edifice with a finely proportioned series of apses at the west end and a sturdy octagonal tower surmounted by a slate-covered spire. The south doorway is one of the finest sculptural ensembles in the region, with an elaborate and imposing tympanum showing Christ in Glory and beneath, a double lintel of apocalyptic monsters, and striking though now rather mutilated panels on either side of the porch. The church also possesses a fine treasure, of which an elaborate twelfth-century Virgin is the cynosure. Here Marshal Ney, the Duke of Elchingen, 'the bravest of the brave', and hero of the retreat from Moscow, sought refuge after the Hundred Days. But to no avail, for he was captured and shot. The twelfth-century Penitents' Chapel, the size of a small church, mirrored by the river which runs wide and calm beside it, is also worth a visit.

The Dordogne is joined by the Ceré just below Bretenoux, a bastide founded by the baron of Castelnau in 1277 (that of neighbouring Puybrun was founded by Philippe le Hardi and the Abbot of Dalon in 1282) and above Castelnau in the department of Lot where it turns to run almost due west for the rest of its journey to the sea.

The gigantic silhouette of the great château of *Castelnau-Bretenoux* (not to be confused with Castelnaud La Chapelle in Dordogne) dominates the landscape on a promontory commanding four valleys and three rivers that run into each other. It is in a superb strategic position on the edge of what was the county of Toulouse and on the frontiers of Quercy and the Limousin. Castelnau is first mentioned in the early twelfth century but the earliest extant buildings are those of the Auditoire, second half of the twelfth, and the keep, at the beginning of the thirteenth century. Subsequent additions and fortifications during the Hundred Years War rendered it impregnable, and indeed it was never either attacked or captured. Not indeed until the sixteenth century did it become a family – albeit grandiose – residence, a fact which prevented it from being demolished by Richelieu.

In 1830 it belonged to the Duc de Luynes, but it had started to deteriorate and he sold it to a Monsieur Molin who proposed to demolish it. Although, through the

Jean Mouliérat outside Castelnau-Bretenoux

good offices of an inspector of the Monuments Historiques, Molin was prevented from doing so there was a disastrous fire in 1851 which destroyed the great gallery. The castle was then bought by Monsieur Dubousquet who wanted to transform it into a monastery. Despite Viollet Leduc's efforts to have it restored it was sold yet again, first to the local curé, in 1873, and once more in 1880, before it was finally acquired in 1896 by Jean Mouliérat.

Mouliérat was a successful tenor, who had won prizes at the Opéra and the Opéra Comique in Paris, and created the role of Don José in Bizet's *Carmen* in 1875. He spent three years putting the château to rights and installing his remarkable collection of furniture, works of art and stone monuments. Castelnau became a vibrant centre for archaeologists, writers, painters and musicians. Amongst Mouliérat's visitors were Colette, Rodin, Dunoyer de Segonzac and Pierre Loti.

Mouliérat died in 1932 leaving the entire property to the state on condition that the château was opened to the public. He would surely be pleased to know that nowadays opera performances are given there in high summer.

The next stop of special interest downstream is *Carennac*, a tidy village which springs to life on market days. It is renowned for its *reines claudes*, the greengages which grow so freely in the region, and for its association with Fénelon, who became prior of the Cluniac foundation there in 1681.

In a letter of 22 May of that year Fénelon wrote to his cousin, the Marquise de Laval (who was to marry his youngest brother in 1693):

> Have no doubts, madam, I am a man destined to make triumphal entries ... Representatives of the nobility, the clergy, the monastic orders and farmers for the third estate came to Sarlat to do me homage. I walk majestically accompanied by all these deputies.
>
> I arrive at the harbour of Carennac, where I find the quay black with people. The boats containing the élite of the townsfolk come out to meet us and at the same time I notice that, by an imaginative artifice, the most war-like among the local soldiery, having concealed themselves on that pretty island which you so well know, emerge bravely and salute my advent with much firing of muskets. The air is darkened by the smoke and the ears deafened by the noise of so much exploding of gunpowder. The steed which I then mount, full of noble ardour, is about to fling me headlong into the water, so I prudently dismount. And now to add to the noise of shooting comes that of the beating of drums. I cross the river, the lovely Dordogne, and a whole fleet of boats comes with us. At the landing-stage, a regiment of venerable monks is there to welcome me. These address me in highly eulogistic terms. I reply to them in the same high oratorial style, but modestly. The huge crowd opens to let me pass through; all eyes search my countenance to divine what I may have in store for them. Slowly and with dignified stride, so that all may take a look at me, I make my way up to the castle while a thousand voices acclaim my progress and everywhere the cry arises: 'he will be the delight of this people'.
>
> On my arrival at the castle gate, the king's official representative takes up the tale, and I need not describe to you how exceedingly eloquent he is. Words fail me to give any impression of the exquisite nature of this oration. First he compared me to the sun; not long afterwards to the moon; still later it was the bright stars that were honoured by this comparison. From there we went on to the nebulae and meteors, and finally in happy vein finished up with the beginning of the world. By this time the sun had set and, to fit the comparison between it and myself, I withdrew to my own chamber in order to follow its example.

Fénelon, by Joseph Vivien (Pinakothek, Munich)

'That pretty island', the Ile Barrade, is now named Calypso's Isle, for there is a firm tradition that Fénelon wrote *Télémaque* there. However, it was unquestionably of the river at Carennac that he wrote:

> *[Elle] ne laisse entendre aucun bruit*
> *Que celui d'une onde claire*
> *Qui tombe, coule et s'enfuit;*
> *Où deux îles fortunées,*
> *De rameaux verts courronnées,*
> *Font pour la charme des yeux*
> *Tout ce que le cœur desire.*
> *Que ne puis-je, sur ma lyre*
> *Te chanter du chants des Dieux!*

(The river makes no sound except that of a gentle wave which falls, flows and drifts away; where two blessed isles, crowned with green fronds, delight the eye and satisfy the heart's desire. How I sing to you the songs of the Gods, plucking my lyre!)

There is a fine ensemble of seigneurial buildings next to the church, which has a strongly carved tympanum and a sixteenth-century entombment in the adjacent romanesque cloister. The whole ensemble of medieval and renaissance houses in the village is homogeneous and a small, informative museum about local life is housed in part of the former château.

The Cirque de Montvalent – a semi-circle of hills – adds grandeur to the next stretch of the river and can be admired from the *belvédère* of Copeyre. Beyond the turning to Lacave, where visitors to the caves there can travel on a small electric railway, is the château of La Treyne, an elegant seventeenth-century building, now a luxurious hotel, perched on the very edge of the river bank. The formal gardens, impeccably barbered, and the tiny chapel in which temporary exhibitions are held, are open to visitors.

It is then but 10 kilometres to *Souillac*. Few of the motorists who pound up and down the N20 with their caravans on the way to and from Spain seem to stop for longer than the time it takes to cause traffic jams in the main street as they buy 'bargain' trays of peaches or melons. But recently its energetic mayor has done much to restore some of the buildings and generally smarten up the town. Perhaps it will come more properly into its own when the N20 is transformed into an autoroute and bypasses it. Work has already started on the road but it is not clear when the new bridge, planned to run to the east of the town, will be in place. There is also a very attractive Musée de l'Automate (by the side of the abbey) well worth visiting on a rainy day, and a carriage museum.

The abbey church, of greater beauty even than that of Beaulieu, is worth more than a cursory visit. The monastery founded there in the tenth century by the Benedictines was greatly enlarged in the twelfth and thirteenth centuries and, by the outbreak of the Hundred Years War, had over eighty dependent priories or

The abbey at Souillac

The prophet Isaiah in Souillac abbey

churches. It suffered at the hands of the English, who occupied it twice, but by 1508 it had recovered and was elevated by papal bull to the status of an abbey. It suffered considerable destruction in the Wars of Religion and its restoration took from 1632 to 1712 to complete. During the first year of the Revolution the Benedictines left and in 1790 the abbey church was turned over to the parish. In 1841 it was declared a *monument historique* and has been the object of loving care ever since. Its beauty derives from its harmonious proportions, both within and without, and the delicacy of its cluster of apses.

The romanesque sculptures, completed about 1135, on the inside of the doorway are particularly remarkable and unusual. They were originally on the outside of the church but were moved inside during the seventeenth-century restoration. There are two large figures, one on either side of the door; that of Hosea (as is nowadays thought, though he is often referred to as Joseph), on the left, was badly disfigured during the Revolution, while that on the right, of Isaiah, uses high relief dramatically to produce a figure of swirling intensity. To the right of Isaiah is a carved pillar full of figures and heads and animals whose precise significance is unknown, though the most plausible explanation is that the ensemble represents sin. Pride, the sin of the spirit, and concupiscence, the sin of the senses, are both there if one chooses so to interpret them; but whatever the meaning, it is one of the most amazing pieces of romanesque sculpture and its intricate beauty still moves us. The tympanum above represents the popular legend of Theophilus. His story was one which had great appeal in France during the Middle Ages and concerned a monk who was deprived of his job as treasurer at Adana in Cilicia about 338, by the new bishop. Theophilus set off to find a Jew who put him in touch with Satan who promised to reinstate him if he were to deny Christ and sign a pact to become the devil's disciple. Next day Theophilus was duly reinstated and acclaimed by the people but, rapidly overcome by remorse, he fasted and prayed to the Virgin. Appearing in his sleep, she took pity on him and eventually gave him back the fatal parchment bearing his signature. Shortly afterwards he died in the odour of sanctity.

Art and religion in so happy a combination, continued today with the concerts given in the church during the summer, were not Souillac's only assets. Its inhabitants had built up over the centuries a flourishing entrepreneurial river-based trade which had been in existence long before the eighteenth century when Arthur Young wrote:

> In going down to Souillac, there is a prospect that must universally please; it is a bird's-eye view of a delicious little valley, sunk deep amongst some very bold hills that inclose it; a margin of wild mountain contrasts the extreme beauty of the level surface below, a scene of cultivation scattered with fine walnut trees; nothing can apparently exceed the exuberant fertility of this spot.
>
> Souillac is a little town in a thriving state, having some rich merchants. They receive staves from the mountains of Auvergne by their river Dordonne, which is navigable eight months in the year; these they export to Bordeaux and Libourn; also wine, corn and cattle, and import salt in great quantities.
>
> It is not in the power of an English imagination to figure the animals that waited upon us here, at the Chapeau Rouge. Some things that called themselves by the courtesy of Souillac women, but in reality walking dung-hills.— But a neatly dressed clean waiting girl at an inn, will be vainly looked for in France.

Arthur Young was right about the rich merchants of Souillac. For centuries the river from Souillac to the Atlantic coast had carried a heavy traffic of boats and gave a livelihood along its banks to innumerable small communities of sawyers, boatbuilders, boatmen, hauliers, merchants and innkeepers. Small quantities of cheese, chestnuts and hides came down from the Auvergne, as well as some coal and charcoal, but the main cargo was wood. The wealthy Souillacois had established a two-way trade which enabled them to maintain a fine economic equilibrium. They bought timber for building and furniture, *merrain* and *carrasonne* or *échalas* (vine stakes) from suppliers upstream who unloaded them at the Port du Larroumet. The wood was then reloaded and transported downstream in boats owned or chartered by the Souillacois. These, built in the yards of Mouleydier and Ste Capraise, were more solidly built than the Argentat *gabarres* which were intended to be dismantled and used for their timber content, and could accommodate a cargo of 30 tons. When the *merrain* had been discharged at the end of the journey at Libourne the empty boats were loaded with salt as their main cargo and coffee, sugar and rum to be transported back upstream.

Merrain was oak cut into staves ready for barrel making and was sold by the *millier*. A *millier* was 1000 staves of *longailles* and *fonçailles* (which were the pieces for the top and bottom of the barrel) and was enough for fifty or sixty barrels. The transport vessels, which were also known as *gabarres*, belonged to master boatmen who acted as agents and bankers for the merchants as well as employing the men who worked the boats. They came mostly from the small towns along the river, such as Grolejac, Domme, La Roque Gageac and Beynac. It is pleasing that the tradition of building *gabarres* is kept alive. A woman who learned her craft from an old boat-builder makes them today in a shed at Mareuil with considerable success.

The journey downstream was relatively straightforward and followed a standard pattern. The boats pulled into the centre of the river from the Port du Larroumet into the current which carried them past the Pas du Raysse, then into the calm stretch by the plain of Cazoulès, past the fishing port of Mareuil, past St Julien de Lampon and, speeding up by the dangerous *tombans* of Aillac, to the port of Grolejac. The *malpas* in the Cingle de Montfort, known as the *lac del moussur*, had to be crossed before another stretch of good current took them past Domme and its port of Cénac St Julien. The Passage de Constaty was treacherous as there were shallow islands to be circumnavigated and there could be collisions with boats coming upstream. It was easier past St Cyprien, Siorac and Le Buisson but the river became faster again at Limeuil where the Dordogne was joined by the waters of the Vézère and its traffic. The Cingle de Trémolat (where there is now a small sailing harbour) brought the boats and the men who manned them into Mauzac, where they usually dined and spent the first night. Eighty-three kilometres from Souillac, it had been a good eight or ten hours' journey.

From Mauzac there is a sharp drop in the level of the water and there was a 100-metre stretch of dangerous rapids known as the Saut de Gratusse. There the boatmen had to call in pilots and often unload some of their cargo, at least until the 1840's when the Canal de Lalinde was built. Fifteen kilometres long, it reduced the dangers but did not speed the journey, for going through the locks was time-consuming. The passage on to Lalinde and Bergerac was easier, for the river there becomes slow and gentle, although open to winds so that collisions with the larger boats, the *chalands* operating a brisk carrying trade on this stretch, were now another hazard. After Lamonzie, Gardonne and Le Fleix the boatmen would reach Ste Foy for their second night after having travelled 57 kilometres in the day. On the third day, if their judgement was correct, they could use the tide from Castillon to take them through the loops at Branne and Génissac down the last 62 kilometres to their journey's end at Libourne. Of course it was not always accomplished in three days, but it rarely took more than four; actually the number of days in the year that the river was navigable at all was few. In winter there was too much water; in summer too little. In the years between 1857 and 1873 it was only *marchande*, as it was known, for an average of twenty-nine days a year and from 1878-97 only twenty-seven days.

Salt was a rare commodity in inland areas, so much so that in 1554 Périgord, Quercy and Bas Limousin were classified as *pays redîmés* which exempted them from the full rate of the *gabelle*, the salt tax. So there was a brisk trade to be done and the Souillacois seem to have had some sort of monopoly, at least upstream from their home town. During the eighteenth century they certainly made strenuous attempts to prevent the river being cleaned up above them since any improvements there would have damaged their own commerce.

Libourne, with its access to the river Isle as well, and Bergerac were the two important centres for salt in Périgord. All their trade was in sea salt, yellow, brown or, most expensive, white. The salt was put into bags taken from Souillac for the purpose, weighed or measured by volume and sealed in the presence of the vendor, the master boatman and the customs officer. The boats were loaded with salt, and any other small commissions, and started the journey back upstream. Cart horses were rare in Périgord so teams of oxen, owned by local peasants known as *bouviers-haleurs*, were used as draught animals. The average relay by any one team, of one or two pairs, was between two and six kilometres.

The nature of the terrain was such that the towpath could not run along one side of the river all the way but had to be hacked out in stretches on whichever side was the most suitable; so the boats too had to cross the stream frequently to reach the next relay stage. To do this involved complicated manoeuvres, and possible unloading; a skiff, normally towed by the *gabarre*, had to cross first, pulling on a rope with which the *gabarre* could be hauled across. For example, to get upstream from Domme to Cazoulès, a journey of 35 kilometres, the boats had to cross the river five times, and it required ten separate relays.

There were rules and regulations as always about tariffs and conditions and although the bankside route was not a public way it was loosely controlled by the public authorities. There were of course numerous abuses and squabbles. Gangs of fourteen or twenty retired *gabarriers* would present themselves as hauliers and demand twenty sous (five centimes) a man, thereby doing the *bouvier-haleur* out of his four francs and stinging the *maître de bâteau* for an inflated sum.

29

Although the time required for the journey from Libourne to Souillac could take anything up to three weeks, the dates on a set of consignment notes found in a former salt merchant's house in Souillac show that it could be done in an astonishing five days – that is, at an average of 40 kilometres a day. Only exceptionally, in very dry weather and when supplies of salt upstream were badly depleted, were mules used, as they customarily were above Souillac; then the salt cost exactly double. The salt was unloaded at Souillac's other port, the Port des Cuisines, where the remains of the quays and port installations can be seen mouldering by the few riverside houses.

The opening of the railway line from Coutras to Périgueux in 1857 and that from Périgueux to Brive in 1860 brought this trade to a halt. But although the ports and the riparian dwellers whose economic prosperity depended on the water traffic suffered a sharp decline from the middle of the nineteenth century until after the First World War, the *houille blanche* of the river has, in its hydroelectric works, been exploited once again to serve a wider community.

Today the small sleepy villages that flank the river as it runs through its department are peaceful havens for canoeists, fishermen and campers enjoying perfect summer holidays – modern equivalents of the *gabarriers* making their temporary homes on the beautiful river. Hardly a village from Souillac, through St Julien de Lampon to Grolejac, Cénac St Julien, La Roque Gageac, Beynac, St Cyprien, Siorac, Le Buisson, Trémolat and Lalinde is without its *site verte*. Fewer are to be found beyond Bergerac where the river opens out into a broad, rather featureless plain to run out of the department beyond Ste Foy, towards Montcaret and St Michel de Montaigne. It must surely have been of the stretch from Souillac across to Castillon – that part of the river that is in the department itself – that Montaigne's great friend Etienne de la Boëtie wrote:

> *Laisse, laisse-moy faire et, un jour, ma Dourdouigne*
> *Si je devine bien, on te cognoistra mieulx*
> *Et Garonne, et le Rhône et ces autres grands dieux*
> *En auront quelque envie et possible vergogne.*

(Only allow me [to sing your praises] and one day, my Dordogne, if my guess is right, you will be better known; the Garonne and the Rhone, and those other great gods will feel some envy and even shame.) His wishful thinking has come true, at any rate as far as the English are concerned.

Outside the western confines of the department, they may be forgiven for passing quickly through Castillon La Bataille with its monument to the defeat of Talbot (see page 108) preferring the delights, to the north of the river, of St Emilion, the 'pearl

Bec d'Ambès

of the Gironde', and Pomerol. A sad parenthesis: on a visit to Château Ausone we were told by the *maître de chai* that the oak for making the casks was imported from the United States, displacing the local product from Limousin and Auvergne.

The traveller determined to follow the course of the Dordogne will also find a small detour to the south worth making, for the sake of *Branne*, a charming town that has few visible mementoes of the past, except a nineteenth-century gothic church. When it was in the possession of the Seigneur of Fronsac, it had to pay an annual due of twelve lampreys; later it had to furnish the King-Duke of Aquitaine and three of his knights yearly with a boat laden in summer with rushes and in winter with straw. The town was of such strategic importance that a bridge was built there as early as the twelfth century; the one there today was designed by Eiffel, of tower fame. Now Branne is a centre for excursions in the region and a good stopping place before *Libourne*, an English bastide.

Founded by Roger de Leybourne, a Kentish nobleman who had visited Gascony with Henry III and been on crusade with his son Edward, the English connection is still strong, and in the church of Leybourne in Kent there is a window depicting the gate tower at Libourne and the castle of Leybourne. It was installed in 1948 by descendants of Sir Roger and the citizens of Libourne. There is also a legend that the Black Prince's son, Richard of Bordeaux, was born in Libourne.

Some of the original wall ramparts and a tower, as well as the characteristic *bastide* layout, are still to be seen there but the fifteenth-century Hôtel de Ville and church have both, alas, been restored. There is a small museum of paintings, gems and prehistoric and Gallo-Roman objects on the second floor of the *mairie*. But wine is its *raison d'être* today as it has been for many centuries; under the English occupation it took pride of place after Bordeaux. Indeed it was Libourne and not Bordeaux that handled shipments of wine from Dordogne, and the competition, complicated by Anglo-French politics, from the Libournais to get their wines to England before their Bordelais rivals resembles the rush there used to be to get the first Beaujolais nouveau into restaurants by Christmas of the year it was made. No wonder the Libournais stayed loyal to the English, even after 1453. They also had a considerable secondary trade in salt, and it is not surprising to find them up in arms over the salt tax imposed in 1542. They were savagely punished; 150 men being publicly hanged in one day of repression.

Libourne is now, as in the past when it was intended as a customs point for wine from Périgord, a town thriving on the wine trade and has 21,012 inhabitants. The quayside is lined by the offices and warehouses of some of the great names in the business of Bordeaux.

Beyond Libourne, the Dordogne and the Isle, which traverses so much of the department with it, run together through Bordelais between the two renowned vineyards of the Côtes de Fronsac and Graves de Vayres. The swollen river, with the marshy land of Entre Deux Mers to the south and the Côtes de Bourg and de Blaye to the north, joins the Garonne in a final broad sweep at Bec d'Ambès. Majestic and rightly sung by poets to the very last, the Dordogne finally loses its own identity as its waters mingle with those of the Garonne to become the Gironde. United, they all flow as a wide expanse of tidal waters, bordered by shallow banks disfigured by oil refineries, into the arms of the cold Atlantic.

It is a far cry, and 500 kilometres, from the Pic de Sancy and the thin trickles of the Dore and the Dogne but far from being an end – for all lovers of the river and its department as for Cyril Connolly – it is a beginning:

> I shall land at Bordeaux or La Rochelle and go first to the valley of the Dordogne, that beautiful temperate romanesque corner of France where Montaigne came from, where in the Virgilian countryside white oxen move about the maize-fields and where, in the oak woods above, the edible truffle mysteriously propagates itself, a connoisseur of geese and men.

The Land

The region re-named the *département* of Dordogne (not *the* Dordogne) at the time of the Revolution is virtually co-terminous with the former province of Périgord, and, as in the other provinces of France, its inhabitants retain their ancestral pride. They like to be, and always are, referred to as Périgordin, and never as Dordognais. Whether one should use Périgordin or Périgourdin has been a matter of academic dispute, and heated articles appear on the subject in learned journals. Some sages opine that Périgordin should be used only to describe natives of the former province, with Périgourdin being kept for those of the city of Périgueux. On the whole, though the former is used to describe the land and the latter the people, either is correct. I have consistently used Périgordin, except in quotations, and have the imprimatur of Eugène Le Roy, the best and best-known Périgordin novelist, for the usage.

The department is landlocked, surrounded to the north-west by Charente Maritime (Saintonge) and Charente (Angoumois); to the north and east by Corrèze (Limousin); to the south-east by Lot (Quercy); to the south-west by Lot-et-Garonne (Agenais); and to the west by Gironde (Bordelais). Together with Lot-et-Garonne, Gironde, Landes and Pyrénées Atlantiques, it is part of the administrative region of Aquitaine.

Its geological formation is in three diagonal bands, running roughly from north to south; to the east, at the edge of the Massif Central, are, as one might expect, the primary rocks; to their west is secondary limestone, honeycombed by the riverain network of the Dronne, Auvézère, Isle, Vézère and Dordogne; and tertiary sandy lands run down into the Aquitanian basin towards the ocean. Lying between the mountains and the sea, watered by innumerable rivers which enrich its soil, it is not surprising that this province affords such a glorious variety of scenery. Its beauties were recorded as early as 1223 in a letter from a Périgordin bishop to Louis VIII in which he said, 'This diocese, because of its charm, its fertility and the quality of its water, is called the garden of the Kings of France.'

The department itself is subdivided into a number of areas which take their names from the largest towns, the forests, or, more fancifully, from the tourist board's flights of imagination, but the nomenclature is based on real physical differences, which range from the rolling wooded hills known as *pechs* to the barren limestone plateaux (*causses*) and the lush and fertile valleys. These regions have no fixed boundaries like those of communes or cantons and cannot be closely delimited. Indeed they overlap each other and there may be some argument over which town or village belongs to which area but as generalizations they have some convenience.

Arthur Young noted the change of scenery as he came down from the Limousin:

> Some views of singular beauty rivetted us to the spot; that of the town of Uzarch, covering a conical hill, rising in the hollow of an amphitheatre of wood, and surrounded at its feet by a noble river, is unique. Derry in Ireland has something of its form, but wants some of its richest features. The water-scenes from the town itself, and immediately after passing it, are delicious. The immense view from the descent to Donzenac is equally magnificent. To all this is added the finest road in the world, everywhere formed in the most perfect manner, and kept in the highest preservation, like the well ordered alley of a garden, without dust, sand, stones, or inequality, firm and level, of pounded granite, and traced with such a perpetual command of prospect, that had the engineer no other object in view, he could not have executed it with a more finished taste.
>
> The view of Brive, from the hill is so fine, that it gives the expectation of a beautiful little town, and the gaiety of the environs encourages the idea; but on entering, such a contrast is found as disgusts completely. Close, ill built, crooked, dirty, stinking streets, exclude the sun, and almost the air from every habitation, except a few tolerable ones on the promenade. — 34 miles.
>
> The 9th. Enter a different country with the new province of Quercy, which is a part of Guienne; not near so beautiful as Limosin, but, to make amends, it is far better cultivated. Thanks to maize, which does wonders! Pass Noailles, on the summit of a high hill, the chateau of the Marshal Duke of that name. — Enter a calcareous country, and lose chesnuts at the same time.

The Nontronnais, known as *Périgord vert*, is to the north of Périgueux and shares the pastures and chestnut forests of Limousin and Charente. It is now quietly domesticated, but in 1895, of the 249 wolves killed in France, sixty-seven were in Charente, and eighteen in Dordogne – of which most were in this wild and desolate north-western area where the two departments meet. Today it is a countryside of trees interspersed with large fields and compact farms, and its damp greenness is due to the schist and granite subsoil which keeps the water on the surface. Until recently the economy depended on timber and its derivative industries – cooperage work-

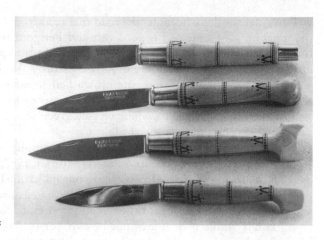

Typical Nontronnais knives

shops, sawmills, carpentry and cabinet-making, mining and such agriculture as could be wrung from the hillsides. Now, although there are some cattle in the east, the west relies more on tourism, and its shoe and slipper manufacture, though even this, faced with competition from Italy and south-east Asia, is in decline.

During the nineteenth century *Nontron* was known for its production of pocket knives with decorated boxwood handles. Their production, though always modest, gave rise to a fair number of jokes, since the ingenuity of the Nontronnais seems to have gone into seeing how small they could make the knives. A contemporary traveller records having seen *twelve* packed into a walnut shell. They are still in production, and indeed the Ecomusée de la Noix at Castelnaud has a few walnut shells on display each containing, alas, only one tiny knife. Pleasantly situated on the river Bandiat, Nontron remains gentle and calm, with a fine view across the valley from its church and château.

The only other town of any size in the area, *Thiviers*, is also grey and undistinguished, especially as it has a hideous château as heavily restored as its neighbouring church, whose capitals are, however, remarkable, and rare in their presentation of the human figure. But small industries, such as building, tinning and nowadays the presence of Hermès, together with the flourishing markets in foie gras, truffles and cheese, liven up its rather drab appearance.

To the east there is a change of terrain, where the red sandstone hills that run down from Brive impinge, and the agriculture changes too. The area round Hautefort is intensively cultivated and produces vines, cherries and walnuts, and has become a market-gardening centre. It is here that one of the most beautiful stretches of the department of Dordogne is to be found, and the discerning tourist will do well to enter the department by the road that runs from Lanouaille to Montignac at the junction as it were of Périgord vert and Périgord blanc. The road twists and turns through gently wooded hills and cultivated plains and it is here that the walnut trees display their greatest glory. Their sturdy trunks and radiating branches sometimes covered with a chocolate-brown lichen stand out starkly etched in winter and in spring, and in summer their clear green foliage and fruit are distinct against the fields of ripening wheat or pale green staves of maize which surround them, making pools of light and shade.

Dordogne is still the second largest walnut supplier in France (the first being Isère) with a commercial production of 4175 tons in 1997; the crop is heavily dependent on the weather and late frosts can do untold harm. The walnut tree, so much a part of the present-day landscape, and concentrated mainly in the north-east and south-east of the department, has been an important economic asset for centuries. Every family would own at least one or two, for the nuts not only supplied nourishment and a cash crop, but the oil extracted from them was used for both cooking and lighting. The wood, made into furniture and used as a veneer in so much fine cabinet-making, was, and still is, much sought after and was for many years the only wood employed in the manufacture of butts for sporting guns, especially in England. The walnut tree, planted at the birth of a girl child for the purpose, would often be sold in due course to provide her dowry.

There are two varieties of walnut grown in the department. The *Juglans regia*, rightly so-called for it is a king among trees, is doubly valuable for both its fruiting properties and its wood but it grows slowly. Consequently *Juglans nigra*, which is a particularly resistant strain, is being planted though it is of less long-term value and its wood is not of much use. *Nigra*, when grafted on to *regia* stock, is more productive but takes thirty to forty years to mature.

The walnut produces both male and female flowers on the same tree – the male on the second year growth, the female on the first – so they are particularly susceptible to frost. Moreover pollination is by currents of air – no bees are ever to be seen on them – and when the pollen coagulates in cold temperatures even a light breeze will not shift it. Nowadays a new variety, the Melanaise, is sometimes planted in small quantities in the orchards to help pollination. Apart from the frost, which only prevents fruiting, though that is serious enough, a new hazard is that many of the trees are suffering from root damage. The roots of the walnut spread wide like its branches, but they lie shallow in the ground and because crops are grown right up to the trees the roots are these days disturbed by the deeper ploughs drawn by modern tractors. Many of the trees which were originally planted on the verges of roads and lanes are also disappearing as the roads are widened, so the tendency now is to plant them in groves or orchards of their own.

Cracking walnuts with a traditional mallet in an old-fashioned kitchen (c. 1960)

One such plantation, the biggest in Europe, is at *Doissat* and covers 162 acres. It was the brainchild of M. Heliant, a director of the Banque Nationale de Commerce et Industrie, and was started in 1959 with *regia* and *nigra* grafted on to *regia* side by side on the American pattern. It has recently been acquired by a new proprietor who maintains it to a high degree of excellence. Nearby is *Belvès*, an attractive small town perched on a hill with gothic and renaissance houses still lining its narrow streets, and a flourishing walnut market. There are also troglodytic habitations which have been furnished to show how they were lived in during the Middle Ages, and a spinning-mill (*filature*) a kilometre away.

Strawberries have been found to be the ideal crop to grow with walnuts since they too are shallow-rooted and do not damage the tree roots. Moreover, while strawberry picking is labour-intensive, so is collecting nuts. Luckily the strawberries are virtually over when the walnuts are ripe for gathering. There are, however, some amazing machines with buffered claws which shake the tree, forcing the nuts to drop in great profusion. The driver has to be protected by an awning, an ironic reversal, if he is a man, of the old saw in French as in English: '*Plus vous battez votre femme, votre chien et votre noyer, plus ils vous offriront.*' Even so, the farmers have some reservations about this method, fearing that the shaking damages the roots. Most of the nuts, which contain 20 per cent water when picked, are dried naturally, and consequently taste a good deal better than the oven-dried variety, and they can conveniently be put into the *séchoirs* which by November are clear of tobacco (see page 50).

There are three varieties of nut: the *corne*, in demand for the table since its inner skin does not stick to the shell which, despite its hardness, allows the kernel to be removed whole; the *grandjean*, known as a nut *de cassage*, sold to pastry cooks, cake manufacturers and used for pressing for oil; and the *franquette*, which combines the virtues of both. The importance of the difference will be readily understood when one realizes that the market price for broken kernels is half that of whole ones. Walnut-cracking is a task which, like its harvesting, is still undertaken by hand and occupies many village women in late autumn and winter. It is still very much a cottage industry; the elderly, with their trays on their knees and a small mallet in their hand, may occasionally be seen on their porches tap-tapping away, though this is becoming rare.

The oil is used to dress salads but is not to everyone's taste for the first pressing has a powerful flavour. It needs to be used sparingly or mixed with a little less idiosyncratic oil. For those who have learned to appreciate it, it is one of the great local products widely available *in situ*. Walnut oil may be bought in tins but for the commercial market much of the flavour has been sacrificed just as with so much over-refined olive oil. A few of the old mills are still in existence and use the machinery that has been operated by the same family for several generations. All the ironwork was made in the local foundry, and, apart from the renewal of some of the

The walnut press at Ste Nathalène in action

wooden components, the presses are much as they were in the last century. The local farmers take their shelled kernels, which are crushed by the millstones powered by the mill race. The cake-like mass is then heated in a huge basin set over a wood fire until the viscous oil runs. The whole is then pressed and the oil stored in stone vats or traded back to the suppliers of the nuts. The remains, known as *torteaux* or *pain de noix*, are used as cattle food and fish bait. Thirty kilos of kernels will provide fifteen litres of oil. The Moulin de La Tour at Ste Nathalène is alas one of the few remaining mills in working order. It sells not only oil but delicious home-made walnut cakes and sweeties. There is now a well laid out and informative small museum, the Ecomusée de la Noix, at Castelnaud.

Périgord blanc – so-called because of its characteristic chalky outcroppings – lies at the heart of the province, surrounding its capital, Périgueux (see page 62), and spreading over to the east. *Terrasson* is one of the more attractive of the larger towns in this region, divided into two bourgs by the Vézère, which is spanned by two bridges – one of which is medieval. The 'old' town has an enormous gothic church containing the remains of St Sour, and a château of which only the fourteenth-century façade is of interest. The old houses, lying steeply raked down the hillside, have slate-tiled roofs which glisten mauve in the sun. A new garden, the Jardin de l'Imaginaire, was opened three years ago.

Formerly the area produced wheat and wine for Limousin but now it concentrates on dairy farming. A large part of it is covered by the Forêt Barade which in the past extended over a much greater area than it does now. By the middle of the nineteenth century, when Eugène Le Roy set so much of *Jacquou le Croquant* in its environs, it comprised the Forêt de Lerm, the Forêt du Lac Gendre and the Forêt de Grandval. He knew it well:

> When we were at La Tuilière, the wood as a whole was not in very good condition. Some areas had been burned down, and the man to whom practically all these forests belonged, a former aristocrat, ruined, it was said, at the time of the Revolution, had cut down many of the trees and had progressively sold the greater part of them for a pittance. But even so, some years later, one came upon thick groves and fine trees in those corners which were uncultivable. In these remote enclaves, these hidden dells, dense copses of gorse and furze and broom and heather, entwined with brambles and fern, grew to the size of small trees. It was in these impenetrable thickets that the wild boar – known in patois as *porcs singlars* – had their lairs, from which they sallied forth at night to ravage the turnips and potatoes growing in the fields around the villages. One never saw them in the daytime unless they were being chased by the count's pack of hounds, or unless a sow, followed by her young, ventured out into a clearing.

Though one is unlikely to see wild boar there now, the forest retains its pristine magic, and one still comes upon thick groves, fine trees and hidden dells.

The western area of the department can be classified in various ways: its northernmost canton likes to call the surrounding district the Verteillacois; Ribérac likes to include the communes of Verteillac, Montagrier and itself under the heading Ribéracois. It is nonetheless an homogeneous economic zone whichever description is used. Cereal and cattle, both raised on relatively large holdings, are its prime products and it has no large towns or industries. *Ribérac*, with a population of 4118 inhabitants, is the largest, and though attractively sited and animated enough, it has little to commend it except its value as a market for local produce and shopping centre for the large number of British residents who own properties in the vicinity.

Nothing is left of the medieval fortress which belonged to the Pons family and later the Aydies; the twelfth-century church is restored and the modern church is boring.

Its one claim to fame is that it was the birthplace of Arnaut Daniel, the troubadour of noble birth whose career prospered between 1180 and 1210. Dante makes Guinicelli, in *Purgatorio*, xxvi, say of him:

> ... He who is singled by
> My finger (he pointed to a spirit in front)
> Wrought better in the mother tongue than I.
> Whether in verses of love or prose romaunt
> He surpassed all.

Brilliant and wide-ranging, Arnaut was, it has been said, the author of verses as unprintable as they were dazzling, though they were recited by, amongst others, St Francis of Assisi. Of himself, Arnaut said:

> I am Arnaut who gathers air
> And with oxen chases the hare
> And ever swims against the stream.

He gravitated, like so many other poets of the brilliant twelfth-century court of Aquitaine to that of Richard of Bordeaux, Eleanor's son. There he was challenged by an English poet who wagered that Arnaut could not surpass him at complicated versification – a dangerous challenge since it was Arnaut who had invented the sestina. Each poet withdrew to his closet. Arnaut found solitary confinement inhibiting to the writing of poetry, whereas the Englishman made his up at great speed and repeated his verses aloud over and over again to himself, little knowing that he could be overheard by his rival. After five days the Englishman asked if Arnaut was finished: 'Yes,' he replied, and they went before the King. Arnaut, as befitted a visitor, was invited to begin, and proceeded to recite his rival's work. Despite this, all ended happily, for the King was delighted by both trick and poem, and duly rewarded them both.

To the south, below the Dronne and reaching to the Isle is the region known as Double. This is still the wildest part of the department and doubtless because of its wildness and desolation there are few buildings of any sort. It has always been a land of forests, of huge chestnuts and oaks and tall pines undergrown with bushes and ferns, and interspersed with small clearings created by the charcoal-burners who made their homes there for centuries. The soil is heavy clay and while the forests stood it was healthy enough, though it gave few much of a living. Such as this living was, it derived from the forest itself and pigs, who fed on the acorns. Only twice a year, for the horse fairs, was the area much frequented. The depredations made on the forests for ship-building at the beginning of the nineteenth century, compounded by the felling of large numbers of trees to make way for railway lines and to produce sleepers, allowed water to accumulate in marshy stagnant ponds. Malaria soon took hold and an already impoverished population deserted its miserable homesteads while it was still fit enough to do so.

Efforts to reclaim the area met with great resistance, but in the 1860's a M. de Belleyme succeeded in engaging Napoleon III's interest, and the money was found. The lead was given by a dedicated band of Trappist monks from the abbey of Port de Salut in Mayenne who were offered, by a philanthropic doctor named Piotay, the land at Echourgnac on which to build a monastery and a model farm. Edward Harrison-Barker, on his visit to the monastery in 1894, quotes the recollections of one of the pioneers who arrived in July 1868:

> There were twenty-two of us in all, *pères et frères*, and two or three weeks afterwards, seventeen were down with fever. You can have no idea what it was like here twenty-five years ago. The country was unfit for human beings. The people went shivering about in the heat of summer wrapped up as they would be in the depth of winter. It was pitiful to see them.

The Trappists set about draining the ponds, replanting vines and raising cattle. When in 1901, under the Third Republic, they were threatened with expulsion from France, so great had been their success that the local peasants said they would resist by force if they, like the Carthusian brethren at Vauclaire, were evicted. However, evicted they were, but in 1923 a community of Cistercian nuns, who had themselves been exiled in 1904, returned from Spain and installed themselves at Notre Dame de Bonne Espérance as their own convent at Espira d'Agly had been sold in the meantime. There are now forty nuns in residence and they make cheese and jam in their intervals from prayer and looking after visitors seeking retreat.

Double is no longer fever- or viper-ridden, but 53 per cent of its area and that of the Landais remains covered in trees and even today the average population is below eleven people per square kilometre. There are some cattle, producing both meat and milk, but its inhabitants hope that the wild beauty of their countryside will attract campers and weekenders to augment their income. Indeed the drive along the Dronne between Bourdeilles and Brantôme goes through a lovely stretch of countryside.

The main towns are Mussidan, modestly industrialized, on the confluence of the Isle and the Crempse; Neuvic and Montpon Ménesterol, which was once famed for the variety and number of its roses. Once again, it is its natural features, such as the rivers Isle and Dronne, that attract. Surely nothing could be greater fun than to emulate the intrepid Harrison-Barker in his voyage down the latter by canoe in 1893. He started at Tocane St Apre with 'a knapsack containing clothes, a valise filled chiefly with provisions, several bottles of wine, one of rum (a safer spirit in France than some others), and another of black coffee, made very strong ...' and shortly found himself under the spell of

> this most charming river. Its breadth and depth were constantly changing. Now it was scarcely wider than a brook might be, and was nearly overarched by its alders and willows; now it widened out and sped in many a flashing runnel through a broad jungle of weeds where the blistering rays of the sun beat down with tropical ardour; then it slept in pools of long green streamers that waved slowly about like Undine's hair. Here and there all about stood the waxen flowers of *sagittaria* above the barbed floating leaves, cool and darkly green. Close to the banks the tall and delicately branching water-plantains, on which great grasshoppers often hang their shed skins, were flecked with pale pink blooms – flowers of biscuit porcelain on hair-like stems.

Landais shares a greater resemblance to Double than to its near namesake, Landes, but it is less wild. Like it though, it is heavily wooded, with maritime pines now encroaching on the native chestnuts, but there are clearings where fruit trees flourish and tobacco grows. It is only in the extreme west, where it is contiguous to Bordelais and as it descends into the valley of the Dordogne, that it becomes more densely populated, though there are few towns of any size or importance.

The area to the south of the river – Bergeracois, now known as *Périgord pourpre* – is by contrast mild and gentle, a rolling plain with vineyards similar to those of Bordelais. Bergerac, though smaller than Périgueux, like it has the feeling of a county town (see page 158). Its economic prosperity has grown from the surrounding vineyards and its proximity to Bordeaux, and the area contains a number of *bastide* towns (see page 94).

Limeuil, a charming village perched on a hill above the confluence of the Vézère and the Dordogne, with its *pont coudé*, is, as it were, a frontier town between three regions – Périgord pourpre, Périgord blanc and Périgord noir. It has clearly been inhabited for many centuries, for remains of a Gaulish settlement were found there in 1909 and its name comes from the roman *lemoialum* – a place planted with elms. The château, now in ruins, belonged to Henri de la Tour, Vicomte de Turenne (the great Turenne's father) who used it as a centre of operations during the Wars of

Isabeau de Limeuil

Religion. It was also the home of Isabeau de Limeuil, a member of Catherine de Medici's flying squad of attractive young women, and the mistress of the Prince de Condé. The village is a mass of tightly packed streets, squeezed between the ramparts, and was until the middle of the nineteenth century a home for weavers and boat-builders. Many of the houses still have the characteristic basket-handle-shaped openings – or *tauliers* – which sheltered the booths on the ground floor. Limeuil also had an arsenal and was, because of its strategic position, an important look-out post. In the valley below, the chapel of St Martin, though its roof is in a parlous state, with many of its timbers stolen, is still being lovingly restored by the Amis de St Martin and can be seen by arrangement. Its main interest for us lies in the fact that it was dedicated to St Thomas à Becket and numbers Richard Cœur de Lion and Hélie de Talleyrand amongst its founders. It was consecrated in 1194 during the English occupation.

Périgord noir, the most luxuriant and picturesque region of the department, lies like an isosceles triangle on its side, with Limeuil at its apex, bounded to the north by the Vézère, with the Dordogne running through its centre, and to the south the departmental border. The dense oak forests that give it its name, the rich alluvial soil and the limestone outcroppings were as tempting to early man as they are to the tourist today, to judge from the number of prehistoric sites that have been found in the north from Les Eyzies to Montignac. It is by far the most attractive – and visited – part of the department. Not only is the landscape varied and colourful, part valley, part wooded hills, but a large number of the most impressive castles and châteaux are to be found there, and many of the beautiful romanesque churches that abound in Dordogne – all this, and Sarlat too.

Apart from the tree-clad hills, the dense forests and the fertile valleys, one of the most characteristic sights in Dordogne is the strip cultivation of the fields. It is still rare to see large fields under cultivation, though this is becoming more common, and even the grazing meadows are small. These *parcelles*, as the narrow multi-coloured strips are known, have a long history.

The big estates which belonged to the nobility and the church under the *ancien régime* survived very largely intact after the Revolution although in many but not all cases their owners changed. Lawyers and ironmasters, shopkeepers and merchants

The confluence of the Vézère and the Dordogne at Limeuil

bought the châteaux and *manoirs*, from which they had evicted both seigneur and priest, and they bought with them the surrounding property. They maintained the system of renting out the farm land known as *métayage* which had been in operation since the sixteenth century. *Métayage* – or share cropping – was a system whereby the landowner rented out his land to a tenant and supplied the agricultural implements, seed and cattle in return for half the produce.

While better than serfdom, *métayage* had great disadvantages. The contract between the landowner and the *métayer* ran only for one year, so that neither party had any incentive to improve methods or strive for greater productivity, and the tenants could be evicted without redress. It is a measure of the immutability of farming habits that not until a law of 1946 was the proportion of produce changed from half each to one-third for the landowner and two-thirds for the men working the land. It is interesting to note that in the department in 1970 75% of the land was farmed by its proprietors, 22% by tenant farmers and 3% by *métayers*. By 1997 these figures had changed to 54%, 45.9% and 0.1% respectively.

If a man had only one pair of oxen, the land that he could work was known as *borderage*. (A *journal*, which measured just over a quarter of an hectare, was the amount he could plough in a day.) However it was more common to have two pairs, when it was known as a *métairie*; it then required two or three men to work it, the women and children looking after the animals. This restricted the amount of land that could be cultivated to between fifteen and twenty hectares. The soil in the department was on the whole heavy and oxen rather than horses drew the ploughs. The land had originally been divided into small *parcelles* to ensure that everyone had a share of the good as well as of the poorer land, and while everyone grew the same crops his *parcelles* were scattered about the commune. In addition to vines, the crops consisted of wheat, rye, barley, oats, buckwheat and maize. A variety of beans and peas as well as beet and potatoes were also grown.

Even the two local agricultural theorists, Marshal Bugeaud (1784-1849) and the Marquis de Fayolle (1765-1841), who did much both in practice on their estates – one at La Durantie, near Lanouaille, and the other at Tocane sur Apre, near Montagrier – and by preaching, thought that the size of the traditional *métairie* was about right, though they both wished to see improvements in their farming. Fayolle was anxious to see greater security for tenure for the *métayer* and a more scientific approach as well as such mechanical aids as better tools used by tenant and proprietor alike. He was a correspondent of the Société d'Agriculture of Paris and wrote an important treatise on agriculture in the department (*ci-devant* Périgord) in year IX (1800).

But even these small areas, Fayolle thought, if properly cultivated, could be made profitable when efficiently organized. When Bugeaud took over La Durantie from his family in 1819 the property consisted of 1000 acres (400 hectares) divided into thirteen *métairies*. By 1835 he had 1750 acres (700 hectares) and when he had brought much of the land under grass and raised his stock to 130 head of cattle, 500 sheep and ten mares, he increased his annual revenue from 1000-1200 francs to 32,000 francs. He and Fayolle still thought that mixed farming – polyculture – was viable and particularly suitable to the terrain, and that an increase in cattle would provide not only meat to improve the diet but also the all-important dung with which to manure the crops. They also encouraged the plantation of root crops. The polyculture is still very evident throughout the department.

Thomas Bugeaud was an interesting character. The fourteenth son of the Marquis de Lapiconnerie, he was born in Limoges in 1784. His parents were imprisoned during the Revolution and his mother died shortly after their release. Thomas was taken to live with his father in Limoges while his sisters were left in the family house at La Durantie. At the age of thirteen, totally unschooled, he ran away from his father and, borrowing money from a servant, walked the 60 kilometres home. Here, in great poverty, he lived the life of the peasants, working with them on the land and acquiring his love for and understanding of it at the same time.

His sisters tried to compensate for his lack of formal education by reading Racine and Molière with him but, by the time he was eighteen, Thomas felt he had to make his way in life on his own. He was rejected by the local ironmaster, M. Festugière, who told him that a gentleman's place was not in a foundry: 'since you are both intelligent and poor, join the army; you'll be a success'. He did, and he was. The army changed the timid boy into a resourceful and hard man. He saw service at Ulm and Austerlitz, and he learned valuable lessons for his own future in Spain where he spent four years dealing with guerrillas. A major at thirty, and devoted to Napoleon, he was promoted to colonel during the first Restoration but went back to the emperor in spite of being instructed to arrest him at the start of the Hundred Days. In 1815 he was fighting the Austrians at L'Hospitalet, and after the armistice was put on half-pay and retired.

Bugeaud went home to La Durantie, where he bought his family out in order to acquire the property for himself, and started to put into practice there some of the order and organization he had learned during his military service. He brought to the stagnant agricultural economy the energy and impetus it required and made innovations which transformed his own estates into a model farm. He encountered great opposition and it was only by example that he began to convince other landowners in the district of the value of his methods. He was as indefatigable with his pen as in the fields, constantly writing treatises on agricultural management to try and convert others to the use of proper tools, fertilizers and open fields on which cattle could graze. He ended the system of *jachère* whereby fields were left fallow in alternate years; he created a market at Lanouaille and formed *comices agricoles* to disseminate information, addressing their members in patois if need be.

His aim was to ameliorate the extreme poverty and stubborn backwardness he saw around him, which was due, he thought, to the fragmentation caused by polyculture. He wrote:

Marshal Bugeaud

My own property is most suited to cultivation on a large scale. I own 1800 contiguous *journaux* excluding the wooded areas. They are worked by thirteen families comprising a total of 106 people; in addition I have twelve servants, male and female, to look after my private land. So you see I have the makings of a company, though I cannot always manoeuvre them as I would wish. Add to this 80 cattle, 10 mares and 500 sheep and you will see I have the wherewithal for a battalion.

All his life Bugeaud saw himself as a *soldat-laboureur* and he continued to write treatises on military tactics as well as on agriculture. In his years of forced retirement he kept up a steady stream of requests to be allowed to rejoin the army, interspersing them with suggestions that the army should be used in peace time to work the land. He finally allayed the fears of the local *préfet* who recommended his return to the army in 1827 but it was not until Louis Philippe came to power that he achieved his aim. He was appointed *général de brigade* in 1831 and at the same time was elected as deputy for Périgord, a position he held until 1848.

Napoleon's '*meilleur colonel de l'armée*' rapidly became better known as the '*géolier de Blaye*'. He was almost immediately given the task of guarding the Duchesse de Berry (Charles X's daughter-in-law) after her arrest for provoking royalist uprisings in the Vendée in 1832. Despite having been a widow for thirteen years, the duchess became pregnant and after the birth of her child was sent back to her native Sicily, freeing Bugeaud for more palatable and suitable tasks. In the meantime French colonial aspirations in Algeria were not being fulfilled and Bugeaud was appointed Governor of Algeria by Thiers. Bugeaud redressed the French defeat at Tafna in 1836 by a brilliant military victory at the battle of Sikkak, and returned to France after the Treaty of Tafna in 1837. This first experience led him to formulate theories about colonization which he succeeded in persuading the politicians to allow him to put into practice when he returned to Algeria in 1840. His campaigns to subdue the Arabs were based on his experiences in Spain some thirty years earlier and his views on colonial policy on those acquired during his fifteen years' exile in Dordogne. He was made a Marshal of France on the eve of the battle of Isly in 1844 but ran into political disagreements with the French government and was recalled in 1847 to a country on the verge of eruption into revolution. He died suddenly of cholera in Paris two years later before his future career could be settled.

Bugeaud was loved by his soldiers, in spite of a nature which had become violent and intractable, and was affectionately called by them *le père Bugeaud*. The *laboureur périgordin*, as he called himself, is commemorated on a plaque in his native village of La Durantie, but his best epitaph is that inscribed on the sword of honour presented to him by the Société d'Algérie of Algiers after Isly: *Ense et Arato* – by the sword and by the plough.

The agricultural methods that Bugeaud and Fayolle pioneered were slowly introduced and there is no doubt that the peasants' lot improved during the middle of the century. However, their main source of income came from their vineyards. A quarter of the cultivable soil of Périgord – 100,000 hectares – was under vines until the phylloxera destroyed them all between 1868 and 1885; by 1892 only 21,200 hectares were cultivated. This was a disaster for the area. The vineyards, being labour-intensive, were densely populated and not only were the peasant farmers out of work almost overnight but so also was the large number of workers dependent on the wine-carrying business, and the artisans who served the whole community. The economic crisis was compounded by the fall in the price of cereals at the same time and many of the landowners were bankrupt. A few who had enough capital bought cattle; a few who lived in truffle-producing areas marketed their produce; a few planted maritime pines, although they were a long-term speculation; some planted walnuts. Many abandoned their land or sold it off. The system of *métayage* began to break down.

Although the flight from the land had begun before the phylloxera, it dramatically increased after 1886. Of the 128,000 people who left the area in the hundred years from 1821, three quarters of them moved out between 1886 and 1921. The countryside was deserted; the peasants barely scratched a living and the additional stagnation caused by the economic crisis of the 1930's induced a mood of despair. The state was slow to intervene. But it did so eventually, albeit at a snail's pace, partly by increasing the number of permits for growing tobacco, which rescued a number of families who would not otherwise have survived. In 1930-31 11,000 farmers in Périgord grew tobacco, but each had only a tiny amount of land devoted to it and that was as usual split into a number of *parcelles*. A total holding averaged a quarter to half an hectare and it was rare for anyone to cultivate as much as one hectare. But it was a good cash crop – as it still is – and it helped towards restoring some sort of economic prosperity to the department.

Today Dordogne is the largest tobacco-producing department in France. Its sturdy stems and full green leaves are to be seen all over the department but most especially in the south-eastern corner. It likes a rich deep soil and is therefore grown in valleys rather than on the hillsides. Until 1961 Paraguay tobacco plants were common but, as they were susceptible to mildew, a hybrid – a cross between Paraguay and Bel, a more resistant American variety is now cultivated. There are three main varieties produced: brown for the Gauloises the French still love to smoke, a yellowish one called Burlet, and increasingly, the blond Virginia. The land on which tobacco is to be planted is worked and fertilized during the winter. The plants are sown in April and May, and harvested from mid-August to early September. In order to get the maximum number of large leaves the flowers have to be removed and, until the advent of chemical sprays, each flowerhead was painted by hand with walnut oil. Throughout July many farmers and their children were to be seen patiently snipping off the flowers before they reached their prime and coating the stubs.

In Dordogne the whole plant is cut and either the larger leaves are stripped and put to dry in small ovens or the whole plant is hung upside down in well-ventilated barns and left there to dry for about forty-five days. Until 1961 the buying and selling of tobacco was a state monopoly but, although it had to be abandoned then because of the stipulations of the Treaty of Rome, the farmers, who all belong to one powerful federation, take their tobacco to SEITA (the Service d'Exploitation Industrielle des Tabacs et Allumettes) for processing. The base leaves go in November and the upper and middle leaves in January. There, over a period of eight days, they are graded and assessed and a week later the local producers' co-operative is paid between 80 and 85 per cent of the total due from the central organization in Paris. The balance is paid in March when the remainder of the crop is delivered and the national balance has been struck.

Over the last twenty years the amount of land devoted to growing tobacco has fallen by about half, with, in 1997, only an area of 1218 hectares devoted to it, concentrated in the Sarladais and the valley of the Isle. Despite a decline of 15% between 1990 and 1995, the total crop in 1997 was some 32,293 quintals of which

Pipes (Musée du Tabac, Bergerac)

just over half was *tabac brun*. There has been a marked increase in the growing of *tabac blond* to suit the changing market, and the price of cigarettes has risen sharply over the last few years in line with western European attempts to reduce smoking.

Tobacco found its way to Europe fairly soon after Columbus's discovery of the New World. Jean Nicot (whence nicotine), who was François II's ambassador to Lisbon, supplied a powdered preparation to Catherine de Medici in 1560 as a cure for her migraines and, for the rest of the sixteenth century, tobacco, known as the queen's herb, was used for medicinal purposes only. It is ironical today to read that according to Olivier de Serres (*c.* 1539-1619) 'its virtues are so great and so manifold that one could properly describe it as the plant for all ills'. Snuff-taking and pipe-smoking, though common earlier in the Low Countries, were not practised in France until 1600 and by the eighteenth century they were widespread. Tobacco was available in *boudins* and *carottes* (groups of six to eight pieces of *boudins* compressed). The first *paquets de gris* appeared at the time of the Revolution, the first cigars about 1830 and cigarettes a few years later.

The cultivation, processing and selling of tobacco was subject to draconian regulations as early as Colbert's decrees in 1624, and the Farmers General maintained rights over them until in 1810 Napoleon made them into a state monopoly. Permission to grow tobacco in Périgord was withdrawn in 1810 and was not restored until 1859. The charming tobacco museum in Bergerac, which sets out much of this fascinating story, is well worth a visit. It has a representative selection of documents, snuff boxes, tobacco jars, pipes, etc.

In the past tobacco was delivered in bundles of twenty-five leaves (a *manoc*) but now the farmers are required to pack it in containers (*cajots*) which hold 25 kilos, and it is these containers which go into the heating and humidifying chambers made of stainless steel for artificial fermentation. After ten to eleven days at a constant temperature of 60 degrees centigrade and a humidity of 80 per cent they are cooled off and unpacked. The whole leaves are then fed into elaborate machines which beat them under steam in order to separate leaf and stalk and can process 230 kilos in an hour. Some tobacco is left to ferment naturally, only needing to be raked over from time to time, but the process takes six months, whereas by artificial means 250 metric tons can be dealt with in ten days or so. The leaves and stalks are then packed separately and kept in stock until bought by national or foreign cigarette manufacturers. It is they who pulverize the stalks, add them back to the leaves and torrefy – that is, roast – them. The tobacco is in fact sold by the producers and not by SEITA, which acts in an advisory capacity, giving technical help, and acting as a middle man between seller and buyer.

Agricultural life in the area is less gloomy now than it was fifty years ago. Increasing mechanization, the use of better quality seed and plants, and of course artificial fertilizers, have improved things greatly, though the amount of work required to obtain even a decent annual financial return is driving the young men from the farms and smallholdings. Of the five departments that make up Aquitaine, depopulation has been most serious in Dordogne, though happily it is now happening at a declining rate. There was a fall of 0.6% between 1962 and 1975 but since then there has been an increase of 3.5%. By contrast the working population of farmers has fallen catastrophically from 73,405 in 1962 to 27,699 in 1975 (-38%) to 23,430 in 1990 (-48%).

Government efforts to persuade farmers to trade their *parcelles* with each other in order to increase the average size of each, a process known as *remembrement*, proved slow and awkward. The implementation of the official policy was not always handled with tact and the landowners resented the fact that lawyers, surveyors and the like made money out of deals they were not in the first place anxious to conclude. Friendly exchanges were subsequently thought to be a more satisfactory way of achieving the end desired, with the government paying any legal charges involved. There is no longer any concerted effort to continue the *remembrement* policy.

Increased productivity has in fact been startlingly noticeable in the whole area. Forty years ago, farmers were still using oxen to plough; now tractors are universal and a great number of other mechanical aids are in use. It is said that the money to buy machinery such as combine harvesters comes from the tobacco crop, though harvesting tobacco itself is still largely manual. There are machines which will fell the tobacco plant and cut the notch in the stem on which to hang it to dry but they are not yet in general use. Mechanization itself without *remembrement*, while going some way towards redressing the imbalance caused by the departure of so many young, has not produced efficiency on the scale that is seen in the Ile de France or the Beauce with their huge wheatfields.

The attempt to introduce new crops such as strawberries, which do well in Dordogne, has been successful and their cultivation is intensive in the area round Vergt, a strung-out, grey little town, and Villamblard. The initial capital outlay for strawberry growing is not enormous and the fruit requires relatively little maintenance during the year. Dordogne is the second largest department growing strawberries (the first is Lot et Garonne) and responsible for 24 per cent of the country's production, with 17,500 tons sold in 1996. Vergt is one of the biggest outlets in France, and its refrigerated market hall is open 24 hours a day from March to November. The strawberries are exported to England and Germany and there is a big drive to sell them in other export markets, especially in Scandinavia, though there they have to compete with Italian produce. One of the most recent successes is the delicious Mara des Bois, which really does have a taste of a wild wood strawberry (*fraise des bois*).

Chestnuts are also a distinctive feature where the walnut does not reign supreme. There are huge groves, which must have been there for centuries, of fine trees whose spiky fruit hang glistening in starry clusters. The chestnuts yielded flour in the past which helped to supplement poor diets, particularly in years of bad harvests, and today a small amount of chestnut jam is produced, though the area is not famed for its *marrons glacés*. Many roadsides are lined with the distinctive, neatly stacked piles of chestnut logs and palings, sometimes left there for years to be used for parquet, roof timbers and sometimes for vine stakes, although acacia is more durable for the last purpose. Chestnut is particularly prized for use in house-building as floorboards or cladding for it has the great merit of not attracting wood-boring creatures.

Just over 40 per cent of the department's 9225 square kilometres is cultivated and just under a third consists of forest. On the whole reafforestation with maritime pines, Douglas firs and walnuts is greater than the de-afforestation required to make clearings for new crops or herds of cattle. Groves of poplars are to be seen all over the department; the trees grow fast, coming to maturity in twenty-five to thirty years and the wood is used for making paper, wooden casks, and roof timbers.

Modernization in agriculture – such as it is – has come relatively late to the area. The 23,430 adult males actively engaged on the land, according to the 1990 census, have an average holding of 47 acres. But despite the slowness with which mechanization has been adopted, methods have changed in the fifty years that have elapsed since Philip Oyler wrote *The Generous Earth*. Published in 1950, it remains one of the best accounts of the region written in English:

At my feet the limestone, which underlies this whole region, ended with a perpendicular cliff of 1000 feet, and I looked out over the Dordogne valley, a mile or more across, to seemingly endless hills beyond, with the wide, clear river, still in places and with mirrored spires of poplars in it, forming islands and small cascades in others. In the valley I could see countless little homesteads, innumerable plots of cultivation. Near the river itself and on the slopes adjoining were lush-looking pastures.

Up the steeper slopes were vineyards, above them woods, which reached right up to the top of the hills, wherever the sides were not too steep for a tree to find footing.

It was a panorama that spelt wealth to me, true wealth. All was bounty and beauty, God-given, and man had not desecrated it ... And as for the way our ancestors lived, there can hardly be any change. The modern mower has been introduced and the threshing drum. The spinning-wheel and loom have almost disappeared, though both were brought out during the years of war, but the ox-team still decides the tempo of life and is responsible for all the cultivation and haulage. The watermills still provide the power for grinding the corn and maize, the brick ovens are in constant use turning out good whole-meal bread, one can still see women spinning with nothing but a distaff, the teazle is still grown for carding, the mattress-maker is still in evidence, making thick soft mattresses for these peasant homes out of their own wool.

The landscape, if not the occupations, happily remains unchanged today.

Caves, Celts and Périgueux

Dordogne is not only renowned for its scenic beauty and architectural delights; it also has a well-substantiated claim, as the hoardings outside Les Eyzies so proudly proclaim, to be the 'capital of prehistory' – a description accorded to it in the later years of the nineteenth century and which subsequent discoveries, mostly in the valley of the Vezère, have not falsified.

Augustus Hare, in *South-Western France*, published in 1890, was one of the first British writers to remark on the new sites.

> *Les Eyzies* (a humble hotel near the station). In this neighbourhood is a group of the most remarkable caverns in France. Very near the station is the entrance to the *Grotte de Cro-Magnon* of the third prehistoric age, where five prehistoric skeletons have been found entire ... at 7k. N.E. is the *Grotte de la Madeleine* of the fourth prehistoric period, where an ivory tablet was found engraved with a representation of a mammoth. At 11k. is the *Grotte de Moustier*, which has given the name of Mousterienne to the first prehistoric period.

Some twenty years later Baedeker's *Guidebook for Travellers in Southern France* also talks of Les Eyzies. He describes it as a 'picturesquely placed village, surrounded and overhung by magnificent rocks. These contain a large number of Grottoes, where remarkable discoveries of bones of extinct animals, human skeletons and implements of flint and reindeer horn have been made.'

A *grotte* is now only applied to a cave, either a deep one hollowed out of the limestone and showing signs of habitation or one which has natural concretions, many in striking configurations. *Abri* is used to describe a shallower aperture which sometimes also shows evidence of man's presence. *Gisement* is used for a stratified accumulation of debris, and the word has no exact equivalent in English. All are of extreme antiquity and are of such archaeological significance that, as Hare pointed out, periods of time in the far distant past have been named from them: not only Mousterian but also 'Tayacian', 'Perigordian' and 'Magdalenian'.

The existence of some, like Combe Grenal near Domme, was known in the early nineteenth century, but their full importance did not become apparent until the explorations of Edouard Lartet and his English banker friend Henry Christy at Les Eyzies, La Madeleine, Laugerie Haute and the Gorge d'Enfer in 1862-63. The discovery of the rock shelter of Cro Magnon, made by accident in 1868 when the railway from Sarlat to Les Eyzies was being constructed, revealed the first burials ever found of upper palaeolithic man, and the name has entered the language of archaeology to describe a specific physical type, just as that of Le Moustier nearby has in describing a specific period of time. Since then more and more caves and rock shelters – in the latter of which early man actually lived – have been found, and the meticulous scholarship that has followed their revelation has been instrumental in transforming prehistory into something like an exact science.

The caves – to use the word in a more generalized sense – not only contained human and animal skeletons, a variety of stone and bone tools and jewellery (now to be seen in the local museums) but also, and most excitingly, the walls of some were covered with engravings, sculptures and paintings of breathtaking beauty. No one is sure why these works of art were created, although many archaeologists think they have a magical or ritualistic significance. For the most part, animals are represented, portrayed in a naturalistic way – though there are some humans and hands not immediately recognizable as such – and at La Mouthe there is a hut-like object whose precise meaning is unknown. The animals include horses, bison, oxen, deer, mammoths, ibex, bear and stag, and the most dramatic and splendid are to be seen in the paintings and engravings at Font de Gaume, La Mouthe, which also has rhinoceros; at Les Combarelles, where there are over three hundred; and in the sculptures at Cap Blanc, near Marquay. There is also a solitary fish, at the eponymous Grotte du Poisson near Les Eyzies, which is surrounded by a row of holes – the marks of the drill with which a covetous and not wholly honest archaeologist was preparing to remove it.

Les Eyzies de Tayac, to give it its full name, is the real centre of the 'cave country'. A small market town near the confluence of the Vézère and the Beune, it nestles under huge cretaceous limestone cliffs honeycombed with caves, many of which can be visited and all of which have some delight to offer. The museum, housed in the medieval château and imaginatively arranged, is in the course of being extended, and the town has four excellent hotels and restaurants so it makes a wonderful centre for an archaeological or speleological holiday.

But by far and away the single most important cave is that of *Lascaux*, which ranks with Altamira for containing the most stunning examples of prehistoric art, and is, alas, now closed. It was discovered by chance by some schoolboys from Montignac in 1940 and until recently was the justified object of many a tourist's pilgrimage. Unfortunately the hundreds of thousands of visitors who flocked to see the paintings and the need for electric light required the installation of air-

Les Eyzies : la Grotte d'Enfer

conditioning which, by destroying the ecosystem, resulted in the appearance of algae and moss as well as calcite which threatened to damage them. The cave had to be closed to visitors but an exceedingly ingenious and convincing replica of part of it has been created, known as Lascaux II, and well worth the visit.

The five main chambers of the actual cave are covered with an enormous number of most vigorous and attractive paintings – in manganese oxide and red ochre – of bulls, horses, deer, bison and rhinoceros. Very few tools were found in the cave, a fact which has led archaeologists to the belief that it was a ritual temple of some sort. But whatever purpose they served, they show early man to have been possessed of the very highest artistic skills.

Montignac itself has many attractive old houses on either side of the river, the remains of a castle which was virtually destroyed in 1398 by Maréchal Boucicaut (the defeated French commander at the battle of Agincourt) and an enterprising museum. The church is modern and possesses one treasure – an ivory Christ given by Louis XVI's sister, Madame Elisabeth to Bousquet, the king's surgeon. Joseph Joubert (1754-1825), whose *pensées* and letters concerned with abstract criticism are of a lucidity and profundity which rank him with Pascal, died here.

The largest decorated cave of all, near *Rouffignac*, has literally hundreds of engravings which draw huge crowds in high summer. The imposing renaissance portal on the church in the village, which was the only building to be spared when the Germans fired the village in 1944, is worth spending a little time in. The caves at

La Roque St Christophe

Pech Merle (near Cabrerets, Lot), found in 1949, have concretions and engravings which, like those at Font de Gaume, belong to the Périgordian period of approximately 35,000 BC; and those at Cougnac (near Gourdon, Lot) has three chambers with fairy-like stalactites and one with paintings of both animals and humans.

There are a number of other caves with no sign of prehistoric man but which should none the less be visited for their remarkable natural features. Le Grand Roc, Carpe Diem and Proumeyssac have extraordinary concretions – stalactites and stalagmites lit with great imagination by their owners. The underground cavern of *Padirac* (in Lot near the pilgrimage town of Rocamadour) has to be visited by boat, and its eerie beauty is highlighted by small patches of vegetation which have found their way to cluster round the electric lamps. To see that of Lacave (also in Lot) one has to travel deep into the hillside by a miniature electric train.

As there are, according to Denis Peyrony, 186 *gisements* alone, showing a wide variety of cultures, there is plenty for the enthusiastic cave visitor – well equipped with woollies, welly boots and a torch – to see, and there is a good deal of attractive and well-written literature in English on them for the more dedicated. One of the most entertaining, though now rather dated, is *The Hungry Archaeologist in France* by Glyn Daniel (1963).

If, to quote Glyn Daniel, cave paintings are the earliest art, megaliths (that is, a group of horizontal and vertical stones arranged to make chambers) are the earliest architecture. But although there is evidence of the continuity of occupation by early man from c.100,000 BC through the mesolithic era (10,000 BC), there is little to show until neolithic times (7500 BC) when stone tools, arrow heads, harpoons and burial debris are found at sites all over the department. There are few megaliths, though there are a fair number of dolmens – that is solitary stones standing as the remains of burial chambers. Far less spectacular than those in Brittany, these stones, so large that one wonders how they were moved without hydraulic cranes, still stand sentinel around the department, alas now often solitary as their fellows were pillaged to make bases for anvils as foundries increased.

Until the last century there was a circle of twelve such stones spaced equidistantly round a thirteenth at Besse, and there were twelve rows totalling 200 known as Les Peyres Brunes near Excideuil. Most of the dolmens that still exist are called Pierre Levée, Peyrelevade or Peyrebrune, and the most impressive are to be seen at Beauregard, Brantôme, Condat sur Trincou, Domme (Giversac), Nojals et Clottes, Paussac St Vivien, Rampieux, St Aquilin, Valeuil and Vitrac. Some have had Christianized myths and others magical properties attached to them: the *allée couverte* at Le Blanc near Beaumont du Périgord was said to have been built by the Virgin to shelter a shepherdess during a storm and Le Roc de Sers, near Faux, a huge millstone (4.6 metres by 2.6 metres), turned nine times by its own impetus when the angelus rang. The stones at Margaux, near Tocane St Apre, were dismantled on the orders of a sleepwalker who reported that they hid treasure.

The burial remains found in the tumuli surrounding or marked by these dolmens and in the *cluseaux* (underground passages or hiding places) have now been studied systematically and we know that neolithic man – living roughly from 7500 BC to 2500 BC – mainly lived in rock shelters (*abris*). There are traces of some of these at Les Eyzies, Commarque, Piégut, Castelmerle (near Sergeac), and at La Roque St Christophe with its staircase hewn out of the cliff.

We are on even less sure ground as we move from the neolithic into the bronze age (2500 BC) and that of iron (900 BC) knowing only that the era of great art declined as new tribes moved into the area from the south of France bringing with them the skills of cultivating wheat and barley and domesticating sheep and goats. Not until the fourth and third centuries can a name be put to these peoples – but it is an enduring one. The Celts, whose symbol was the cock, now used so distinctively on so much French merchandise and advertising, established themselves with a reasonably clear form of territorial and administrative unity for some 300 years.

Remains of Gaulish settlements – for, like Caesar, we call the French Celts Gauls – in their underground shelters and defensive earthworks exist, and the fact that the Gauls' military system slowly became more sophisticated is evident at Camp de la Boissière near Périgueux where something like a fortress has been excavated. The Gauls are known to have lived in small stone huts now called variously *bories, garriottes, causelos* or just *cabanes*, although claims that those at St André d'Allas

One of the cabanes *at St André d'Allas*

Petrocorian denarius

pre-date Roman Gaul seem fanciful, especially as the locals say that they were restored for a film, and one woman remembers her grandfather building one. Some Gaulish sculpture has been found at Condat sur Trincou; there was a sarcophagus built into the rock known as La Ribeyrie at Fongrenon and eight different types of coin from before the Roman occupation have been found.

The Petrocorii, the Celtic tribe which settled in the area during the fourth century BC, have given their name to both the province and its capital city. The Petrocorii were known to Strabo, the geographer writing at the beginning of the first century AD, for their excellence in metalwork, and indeed remains of their forges have been found. They were amongst the tribes beaten by Caesar when he mounted his invasion of Gaul in 58-52 BC. His campaigns in the region were hindered by Vercingetorix whom he finally defeated in 51 BC at the battle of Uxellodunum, the site of which is thought to be at Puy d'Issolud, Vayrac, just outside the confines of the present department. Caesar, doubtless exaggerating as usual, claims in *De bello Gallico* that he beat 5000 of the Petrocorii when they went to the aid of their leader. *Le coq s'effaça devant la louve.*

Gaul was romanized fairly rapidly, and under Augustus the central part became known as Aquitania. The area to the far south-west was inhabited by the Aquitanii tribe taking the name of Novempopulania. Aquitania was later subdivided into First and Second Aquitania, Périgueux, or Vesunna as it was then called, being in the latter; and between 16 and 13 BC it covered the area from north of the Garonne to south of the Loire. As usual the Romans maintained the administrative structure of the Gauls and there was little change from 27 BC right up to the time of Diocletian in AD 285, apart from that made in Caracalla's edict of 212 when Roman citizenship was made open to all. The distinction between the *municipium* (town) and the *colonia* (countryside) was removed and a new entity based on local peoples which combined the town and the surrounding countryside was devised under the supervision of a prefect who later took the name of count.

Unlike Provence, which was colonized by the Romans much earlier, Dordogne has relatively few Roman remains of great interest except at Périgueux from which radiated a series of roads whose traces can still be followed. Over fifty sites with Gallo-Roman foundations have so far been discovered of which those with walled enclosures (as opposed to mounds or ditches) at Le Bourdeix Puydivers and Abjat, St Méard de Dronne and St Médard d'Excideuil may be seen. The château de la Rigale at Villetoureix incorporates a Gallo-Roman tower in its walls, and there was a fine villa at Montcaret, the remains of which are well worth visiting. At present the Musée Tauziac only houses explanatory display panels, as the collection of objects excavated and collected by M. Tauziac, who left it to the state, are being scientifically examined and classified. It is hoped that they will be exhibited in the Musée in a year or so. Other objects, such as the bronze figure from Le Canet near Port Ste Foy have been found, and many of them are in the fine collection in the museum at Périgueux.

It is to *Périgueux*, Vesunna Petrocorium, that we must turn for any extensive Roman architecture. It was an honour for the city, built like Rome itself on seven hills, to be known by both names, one Roman, the other Gaulish. The city had 20,000 inhabitants who were served by the usual sophisticated Roman water supply. Water for both the public and private baths was taken from the Source de Grandfont in the valley of St Laurent sur Manoire and the hot spring of Ste Sabine; it was piped underground across the river Isle by the mill of St Claire along an aqueduct 7043 metres long. Both the aqueduct and the baths were, according to a finely inscribed tablet, given to the city by Lucius Marsullius Æternus, one of the governing magistrates (*duumvires*). The baths no longer exist, having been quarried for the medieval Château Godofre, itself destroyed in the eighteenth century.

There is plenty to admire in this city (map in inside back flap) and it makes good sense to split sightseeing into two or three circuits. It is obviously sensible to start with the Roman and Gallo-Roman remains which all lie in the lower town in the plain. The amphitheatre – known as the Arènes – was one of the largest arenas in Gaul, comparable to those at Nîmes and Arles and could seat 20,000 people. Little of it now remains as in the Middle Ages the counts of Périgord built their château de la Rolphie on the site, using its stones as a quarry. Marble statues of Diana, Hercules and Jupiter were found in it in the seventeenth century but these have all disappeared, as has the château. The central area is now a charming garden created in the nineteenth century with a little pond which delights small children.

The Porte Normande, one of the four gates of the Roman city, was originally built in the third century from stone quarried from local villas and temples but its name derives from the belief that it was burned during the Viking raids of about 841. It, and vestiges of the Gallo-Roman wall which was originally 800 metres in circumference and pierced by twenty-four towers and four gates, are all that remain of the third-century defensive fortifications.

The Tour de Vésone is just across the road; only half a stone tower 27 metres high

Stele of Claudius Placidus (Musée de Périgueux)

and 20 metres in diameter remains but that is very impressive. It may have been the *cella*, the most sacred part of a temple, built by the Romans at the end of the first century, just as Vesunna herself may have been a Celtic water goddess. This however is pure conjecture, as is the suggestion that the tower itself was once marble clad, a theory put forward because of the bronze frieze which decorated its upper reaches. It is not even certain if it was originally roofed or open to the skies (as it is today) for the Gauls to watch the auguries. Its enormous stone blocks were dismantled to be used in the construction of the defensive wall. Excavation has shown that it was surrounded by a number of buildings and that the forum, from which statues have been recovered, lay in front of it and led to another large public building to the south-west. The church of St Etienne de la Cité was built on the site of a temple of Mars with the Porte de Mars opposite.

The Château Barrière was constructed on the wall and belonged to a family of that name in the Middle Ages. It later belonged to the Abzac de Ladouze family and was refashioned during the Renaissance. After its destruction by the Protestants in 1575 it was not rebuilt.

The Maison Romaine or Villa Pompeius, just beyond the ruins of the Château Barrière, was rebuilt in the first century on foundations which revealed frescos unique in Roman Gaul for their antiquity, and continuously rebuilt over the next three centuries. The villa, typical of its kind, was built round a courtyard, and contained a series of baths, with a double staircase to the first floor. It is thought that it

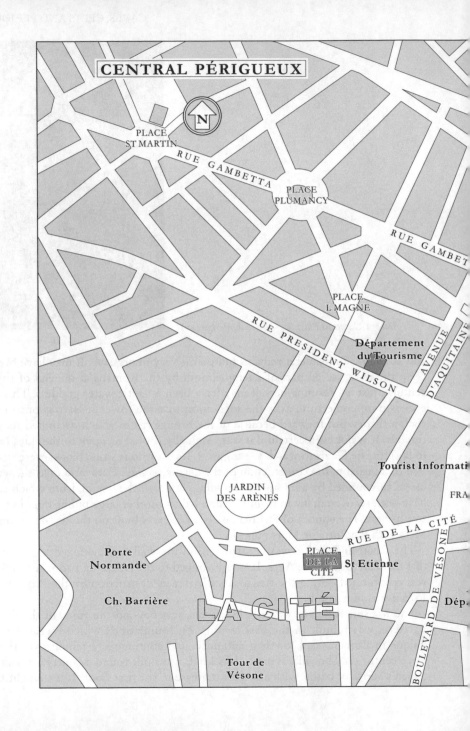

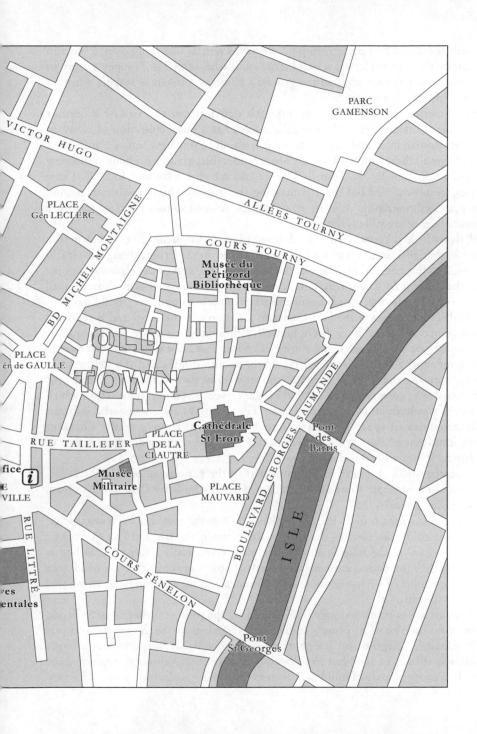

was built for Caius Pompeius Antiquus, who was not, as once supposed, a relation of Pompey the Great. He was a rich Petrocorian who served in Pompey's army in Spain and whose family adopted the general's name as a token of respect when its members became Roman citizens.

The museum, rebuilt in the nineteenth century on the site of a former Augustinian convent (hence the central cloister) has a large collection of many of the Gallo-Roman finds and fragments but it is about to undergo radical transformation because all these objects, and they are considerable, are to be rehoused in a new museum being built by the Tour de Vésone and scheduled to open in 2000. These galleries are now closed but those containing the many prehistoric objects, natural history and ethnographic collections, paintings, sculpture, odd items of furniture and some faïence are still on show.

Relatively little is known about the development of Périgueux after its destruction by the barbarians, despite having been evangelized by St Front, though it clearly continued to flourish and maintain its position until the end of the eleventh century when the present St Etienne de la Cité was built. This magnificent church, until 1669 the city's cathedral, stands hemmed rather crudely in by dreary buildings on a main traffic artery. It was the first Christian sanctuary in the town and is reported to have been consecrated by St Front himself, although his dates are so disputed it is impossible to be sure. It originally consisted of four bays in a row each surmounted by a dome, and a three-storey belfry. Three of the domes and the belfry were destroyed during the Wars of Religion and now only two of the bays remain; the furthermost was constructed at the end of the eleventh century and that by which one enters was built about fifty years later. The two bays are a wonderful contrast in the geometry of space where two cubes are treated to give totally different impressions: that of the nave is still, dark, massive and contained, whereas that of the chancel is luminous and elegant.

The nearby small chapel of St Jean attached to the convent of Ste Marthe is elegant too; it has delicate Renaissance tracery and was built by Guy de Castelnau, bishop of Périgueux in 1521.

The present isolation of St Etienne makes obvious the fact that Périgueux originally consisted of two towns – La Cité in the plain of the Isle and Puy St Front a little to the east on the hillside above. The two were deadly rivals until as late as 1240 when they decided to amalgamate in order better to protect their own interests against the counts of Périgord, the kings of France and the Church, who all wanted to control the city.

The Church was commandingly represented by the present cathedral of St Front. A chapel on the site of St Front's tomb was erected in the sixth century and was much visited by pilgrims on the route to Compostella. A new and much larger church was started in 1047 but fire destroyed most of this about a hundred years later when another spate of building, on an even grander scale, took place. This new

Cathedral of St Front (c. 1910)

building was, a rarity in Périgord, laid out in the shape of a Greek cross with five cupolas, influenced no doubt by the church of the Holy Apostles at Constantinople, and St Mark's, Venice. But what we see today is almost entirely a reconstruction carried out between 1852 and 1890 by Abadie, who subsequently became the architect of the Sacré Cœur in Paris, and his colleague Boeswillwald.

The church is enormous and has a grey coldness quite out of keeping with the warmth we have come to expect from churches in Périgord. The most impressive view of the whole ensemble is to be seen from across the Isle where the truth of Foçillon's remark that 'the domed churches of Aquitaine superimpose oriental silhouettes on Gallic horizons' becomes startlingly clear. The massive belfry rising in arcaded tiers and topped by a pine cone surmounted by a stone angel still majestically dominates the skyline. On market days it even achieves a sort of humanity when the *place* in front of it is jollied up by the gaily coloured parasols shielding the fruit and vegetable stalls.

Apart from its Roman remains and these two churches, Périgueux has many pleasures to offer. It is a bustling city which never seems overcrowded and which maintains a graceful urbanity in the midst of the calm surrounding countryside. The narrow cobbled streets in the old part of the town, now sensibly closed to traffic, are lined with small shops which have been converted to sell high-class food, clothes

Stairway, rue de la Sagesse, Périgueux

and antiques and afford constant glimpses of the town's medieval and renaissance past.

The Tour Mataguerre is the only remaining late medieval tower, and dates from 1477. Its name is reputed to derive from the eponymous captain of the English garrison at Auberoche held prisoner there for seventeen years. Round, on a polygonal base, it is crowned by machicolations and fleur de lys carvings sculpted by François Molharo.

The Moulin du Chapitre, precariously cantilevered, is one of the few other medieval buildings preserved, as is the Maison des Dames de Foi in the rue de Farges, likewise of fourteenth-century origin. It originally belonged to the Templars at Andrivaux and both Sir John Chandos and du Guesclin, after he had recaptured Chancelade from the English in 1370, were reputed to have lodged there. It was transformed into a convent in 1680, hence its name, but was closed in 1789.

The Place du Coderc takes its name from the *langue d'oc* word for pasturing, for it was a communal open space where the inhabitants raised their pigs in spite of prohibitions, repeated constantly from 1329 to 1657, because it was so insanitary in the middle of the city. Note the number of small shops throughout the department which are still run by Co(u)dercs.

Constantly attacked by the English, and gripped by endless internal disputes, Périgueux nonetheless became a prosperous city during the fifteenth and sixteenth centuries and the wealthy burgesses took to building elaborately decorated mansions as an outward manifestation of their success. Several of the houses are still intact – or at any rate have been scrupulously and recently restored to a very high standard – and most of them are carefully labelled to help you on your walk round the city. Good examples include the Maison Estignard at the angle of the place du Coderc, a fine ensemble, its door surmounted by a tympanum carved with a salamander and an interior spiral staircase; the Maison Lapeyre said to have lodged Marguerite of Navarre after her divorce from Henri IV; the Logis St Front is another Renaissance ensemble and has a good gothic doorway. The Galerie Daumesnil is an example of sensitive restoration; the Hôtel Abzac de La Douze with its octagonal towers was fortified in the fifteenth century but had earlier foundations.

On the corner of the place St Louis and rue Eguillerie is the house known as the Maison du Pâtissier with an elaborately carved doorway above which is a Latin inscription:

> Remember that you must die. Let him who likes to speak ill of the absent know that this house is forbidden to him. The greatest glory is to upset the wicked. This house built in 1518 with the good will of the All High.

Other examples of sober elegance and rich decoration can best be seen in the doorways and staircases in the rues de la Miséricorde, Aubergie, Calvaire, Sagesse and Limogeanne – all within a small area to the north of St Front. Both the Place de la Vertue and that of St Louis are charming squares and the Maison des Consuls, a sixteenth-century complex which consists of the Maison Lambert, the Maison des Consuls properly called, and the Hôtel de Lur is to be found down on the *quai*.

Périgueux obviously fell on evil days in the seventeenth and eighteenth centuries; in 1789 the population was only 5700, but by 1850 it had doubled and by 1890 reached over 30,000. The three native sons of whom the city is proudest are Lagrange-Chancel, Daumesnil, whose birthplace is in the rue de la Clarté, and the cartoonist Georges Goursat (1863-1934), who called himself SEM and whose work is displayed in the museum at La Cassagne.

SEM, self-portrait

General Daumesnil

François Joseph Lagrange-Chancel (1677-1758) was the author of rather poor tragedies on Greek themes, but is better remembered for his *Philippiques*, satirical verses on the Regent which earned him imprisonment. He lived for a time in the Hôtel de Ville, and died at Razac sur l'Isle, after escaping from the island of Ste Marguerite to which he had been banished. The Duc de St Simon said of him 'everything true or false that hell could spew forth was there expressed in exquisite verse, in the style of great poetry, and with all imaginable elegance'.

Pierre Daumesnil was also born in Périgueux, in 1776. He was one of the trio of colourful Périgordin generals who fought in the Napoleonic wars (the other two being Fournier-Sarlovèze and Bugeaud). He was the son of a Norman draper, and got into a scrape when he was sixteen, killing a soldier in a duel. He took flight to join his brother's regiment at Toulouse, and having served in Spain under General Dagobert, returned to Périgueux, where no action was taken against him. A fanatical devotee of Bonaparte, he set off with the army of Italy determined that his mission in life was to protect his hero, and indeed he saved Bonaparte's life three times during the battle of La Favorite and a fourth time at the Pont d'Arcole.

Daumesnil was also with the army in Egypt but he and a few friends insulted some officers in Cairo and, as they were still in the ranks, they were condemned to death. Bonaparte intervened and promised Daumesnil his life but when he asked for those of his friends too Bonaparte demurred. Daumesnil was forced to witness their execution but did not himself languish long in prison, for he was at the battle of Aboukir where his valour was so prodigious that he was promoted to brigadier. He saved Bonaparte's life yet again, returned to Paris with him on his flight from

71

Egypt, and fought at Austerlitz, Jéna, Eylau and in the Spanish campaign. He was promoted to colonel-major at Eckmühl, where he had two horses killed under him, and at Wagram his leg was so badly damaged that Larrey, Napoleon's surgeon, had to amputate it. Napoleon rewarded him with a sixteen-year-old wife, a directorship of the Banque de France and the position of commandant of the château of Vincennes, then both a state prison and a huge arsenal.

When in 1814 the Allies advanced on Paris, Vincennes was not attacked but after the Hundred Days the terms of the armistice stipulated that its 2 million arms were to be handed over. Daumesnil refused, saying he would rather blow them up and, despite entreaties from Talleyrand, punned that he would yield Vincennes only when his leg was given back to him: *Je rendrais Vincennes quand on me rendra ma jambe*.

He subsequently withstood a siege for 120 days, by which time the Allies gave up and the arms were left in the possession of the French. Daumesnil was relieved of his governorship by the Bourbons after Waterloo. He spent the next fifteen years in retirement but when the 1830 Revolution broke out he hastened to the barricades to be greeted by Louis Philippe: 'General, Vincennes awaits you!' Back he went, but for a short time only; cholera killed him in 1832, aged fifty-six.

It is particularly fitting that Périgueux should house one of the best small military museums in France, which despite its restricted opening hours out of season is worth some effort to see.

Churches, Castles and Bastides

There is little to link the few fine Roman ruins and the evocative but romanticized Gaulish huts we can still see in Dordogne with its crowning glory – the romanesque churches that are to be found in almost every town, village and hamlet. Nor is there much evidence of, and certainly no monument to, the intervening centuries, for they were a time of destruction and confusion. Tribe after tribe of barbarians poured into Europe from the east during the fifth century, and Aquitaine was as ravaged as the rest of Europe. In France the Visigoths were in their turn supplanted by the Salian Franks and even though their leader Clovis achieved some sort of mastery, no one is clear to which of his four sons Périgord fell after his death in 511. But the loose central control gave the dukes of Novempopulania and southern Aquitaine a free hand and during the seventh century the land between the Pyrenees and the Loire became virtually independent.

Pépin of Héristal, palace mayor of the last of the Merovingians, those kings known as *les rois fainéants*, tried to bring the dukes of Aquitaine back under his wing, but to little avail and under his successors Périgord stayed the centre of hideous conflict. Charles Martel's son, Pepin the Short, made Périgueux his head-quarters and he is reputed to have visited the monastery at Sarlat, though it is unlikely to have been in existence so early. A similar desire for prestigious origins is doubtless responsible for crediting the foundation of the abbey at Brantôme to Charlemagne himself, though he certainly did spend much time in Périgord. The early abbey buildings there, like those of Sourzac and St Astier, were destroyed by the Normans who took their marauding habits up both the Dordogne and the Isle, attacking Montpon, Mussidan and Périgueux while they were at it. Few Carolingian artefacts have been found in the department, save for some skeletons, pottery and jewellery in a huge cemetery at Bézenac. The ninth century saw relative peace and prosperity in both church and state, if such it can be called then, and gave birth to a great wave of religious foundations. Ralph Glaber, a chronicler writing in about 1047, spoke of the 'white robe of churches' that covered France and Italy, and during the next two hundred years, over a thousand churches, abbeys, priories, commanderies and preceptories were built in Périgord alone. Some were large, some were small; some are dilapidated, some are restored; but virtually every commune today has some monument to that sturdy and humane style of architecture, so expressive of the medieval spirit, that we call romanesque and the French *roman* (Roman is *romain*).

There is a dearth of information about the precise dates when the building of these churches began, or when they were rebuilt after the original foundations had been destroyed by the Normans but Paunat was consecrated between 979 and 991, St Astier was rebuilt in 1010, and by 1047 St Front at Périgueux was complete. With the exception of St Front, which stands by itself in size and its obvious derivation from Byzantine sources, there is a loose family resemblance in Périgordin romanesque though perhaps no style as distinctive as that of the Limousin or Auvergne. Most of the churches have similar plans and elevations; most have the same kind of apse and belfry; many are domed and have blind arcading; many were fortified, and all were built of the local materials that are so plentiful and which are still used today for domestic building and restoration. Their limestone glows golden in the south and rosy pink in the north and north-east from the schist and granite.

The priory at *Merlande* best exemplifies this early period of ecclesiastical building. It is isolated, tucked away in a small clearing in the Forêt Feytaud and it is reached by travelling across seemingly uninhabited and wild stretches of land. Over-hung by the trees of the forest, it stands small and quiet, witness to men who wanted to escape the cruelty and rapacity of their times. It was founded by the monks of Chancelade, eight kilometres away, but now only the church, well restored, and the ruins of some of the monastic buildings are extant. The present chancel was originally a chapel built in the mid-twelfth century, and was later enlarged by the addition of two dome-roofed bays. One of the domes was destroyed about 1170 by English troops and was replaced by broken barrel vaulting; and the church was further damaged during the Wars of Religion when the defensive outworks, still there, were constructed. The capitals in the chancel are, as so often in these churches, particularly worthy of note. The prior's house has been turned, rather charmingly, into a private residence and looks for all the world like an advertisement for a *maison secondaire*. *Chancelade* too, despite later additions and perhaps because of impeccable restoration, retains its twelfth-century feeling. An abbey founded in 1192 by a monk from Charente, it was later inhabited by Augustinian canons. As church organization developed along its own lines so did the monastic movement and the attitude towards collegiate life. Cathedral clergy, known as secular canons since they lived in their own houses on a stipend, slowly became part of monastic communities and in the eleventh century a new order of Augustinian canons was founded. They adopted a rule based on a letter to his sister by St Augustine (or one of his friends) and because they adopted a life based on a rule they became known as Regular Augustinian canons and in due course differed little from other monastic orders. They were particularly active in Périgord.

Only the lower walls of the church at Chancelade are romanesque; the five-bay nave, which originally had a broken arch vault, was re-roofed with ogee vaulting in the seventeenth century, and the flat-ended chancel, with its two bays, has frescos depicting St Christopher and St Thomas à Becket. Of the other conventual buildings there remain two towers, a gable decorated with a curly cabbage pattern, a large wash house, a barn and an abbatial building known as the Logis de Brantôme. A painting of the Flagellation of Christ, formerly attributed to Georges de la Tour but more probably by a painter of the Dutch School, hangs in the church. The village also contains one other romanesque gem – the tiny but exquisite chapel of St Jean – glowing like a topaz in the morning sun. Now deconsecrated, it was the chapel to the abbey. The exterior features are the semi-circular apse and a fine doorway surmounted by the paschal lamb. The interior consists of a nave of two bays with broken arch vaulting, and a three-bay apse with a semi-dome, which can now only be seen on winter Sundays when Mass is celebrated there rather than in the church which is too large to heat.

The Benedictine order, founded in 480, with its austere but not ascetic discipline, was the most successful and enduring form of western monasticism. Eventually its inevitable accumulation of land and wealth led to a laxity which prompted St Bernard to found a reformed order at Clairvaux in the second decade of the twelfth century. It was the monks of his order, the Cistercians, who founded the abbey of *Boschaud*, which like Merlande is tucked away, not far from the village of Villars. The name derives from Bois Creux or Bosco Cavo. Although the buildings are in a ruinous state, they have been partially restored and one can wander round at one's leisure admiring the purity of line and simplicity of design associated with the Cistercian movement. In contrast to the black habits of the Benedictines, the Cistercians wore white to emphasize their purity and such was their appeal that, by the time of St Bernard's death in 1153, 343 new houses were in existence. Their buildings reflect their aims and ideals; they are severe and little decorated.

Of the four Cistercian churches in Périgord, only Cadouin survives in anything like its original state. Boschaud is in ruins; Le Dalon, once as large as Cluny, was dismantled in 1812 and only the four chapels of the west transept and a chapter house furnished as the abbot's lodging in the seventeenth century remain; Pérouse was completely destroyed during the Wars of Religion. *Cadouin* abbey now stands on a proud *place* with its covered market in a village which was once at the crossroads of faith. Founded, as was common, in a clearing in the surrounding woods, by Robert d'Abrissel in 1115, its first abbot was Géraud de Salles. The church took only thirty-seven years to build and was consecrated in 1154. Rather curiously its style seems to have affinities with the churches of north Italy, though the textbooks link it with the style then prevailing to the north, around Angoulême or in the Saintonge.

The western façade is divided into three with a simple row of blind arcading

Cadouin in the 19th century

running across the top, and its lack of decorative devices betrays the Cistercian dislike of luxury and ostentation. The spire, with its chestnut shingles, is unusual for the district, though of a type seen on other Cistercian buildings. The interior, consisting of a nave and two side aisles is also plain and unemphatic; the modest use of palm leaf and acanthus foliage round the arches in the apse dates from the eighteenth century.

During the Middle Ages the abbey's great claim to fame and riches lay in its possession of its relic – the head shroud of Christ. The shroud – a fine linen sheet with two bands of embroidery – was reputedly discovered at Antioch by Adhémar de Monteuil, who was bishop of Le Puy and a papal legate on the first crusade. He gave it to one of his chaplains who, dying on the return journey from the Holy Land, entrusted it in turn to a Périgordin priest who on his return home took it to the chapel at Brunet, near Cadouin. A few days later and in his absence, fire destroyed the village and the chapel but the coffer containing the shroud was miraculously spared. The monks from Cadouin took it to their abbey for safe keeping and the priest, unable to bear being parted from his treasure, joined it and them and died in the abbey in about 1135. The possession of a relic of such venerable antiquity and of so personal a nature was of inestimable value to the abbey and when, over 200 years later, the monks were fearful for its safety on account of the English soldiery, it was taken to the church of Taur at Toulouse. When it was first displayed there 30,000 pilgrims flocked to see it. Arguments over its rightful ownership persisted throughout the fifteenth century; four Cadouin monks posing as scholars

The cloister at Cadouin

broke into the sanctuary at Taur and stole away with it. Despite an order from the king for it to remain at Cadouin the monks were so frightened of reprisals by the Toulousains that they hid it for seven years in the Cistercian abbey at Aubazine. The arguments raged until 1468 when it was assigned to Cadouin in perpetuity; it was to hang from the chains dangling from the vault in the apse.

The renewed prosperity of the monastery – in part aided by the return of the precious shroud – led to a new wave of building and it was in these middle years of the fifteenth century that the cloister was rebuilt. Money was forthcoming from Louis XI, Charles VIII and Louis XII and the two latters' joint queen, Anne of Brittany, and the cloister walk leading from the twelfth-century chapter house is known as the royal gallery.

The rich decorations in the cloister allude to Christian myths and include subjects from both the Old and the New Testament with imagery enriched from medieval poetry. There are four especially interesting capitals which include Lazarus and Job, and a group of satirical statues emphasizing the temptations presented by women. The abbatial gallery has some amusing sculpture depicting the monks themselves and the deadly sins. The southern gallery was entirely reconstructed in 1908 and holds little of interest except for two fine doors at either end known as the doors of France or of François I. The eastern gallery is less lavishly decorated and is not very well preserved.

As part of the religious revival that swept over Europe in the middle of the nineteenth century it is not altogether surprising that the annual pilgrimage to the abbey was re-introduced, and on 5 September 1868 10,000 pilgrims and 250 priests joined in a celebratory procession to venerate the shroud, now exhibited in the museum adjacent to the abbey. But in 1933 its authenticity was seriously questioned, and it was established from the nature of the characters on it that at least the borders must have been woven in Egypt under the Fatimids, probably during the eleventh century; a conclusion confirmed again in 1982. A particularly well-attended pilgrimage, which included a cardinal, took place in September 1933; but it was the last, for the next year the Church announced that there would be no more. It was a sad blow for many of the inhabitants of Cadouin who lost part of their means of livelihood and their resident doctors, lawyers and even their tax office. There is now, however, a Bicycle Museum (Musée de la Vélocipède) to attract new visitors.

Cadouin lies, like so many of the great abbey churches with their outlying buildings and huge living complexes, in a carefully chosen site. Proximity to water must have been the first priority; though it would seem that the proliferation of names in Périgord ending in *ac* owes more to a shortening of the common Latin suffix for places *acum* than to a contraction of *aqua* for water. New ground literally had to be broken; the forests that supplied timber for the roofs and the only fuel had to be cleared, but, however inaccessible the chosen spot might appear, the fame of the foundation spread and no community was immune from attack. Hence, during the ubiquitous building spree of the early Middle Ages, the emergence of those great fortified churches which in Périgord are in a class of their own. The villages of Trémolat and Paunat were close to the main artery of communication – the Dordogne and its valley – and both were therefore particularly vulnerable. Their churches consequently share a sobriety and lack of decoration that makes them austere, and that of *Trémolat* could even be described as forbidding.

A church was originally built there in the seventh century to commemorate the miracles which took place at the tomb of the parents of St Cybard (one of the many local anchorites) and it later fell into the hands of twelve monks from Angoulême who founded a priory in 982. The massive high belfry porch was built for the Benedictines in the twelfth century, and the classical portico was added in the eighteenth. The belfry itself was a keep and there is a huge defensive chamber in its vaulting. Measuring 350 square metres, the church could accommodate the entire population of the village as well as its monks. There are the remains of gothic frescos along the walls and the chains hanging from the chancel ceiling suspended a reliquary containing the infant Jesus' shirt.

The church is so damp and gloomy now and so difficult to heat that services in the winter are held in the tiny chapel of St Hilaire in the cemetery. This has been most elegantly restored and has modern stained-glass windows. A hand and fish glow in strong medieval colours and have a direct appeal – living proof of the strength of the post-war Catholic revival in France, and a splendid example of the best kind of contemporary art. The village is vaguely proud of them; local enquiry only elicits the response that they were made by 'an artist from Paris', whose name escapes the grocer. Perhaps it doesn't matter and the artist may be willing to share the anonymity of his predecessors, the masons who built the original chapel. But the village of Trémolat itself emerged from its anonymity when the film of *Le Boucher* was made there by Claude Chabrol (his real name), a native of Dordogne. The school, opposite the church across the square with its pollarded plane trees, is in reality no trap for a frightened schoolmistress but a functional piece of late nineteenth-century utility architecture. Just beyond the village with its charming old houses is the famous *cingle* in the river. The word derives from *cingulum*, a belt, and at Trémolat the Dordogne makes one of its swirling great loops encapsulating in it one of the most typical of the valley landscapes – strips of green and russet and gold running into the pellucid river water. There is now an attractive small marina there.

The nearby church of *Paunat* too was once part of a Benedictine abbey probably originating in the eighth century. It was given to St Martial of Limoges in 804, sacked by the Normans and re-established by Bishop Frotaire who was present at its consecration. It was modified in the fifteenth century, but remains a church built not only to glorify God but to withstand attack and succour its faithful.

Nowhere is this need for defence more massively evident than at *St Amand de Coly*. The church juts out from the hill from which it is hewn like a living embodiment of Jehovah, the Old Testament god of battles. Huge and sombre in its grandiose austerity, it is one of the most impressive of the great fortified bastions of medieval Christianity. Said to have been founded by St Amand in the seventh century, the buildings we see date from the first half of the twelfth, when the whole abbatial complex was undertaken. Its first abbot, buried in the church, died around 1124 and some time later it was occupied by Augustinian canons. The defensive porch, which is actually fourteenth century, stands out of a façade of a type unique in Périgord in which a huge arch pierced by a large window is cut out of the wall and capped by a hip-roofed defensive chamber. One gasps with astonishment as one steps out of the blazing sun reflecting on its golden exterior across the threshold to be greeted by a pale cavern. The altar lies 41 metres away up a steep slope – a rise of 4 metres from front to back – and in the fall of the year is decorated with branches of broom to celebrate the feast of St Hubert, patron of hunting and autumn sports.

Nowadays the church is less damp but the cool cavern has lost none of its powers of surprise, with an occasional mossy pillar soaring up to the dome above the crossing. The modern stained-glass windows, made up in delicate pale colours to a simple geometric pattern, have been, as in so many of these restored churches, thoughtfully designed to harmonize with and enhance the severe but sophisticated perspective. The church has remarkable acoustic qualities, though with too long a reverberation

St Amand de Coly

period to please professionals, as one can discover by intoning a little private plain-song or happening upon a portable organ being tuned up in preparation for one of the concerts which have now become a regular event throughout the summer season. It is pleasing to find music being worshipped as a new religion, and the abbatial buildings housing numerous small craftsmen and artisans.

Amongst the other fortified churches, those at both *Grand Brassac* and *St Privat des Près* also excite admiration. The former, huge outside and surprisingly small inside, was built in the twelfth and fortified in the thirteenth century. It has a single nave surmounted by three domed openings and fine sculpted figures of various dates over the side porch, but maintains its fortress-like appearance. St Privat is one of the finest domed romanesque churches in Périgord. Its impressive and harmonious saintongeais façade has an upper row of blind arcades and is pierced by a massive doorway with nine rows of recessed arcades. It was noted in the cartulary of St Saure in 1108 as a Benedictine priory, and its fortification was doubtless due to its geographical position on the borderland between Guyenne and Angoumois rather than to its proximity to the river.

In general, these Périgordin churches have a single nave and are rectangular, though Paunat and Trémolat are in the shape of a Latin cross (St Front is unique in being in that of a Greek cross); and out of 600 churches only four have side aisles. Barrel vaulting predominates and there are innumerable domes, supported on pendentives and squinches, which vary in diameter from 2 to 15 metres. The roofs, supported by oak or chestnut beams, were originally covered in the stone tiles known as *lauzes*, though today many of them have been re-roofed with terracotta or slate tiles.

The decoration on the whole is simple and nearly always architectural rather than sculptural. Such sculpture as there is is to be found round the arches, exceptionally round an elaborate doorway, and in capitals and corbels. In these animal and vegetable imagery are frequently intertwined in convoluted and, to us, often meaningless combinations, though when, rarely, they depict the human figure their vigour and gaiety are overwhelming.

A rare and exceptional example of this decoration is to be found in the church of St Martin at *Besse* down in the south of the department, between Prats du Périgord and Villefranche (not to be confused with the smaller Besse, a village to the west of the main road from Périgueux to Villeneuve sur Lot). It lies hidden away once again in a thickly wooded valley. It is small and the very antithesis of severe, and is unusual in that its belfry porch has a highly worked and decorated portal. The doorway is flanked by a pair of pillars on each side, each supporting carved capitals and there are two rows of sculpture in the arches above. The lower row, rising from two rampant beasts on the left, consists of decorative leaves with a crude paschal lamb in the centre. The upper row is full of lively figures carved in a rustic style: St Peter and Isaiah, Adam and Eve naked before the fall and clothed after, St Eustace as a horseman shooting a stag bearing Christ between its horns, the Virgin and Child, and St Michael slaying the dragon jostle one another in friendly pursuit of their aim: to represent man's sinfulness and redemption through the intercession of the angels and Christ's mother. The nave combines eleventh- and twelfth-century work but the transept and choir were added in the sixteenth century.

The church at Besse shares with that at *Bussière Badil* its decorative features but in other respects Bussière Badil could hardly be more different; it is situated in the middle of the town, it is large and pinkish and very unlike the majority of Dordogne romanesque churches. Founded in the eleventh century by Benedictine monks from the abbey of Cluse in Piedmont, it was extensively restored in the fifteenth century when the Pompadours, who furnished several local bishops, added their armorial bearings to the carvings of soldiers and page boys in the decoration. The sculpted capitals are of particular interest as are those at *Cénac*, where there is a fine and interesting church set just outside the town on the road to St Cybranet. It was founded by Aquilanus, Abbot of Moissac about 1090, as a priory and built in the twelfth century. Its prior was excommunicated by Bertrand de Got (Pope Clement V) when archbishop of Bordeaux in 1304 for refusing him entry. The main apse is harmoniously counter-balanced by minor apses, and a small round tower rises graciously between them. The nave and transepts are heavily

The church of St Martin, Besse

restored but the capitals in the chancel are very splendid. The corbels are more elegant than usual and the moulding is delicate. There are thirty of them and the sculptures are of a different order from those at Besse. More refined and displaying greater technical skill, they include a fine bestiary of lions, birds, rabbits, monkeys and Old and New Testament scenes including Daniel in the lion's den and the raising of Lazarus.

Among the hundreds of other romanesque churches virtually all have some attractive feature and most are worth looking at if one has the time, taste and inclination; only a few will disappoint and, despite the enthusiasm of purists and the historians, *St Avit Sénieur* is one such. Even with a fine autumnal sun warming its venerable stone, the presence of elderly black-clad villagers sobbing round a funeral cortège only added to the gloomy and depressing first impression it made.

Perhaps it was this, and the fact that it was never completed, together with the poor nineteenth-century restoration that left me feeling disappointment. Of course it is of interest and others may find it more to their liking. The altar was consecrated in 1117 by Guillaume d'Auberoche, Bishop of Périgueux, and the body of St Avit, a soldier turned hermit after whom it was named, was moved from his tomb nearby into the church a year later. In 1295 it became a chapter for the Augustinian canons, and it was fortified in the fourteenth century. In the fifteenth it was annexed to the abbey of St Cyprien and in 1685 became attached to Sarlat cathedral. Only the two massive square towers and the sentry path inside the church remain of the fortifications and the only evidence of the former abbey to be seen is the ruins of a cloister and part of a chapter house.

By contrast, the church at *La Chapelle St Robert* has peculiar charm. It seems deserted and, though it is in the village, the grass grows up to its walls – sad because it has a simple and sturdy beauty worth restoring. It was founded by Benedictine monks from the magnificent church of Chaise Dieu in Auvergne on land given to them by a rich bourgeois, Frotaire de Terrasson, and dedicated to one of their brethren who died in the odour of sanctity. It has a fine two-storey bell tower which dominates the sleepy village. Today the area round it and the neighbouring town of Javerlhac is a haven of peace and a centre for fishing since the river Bandiat is unpolluted. It used however to be the home of many foundries and that of La Chapelle St Robert was one of the most important metallurgical establishments in France, supplying the naval station at Rochefort.

The beauties of *St Léon sur Vézère* are even more congenial, with quiet streets, an enchanting manoir and a fine château. The church is the very acme of perfection. It is built on a flat spur, practically in the river Vézère, and stands, reflected and reflexive, like a defenceless younger sister to the weighty St Amand de Coly. A Benedictine priory church, belonging to the abbey in Sarlat, it was built on the ruins of a Gallo-Roman villa from which coins and burial objects have been excavated. The most striking feature of the church is the exquisite balance of its proportions;

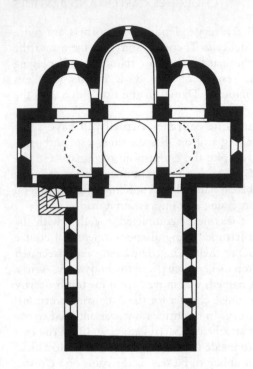

Plan of St Léon sur Vézère

entirely harmonious, the square belfry, topped by a stone-capped spire, surmounts the crossing of two small transepts, the wide flat-roofed single nave and a three-bay apse. The east end, seen through the pelargoniums on the terrace of the facing house and the lime trees, with its combination of honey-coloured stone and dark roofs is an object lesson in solid geometry. Never have the square, the cylinder, the circle, the cone and the trapeze seemed more enchanting.

The interior too is simple, achieving its results with little decoration and relying on vistas framed by a rectangular proscenium of rounded arches of varying sizes. Little disturbs the contemplative calm, though fugitive frescos still remain on the chancel ceiling, and a few well placed stone sculptures have been ranged round the walls. The god of battles has laid down his sword and taken up a golden slide rule.

A curiosity is to be found in the small chapel in the cemetery. An inscription in occitan over the door refers to the occasion when a servant, passing, fired an arrow at the crucifix standing at the entrance and promptly dropped dead but with his head turned back to front. This was in 1233. In 1890 a tomb excavated by the local archaeological society was found to contain a skeleton with the skull turned back to front.

Of the small beauties four may be singled out. *Carsac* is a very fine twelfth-century church, particularly well restored in the early 1940's. It contains not only good capitals and a powerful Blakeian carving of God the Father over the door to the sacristy, but interesting modern stained-glass windows, and stations of the cross carved by Léon Zack to a text by Paul Claudel. The domed church of *Chenaud*, on the banks of the Dronne, consecrated in 1100, has a square bell-tower and trefoil apse. It was a priory dependant on the abbey of Baignes. The decorations are remarkable, though the façade and nave are nineteenth-century restorations. Note the renaissance-style pulpit, dated 1651.

The fortified church at *Cherval* has a single nave surmounted by four domes and a solid, even heavy, belfry. The bareness of the exterior is in contrast to the inside decorations (though the north chapel is modern) and the area between the vaulting and the domes served for a hiding place and defensive post. The church at *La Chapelle Gonaguet*, also of twelfth-century foundation, was heavily restored in both the fourteenth and sixteenth centuries and is also of note for the fact that Victor Hugo makes Jean Valjean in *Les Misérables* sojourn here.

Building on a huge scale in the eleventh and twelfth centuries was not of course confined to churches and abbeys. While the Capets, the first true kings of France, were concerned with consolidating their hold on the crown and the lands in and around the Ile de France which constituted the royal desmesne, the local bold bad barons were doing the same nearer home, and that meant building castles.

The complications of the succession to the county of Périgord from Wilgrin (d. 886), Aldoin, to Guillaume Taillefer and his nephew Bernard, with bastards and legitimate sons gouging each other's eyes out, incarcerating or murdering each other, make tedious and nauseating reading. But one of them, Adalbert, has a place in all French history books, for it was he who, while besieging Tours in 990, replied to the newly elected king's question, '*Qui t'a fait comte?*' with the pert answer, to which Hugh Capet is not known to have responded, '*Qui t'a fait roi?*' But nothing remains to show us how Adalbert and his peers lived in Périgord, for documentary evidence for the early *châteaux forts* (fortresses – as opposed to the châteaux – which really have no equivalent in English) in south-west France is scant and none actually exists for any building before 1100. It is interesting to note that for the pre-1200 period only 110 castles are known to have existed in the whole of Gascony whereas there were 70 in the much smaller area of Burgundy before 1186.

Aquitaine was one of the six great feudatories owing homage to the king of France and it was the strength of this bond that exacerbated the struggle between the Capets and the Plantagenets, as each sought to extend their domains. The counties of Maine and Anjou, to the north of Périgord and beyond Poitou, were consolidated early in the twelfth century by Fulk the Young and inherited by his son Geoffrey, who earned the sobriquet of 'Plantagenet' from the sprig of broom he wore in his helmet. In 1127 Geoffrey married Henry I of England's daughter

Matilda, the widowed empress. On Henry's death in 1135, his only son having drowned in the White Ship, his grandson Stephen claimed the throne of England, but Geoffrey pressed his wife's claim to Normandy and to the English throne. Of the rival claimants Stephen won but he agreed that he should be succeeded by Henry and Matilda's son, Henry. On Geoffrey's death in 1151 Henry succeeded to the counties of Anjou, Maine, Touraine and Normandy and a year later he married Eleanor of Aquitaine.

It was a bad day for the Capetian monarchy – and for Périgord. Eleanor, brought up at her troubadour father's court in Bordeaux, had been married at fifteen to Louis VII in 1137, had been on crusade with him and had borne him only two daughters. She found his piety little to her taste, and the pope was persuaded to annul the marriage on grounds of consanguinity. She took with her to Henry, only two months after her divorce, not only her vivacity, cultivated tastes and pugnacity, but also the duchies of Guienne and Gascony, viscounties and counties - including that of Poitou - and overlordships of virtually the whole of the south-west of France. With his own inheritance and this marriage, which was to be so turbulent, Henry became the largest landowner in France but, by the legal niceties of the time, when in 1154 he became king of England, he owed homage to the king of France for all his French possessions. Louis, maintaining that Henry had not sought, as his vassal, permission to marry nor answered his summons to appear at court, declared Henry's French property forfeit and him a rebel. In due course Louis renounced his

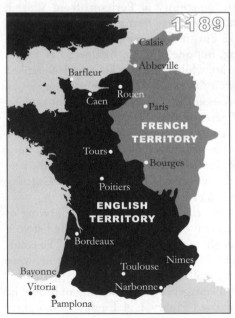 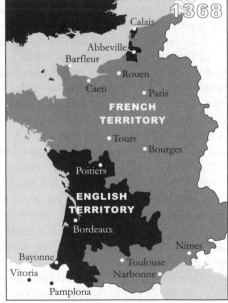

claim to the duchy of Aquitaine, which included Périgord, and in 1169 Henry gave it to his son Richard, then aged twelve. Richard and his mother Eleanor ruled the duchy from 1169-73, a period during which all Henry's sons were in rebellion against him and when many of the skirmishes took place in Périgord.

In the meantime the counts of Périgord had been pursuing much the same policy as their kings; they succeeded in establishing their hereditary title and increased their land holdings through marriage. Hélie III (1086-1104) was succeeded by his brother Adalbert III, whose sons Guillaume Taillefer and Hélie IV were followed by Boson III. Their fortunes were inextricably mixed with the Anglo-French struggles for supremacy and they sided with both kings at various times.

Philippe Auguste succeeded to the French throne in 1180 and upheld Henry's sons in their continuous revolt against their father. Henry's eldest surviving son, Henry Courtmantel, the Young King, died in 1183 in a house still to be seen in Martel, a charming town in nearby Lot, and Richard Cœur de Lion became his father's heir. Richard, hated throughout Aquitaine for his ruthlessness and acts of terrorism, fought both his father and later the French king, with whom he was at war when, in 1199, he was killed at Châlus (just outside Périgord) by an arrow shot, it is said, by a man from Gourdon. He was succeeded by his brother John, known from his youth as 'Lackland' since his father did not make over territories to him as he had to his brothers. John continued the feud with Philippe and proceeded to lose Normandy, Anjou, Maine and Touraine – thereby *earning* his sobriquet – though he managed to keep Aquitaine for the English crown. Archambaud I, Hélie V's successor as the count of Périgord, continued the policy of changing sides and did homage to the French king for the county in 1212 and to the English king in 1214.

When Henry III succeeded John in 1216 he was only nine years old and it was not until 1224 that he felt strong enough to demand the restoration of the lands confiscated from his father. Louis VIII, who became king of France in 1223, replied by invading the lands Henry still held and by 1226 the English were deprived of all save only Gascony and Bordeaux. Warfare continued, broken by occasional truces and treaties, until 1259 when the Treaty of Paris was signed, resulting in thirty-five years of peace.

The confusion of terms like Aquitaine, Guyenne and Gascony may be worth a small digression, at least to describe Gascony. Professor Maurice Beresford has made it elegantly clear:

> The name Gascony derived from the Vascons who plundered and settled an area extending north from the Pyrenees almost to the Garonne. Its history in early medieval times is obscure. In the period after the break-up of the Carolingian empire it was ruled by an independent line of dukes who annexed the counties of Bordeaux, Agen and Bazas, though never very securely. This duchy of Gascony was

united during the eleventh century to the duchy of Aquitaine which was centred upon Poitou, and these united duchies were inherited by Eleanor. After Henry's accession to the English throne, the kings of England ruled (in so far as they did 'rule') the territory of Gascony as dukes of Aquitaine.

For administrative purposes in the late twelfth and early thirteenth centuries their duchy was divided into Gascony in the south and Poitou in the north, and when Poitou was lost to the French only the southern territory (and not all of that) was left to Henry III as king-duke. The treaty of 1259, in which Henry accepted the loss of Poitou, acknowledged and gave currency to the name 'duchy of Aquitaine' for those territories which still remained subject to him in the south.

Although the style of Edward I was always 'duke of Aquitaine', contemporaries tended to use 'Gascony' to describe all the lands that he held in south-western France. Thus the rolls in the English chancery that recorded the letters relating to southern France were called 'Gascon Rolls', and the wine that came to England from Bordeaux and Bayonne was called Gascon also.

It was during the troubled period from 1216 to 1337, which has been called the first hundred years war (as distinct from the Hundred Years War which started in 1337), that at least a thousand castles were built in Périgord, all on rocky heights dominating strategic positions on roads and rivers. But only a handful remain in Dordogne and these were mostly enlarged or rebuilt later. The only extensive twelfth- and thirteenth-century remains of *châteaux forts* are to be seen at Castelnaud, Beynac and Biron.

The château of *Castelnaud* lowers above one of the most magnificent stretches of the Dordogne, its silhouette the very epitome of military power in early medieval times. How uncomfortable life must have been in those days of constant if intermittent warfare, and how many men, one wonders, must have toiled up the cliff with blocks of dressed stone to complete this powerful fortress. Its history, like that of Beynac facing it across the river, is inextricably mixed up with the English occupation. Taken by Simon de Montfort in 1214, retaken by its seigneur in 1215, burnt by the archbishop of Bordeaux, it was 'lent' to the Duke of Aquitaine after the Treaty of Paris, provided that he would give it up or have it destroyed should the King of France so wish. He clearly did so wish, and very soon, for in 1262 Henry III had to install himself at Castelréal instead of at Castelnaud; and by 1310 Edward I was complaining that it was being used by the French king.

It was inevitable, given its strategic position, that the château should remain the centre of argument and that it should suffer from the endless squabbles between the two rival owners but by the sixteenth century and the Wars of Religion it became the setting for a tale Alexandre Dumas would have been hard put to invent.

Geoffrey de Caumont, a younger son of the house, had gone into the church and become abbot of Clairac in Agenais. His sympathies however lay with the Huguenots and on the death of his elder brother he inherited the family property and left the church. He moved to Castelnaud in 1572 and died there, poisoned by mushrooms. His wife, Marguerite de Lustrac, always known as Mme la Maréchale (because of her previous marriage to the Maréchal de St André) gave birth to his daughter Anne some three months later and her godfather was Geoffroy de Vivans (see page 101).

As one of the richest heiresses in France, her elder brother having died, it was inevitable that Anne should herself become the subject of conflict. Her aunt had married the Sire de Cars, a staunch Catholic, and it was he whom Henri III designated as the girl's guardian. Jean de Cars was therefore anxious that his son, the Prince de Carency, should marry Anne but the seigneur of Biron also had his eye on her. Learning from servant informers at Castelnaud that the castle was undefended, Jean de Cars simply arrived and kidnapped the child. She was forcibly married to the prince at the tender age of seven and, despite complaints by her mother at the royal tribunal in Paris, the marriage was held to be valid. Five years later, the young husband, now aged eighteen, was challenged to a duel in Paris by the equally young Charles de Biron and killed. Anne was a widow at twelve. Jean de Cars, nothing daunted, immediately suggested that she should marry his second son. But this time Mme la Maréchale, supported by Geoffroy de Vivans and the Duc de Mayenne, also after the unfortunate girl's fortune, was able to prevent it. The girl was seized by force once again, from the château of La Vauguyon, and married to Mayenne's son in Paris. He was only nine! The arguments continued until Henri III sent Anne to the Duchesse de Nemours to be looked after, where in the deeply religious atmosphere of the princess of the house of Lorraine, she became a Catholic. Kidnapped for a third time at the age of eighteen, Anne was married, for the third time, to François d'Orléans, Comte de St Pol.

But happiness was not to be hers. The count was wildly extravagant and Anne left him, taking with her the son of this union. A page to Louis XIII, the boy was killed at the siege of Montpellier and his distraught mother founded and retired to the convent of the Filles de St Thomas. Her mother disinherited her and Castelnaud was given to her nephew Jacques de Caumont, thereby enabling it to remain in the Caumont La Force family.

The château has been extensively – and expensively – restored in recent years and now contains the second most important collection of arms and armour in France. All are magnificently displayed with clear captions and many of the weapons and military siege equipment have been put back into working order. In high season there are realistic demonstrations with visitor-participation.

Beynac, home of one of the four baronies of Périgord, glares across the river at Castelnaud, challenging from its own dominating heights its rival, with whom it has shared a known existence and similar history since the twelfth century. It belonged to the Beynac family and was seized in 1195 by Richard Cœur de Lion who gave it to a particularly brutal captain, Mercadier. It then became the subject of endless disputes, lying as it did on the frontier between the English and the French and it was partially demolished in 1214 by Simon de Montfort who took it since its owners were suspected of Albigensian sympathies.

But despite being the scene of constant warfare right through the Wars of Religion much of it still stands, a huge complex, within a curtain wall, standing proud above the river – another example of elaborate thirteenth-century military architecture.

Inside, the château has undergone extensive restoration, or rather, in most cases, as the guides freely and rather disarmingly admit, reconstruction. But it has been done scrupulously, with the constant guidance of the Beaux Arts. On their advice, a wooden spiral staircase has been reconstructed. Made from slabs of solid fifty-year-old oak, it took eight years to make, and each step, both tread and riser, is sculpted so that no newel post is required. The cobbled floors, known as *pisé*, have similarly been replaced with care. Each stone, 15 x 20 centimetres, came from a site in Périgueux known to be of fourteenth-century origin. The Salle des Etats (so called because it was where the Périgordin Estates, a local parliament, met), is impressive, and there is a curious fifteenth-century fresco in a small oratory leading from it. The kitchens too have been restored. Part of the château was rebuilt in the seventeenth century and the rooms, some of which have interesting new stained-glass windows of local people and scenes, are now on view. Apart from state and departmental subventions, which have been enormous over the last twenty years, many of these restorations are in part financed by film companies who find the settings irresistible for costume dramas.

The village church and that of nearby *Cazenac* are also of interest as is the Parc archéologique which houses a reasonably convincing recreation of the daily life of peasants from the neolithic period to 50 BC.

Less well known, but worth an expedition, are the ruins of the château of *Commarque*, near Marquay on the Beune. Plans are afoot to open it to the public. At the beginning of the twelfth century Gérard de Commarque gave all his goods, including the castle, to the Templars. Subsequently it came into the hands of the Hospitallers who enlarged it and later sold it to the baron of Beynac, who gave it to one of his sons. By 1406 it was in English hands. There is some disagreement as to how it finally came to be destroyed; the king called for its demolition in the sixteenth century, but local legend has it that it was destroyed by fire. However it was destroyed, the present ruins give a good idea of its huge size and brooding power. Its dominance is enhanced by the view from its gaping windows of the small

Beynac

château of Laussel across the valley, which, restored and inhabited, tranquilly maintains its privacy and domesticity.

It is difficult to know whether the château of *Biron* should be considered primarily a medieval or a renaissance building, but its well-documented early history justifies its inclusion here. The great castle looms over its charming small village, with an interesting little church, Notre Dame du Bourg. An imposing pile, despite Viollet Leduc's restoration work in the last century, the château is of interest partly because so much of it is still extant and partly because it is so enormous. At the confines of Périgord and Agenais, it perches on a rock surveying a wide horizon. Mention is made as early as 1076 of a castle on the site belonging to the Gontaut family. The Albigensians took it in 1211 and, when it was re-taken by Simon de Montfort in 1214, Martin d'Algais, one of John Lackland's captains, was killed and brutally dragged round the village by his heels. In 1222 Louis VIII gave it back to the Gontaut family, whose seigneur, Henri, played the English and French off against each other. From 1239 to 1294 it was in Plantagenet hands.

The square tower overlooking the lower courtyard and the staircase gateways date from this early period; Simon de Montfort destroyed the keep. The importance of its position made it of strategic value during the Hundred Years War, and from 1345 when Derby took it for the English, it see-sawed back and forth between the two kings. The last assault took place in 1463 and allowed the Gontauts, fourteen generations of whom lived there, to pursue more pacific ends and rebuild with fewer interruptions. There had been some additions in the fifteenth century, but the renaissance wings put up by Pons de Gontaut virtually doubled the existing château, and in the seventeenth century yet another wing was added. To walk round Biron is to undergo a visual history of architecture in the most painless way.

Head of the oldest of the four seigneuries of Périgord, Biron's lord was the premier baron of the province. Armand de Gontaut-Biron, its most distinguished owner, was very much the new man of the Renaissance. His career and his sympathies with (though not belief in) the Protestant religion were formed when he went as a boy to François I's sister, Marguerite, at the court of Nérac. He quickly rose in the army, for he was a brave and dashing soldier and distinguished himself in the Italian campaigns. He was wounded in the foot at the siege of Fort Mézin and limped for the rest of his life. He kept very detailed notebooks of his military experiences and wrote treatises on the art of war, which became well known under the title of *tablettes du boîteux*. Although his Huguenot sympathies earned him disfavour amongst the extreme Catholics, he was protected by Catherine de Medici and was an ideal person to negotiate peace terms with the King of Navarre. He was made governor of La Rochelle, a marshal of France in 1577, and lieutenant general of Guyenne. He served with Henri IV at the battle of Ivry in 1590 and was killed

Charles de Gontaut-Biron

dramatically two years later at the siege of Epernay by having his head blasted off by a cannon ball in 1592. Though his progress through life appears to have been that of any run-of-the-mill career-soldier, he was of a different stamp from most of his peers. Essentially a humane and intelligent man, he was not, according to Brantôme, a cold-blooded killer, and 'though the perfect warrior, he was a man of the world'.

Armand's son, Charles, also came to a nasty sort of end but by less glorious means. He too had a successful military career, and became a marshal of France, and governor of Burgundy, and in 1598 Henri IV elevated his barony to a duchy. But Charles became involved in a plot with the Spanish in Milan against Henri IV to whom he was betrayed. The king offered to pardon him if he confessed, but he refused and was beheaded at the Bastille in 1602.

The tombs of two members of the family are now to be seen in the chapel, which was built on two floors in the early sixteenth century. The lower church was used by the villagers and the upper was for the exclusive use of the family. It is a fine renaissance building and the tombs – of Pons de Gontaut, who erected the chapel, and his brother Armand, who was Bishop of Sarlat – are magnificently sculpted and wrought. It is sad that the two other gems of the Biron family, a pietà and entombment by a Périgordin artist, should now be in the Metropolitan Museum, New York.

Permission to build the chapel at Biron was obtained by Pons when he was in Italy from Pope Alexander VI, who addressed his bull to the abbots of nearby Cadouin. Subsequent generations of the family included two more marshals of France, one of whom went to the guillotine in 1793. The château now belongs to the department.

Although not strictly medieval, the château of *Bonaguil*, just beyond the southern tip of the department, near Fumel, deserves a special mention. Dubbed the *château fou*, it is the epitome of the fortified castle and feudalism's swan-song. In 1477, its creator, Bérenger de Roquefeuil swore an oath that he would 'build a castle which neither my villainous subjects could take, nor the English either if they should have the audacity to return, nor even the most powerful soldiers of the King of France'. He spent the next forty years doing just that and built a castle so impregnable that no one ever even tried to take it. Consequently it remains in a perfect state of preservation and is of the greatest possible interest because it embodies every form of defensive military device then known, with, as it were, knobs on. One of the great pleasures when visiting the castle is the way in which the guides pretend that one is part of an invading army.

Of other châteaux, *Montfort*, perched like an eagle above its own *cingle*, looks romantic enough from a distance but being mostly a nineteenth-century reconstruction loses much of its credibility at close quarters. It is no loss that visitors are no longer allowed in even to see the good Louis XIII furniture in the interior, but a walk round the ramparts might be considered worth it for the view alone. (The infamous Simon de Montfort, who led the crusade against the Albigensians in the twelfth century and who died at the siege of Toulouse in 1219, should not be confused with his third son, also called Simon and also Earl of Leicester, who headed the baronial revolt against Henry III of England.)

The château of *Fayrac* also preserves a fairy-tale aspect, lying low in a bend of the Dordogne, feminine and cosy as it faces the grim virility of Beynac, guarding its privacy with success. Remains of the fourteenth-century buildings are extant in the interior courtyard reached by a drawbridge, and it is these late medieval, albeit restored, aspects that the motorist sees. There is also a restored pavilion in the classical style not visible from the road.

Châteaux and churches, remarkable and numerous though they are, are not the only architectural delights the province has to offer, for the late thirteenth century saw a new building phenomenon in the region.

Périgord, for so long a frontier area during the years of the English occupation of Gascony, is particularly notable for having a number of well-preserved *bastides*. The reasons for the creation of these towns in the department and its near neighbours to the south and west between 1250 and 1350 have now been established as economic rather than defensive. The name is derived from the word *bâtir* – to build – rather than from one with more military connotations. Some 140 of these 'new towns' were built or planned during that century and some, including one of the best preserved, are still to be seen in Dordogne. They form a distinct group of towns all laid out on the same clearly defined plan. Many of them were built by

Louis IX's brother, Alphonse de Poitiers, and many by Edward I, who found them a useful way of both augmenting his revenues and increasing his political power. With the growing importance of the wine trade in the area and the higher degree of agricultural specialization it entailed, market towns were of great economic use and their creation afforded an opportunity for rural serfs to escape from feudal bondage into relative freedom.

The sites chosen for these new towns were always in areas where the land, though not previously cultivated, was suitable for exploitation. It was acquired by the king or his agent from its owner, lay or ecclesiastic, by an act known as *paréage*, whereby they became co-seigneurs. The prospective inhabitants were tempted by privileges and franchises and they were also directly protected. The seigneurs, who could in return reasonably count on their support, could hope to augment their power and, in due course, their revenues. Obviously only ambitious and hard-working people would be willing to break new ground and the whole enterprise was an expression of economic vitality.

The intention of establishing a new town – many of which were quite simply called Villefranche or Villeneuve – was announced by a public crier, and accompanied by trumpet fanfares; the herald would describe the site and list the privileges to be accorded. These were considerable, and the English were more generous than the French. In many cases, though not in all, one of the most attractive was exemption from military service – at least for ten years while the site was being developed. The inhabitants were required to build the town with their own hands, local materials being made freely available to them. Planning permission was strict and uniform; the gridiron pattern ensured both the best and fairest allocation of space, for each family was given an identical plot within the town, at its extremities (for a kitchen garden) and in the surrounding countryside (for cultivation). Of course the grid pattern had to be flexible to cope with the contours of the site. The houses, mostly built of wood, were in general the same shape and size although the seigneur might reserve a larger one for himself in the central square. Houses were separated by gaps, known as *androntes*, sometimes only 25 centimetres wide, which not only made the most economical use of space but also served to reduce the fire hazards.

Four large main streets, crossed and paralleled by smaller ones (known as *ruelles* or *carreyrous*), ran the length of the town to the main gates. The church, usually of a fair size, and the administrative offices would be placed in a large central square which was ringed by a row of merchants' houses with galleries (known as *cornières*) and contained a covered market place. Trading rights were carefully regulated and each town was assigned its own weights, measures and currency. Iron, copper, cloth, leather and medicines were the main commodities apart from agricultural produce and there were weekly markets. Weighing scales for grain, walnuts and chestnuts can still be seen at Villefranche du Périgord and Monpazier, and the building which housed the mint is still in existence at Domme. Each town elected its

Eymet – a typical bastide

own governing body of *jurats* and had its scribe. It is from the constant written applications to both kings' representatives that we discover that requests for fortification came mainly from the local inhabitants. The Gascon Rolls (in the Public Record Office in London) are a prime source of information for this medieval period of Périgordin history. Many guide books still persist in claiming that the aims of the founders of the *bastides* were primarily military despite a great deal of recent research which conclusively proves this not to be so. Most of this evidence is too detailed to go into here but one of the most telling facts is that few towns were fortified before 1279 and in some cases it took as long as forty to seventy years before the seigneurs built anything resembling ramparts on the outer ditches.

This confusion is analogous to that in even the most up-to date tourist literature which, in the matter of which château or which town belonged to whom – English or French – at any given time, blatantly contradicts itself. It seems a matter of little concern for the casual visitor to do more than be aware that they changed hands frequently. C. Petit Dutaillis said, with some accuracy, 'English Gascony, with its quarrelsome archbishop and bishops, its pillaging nobility, its towns jealous of their liberties and riven with internecine factions, presented a picture of anarchy which the English government was unable to quell, but it resisted all French interference.'

This 'anarchy' is evident when one tries to establish a clear picture of the details of ownership and loyalties of the many seigneurs and their new towns. However, there is no disputing who founded which *bastide*. On the French side sixteen, most of them actually outside the strict confines of the present department, were created by Alphonse de Poitiers. Alphonse, born in 1220, was Louis XI's third brother, and in 1237 he married Jeanne, the only daughter of Raymond VII, Count of Toulouse. His grandfather, Raymond VI of Toulouse, had acquired Agenais (in which Ste Foy was situated), Rouergue and Quercy on his marriage to Henry II of England's daughter, another Jeanne, to whom they had been given as a dowry. Alphonse, therefore, on his father-in-law's death, acquired the title to these areas and the county of Toulouse, as well as to the counties of Poitou and Auvergne which his brother gave him as an *apanage* – that is, a grant of land to a member of the royal family on terms of relative independence. The Treaty of Paris had stipulated that if Alphonse and Jeanne were to die childless – which they did, of plague in 1271 within a few days of each other at Genoa on their return from the Tunisian crusade – their properties should revert to the duchy of Aquitaine, that is to the English crown. It took eight years for Agenais (included in the area to revert under the Treaty of Paris) to be returned to the English, but when in 1279 it was handed over, of course the Alphonsian *bastides* then changed hands too.

Monflanquin, Villeréal (Lot et Garonne) and Villeneuve d'Aveyron (Aveyron) have few interesting remains though they are pleasant towns. Of those within Dordogne, St Louis has nothing, Castillonès is heavily and hideously restored and Villefranche du Périgord retains its *halle*, its measuring utensils and some of its arcades. *Ste Foy*, still full of medieval houses, was created by Alphonse de Poitiers in 1255 by an act of *paréage* with the abbot of Conques, where there is a remarkably fine church to the south, in Aveyron. *Eymet* is a lively market town, specializing in tinned *foie gras*, fruit and vegetables, which has preserved its half-timbered *halle*, with a second storey reached by a wooden stairway leading up through its finely tiled red roof, and its arcading. It also has an attractive château with a small museum and the town was known in the past for its manufacture of pearl funerary wreaths.

Of the bastides built by the English between 1260 and 1281 there is little of special interest to see at Fonroque, Roquepine or Villefranche de Lonchapt. *Lalinde*, founded by Jean de la Linde for the English, lies flatly by the river and is a busy rather grey little place. Its grid pattern still dominates its layout but only part of one medieval gate remains. *Molières*, with a huge church, is a charming if windswept village which was never completed. Guillaume de Toulouse had been ordered to build it but had to borrow money to do so and as late as 1316 London was complaining about the expense and querying the necessity for its completion. Work stopped shortly after 1318, and in some senses it looks as though nothing has happened there since. There is a small but interesting museum there now devoted to the walnut in the 'Pays des Bastides'.

Monpazier, on a plateau dominating the Dropt, on the other hand, is a showpiece *bastide*. It was founded by Edward I's seneschal Jean de Grailly in 1285, by an act of *paréage* with Pierre de Gontaut, seigneur of Biron. It is worth noting that its name is now thought to derive from Mont de la Paix rather than Mont Passier (*passager*) – another indication that the creation of *bastides* was not primarily military. The central market square, which is still used on market days, has a covered market hall still possessing its medieval measuring vessels. It is surrounded on all four sides by galleried houses with their arcades running all round. Many of the old houses themselves are well preserved, as are four of the six original gateways and much of the ramparts. One house, of three storeys, built in the early fourteenth century, is known as the Maison du Chapître, though it was probably used as a tithe barn. The church, while preserving in general its late thirteenth-century character, was modified in the fifteenth and sixteenth centuries. Monpazier is curious in that the limits of the town exactly coincide with those of the commune, making it one of the smallest communes in France.

The other English bastide of note and well worth a visit is *Beaumont de Périgord*, founded by Lucas de Thaney, Edward I's seneschal of Guyenne in 1272. It was built

The central square at Monpazier

in the shape of an H in memory of Edward's father Henry III who died before it was constructed. Only part of one of the sixteen original gateways is in something like its pristine condition; part of the central square with its angle irons (*cornière*) is still visible and there are some fine houses with fifteenth-century additions. The *halle* was demolished in 1864. The church however is remarkable; it is a good example of thirteenth-century defensive ecclesiastical architecture, despite nineteenth-century restoration. The porch and the balcony above it are elaborately decorated and the contrast with the four massive towers at each corner of the building is surprising. Together with the high solid walls they give the feeling that the church would indeed be a safe place in times of invasion.

Domme is the bastide *par excellence*, although in high summer it is made hideous by the invasion of innumerable tourists. Sometimes called the 'Acropolis of Périgord' and classified as a *monument historique*, Domme sits high on a cliff above the river Dordogne. From the valley only a short row of modern houses breaks the skyline on the top of a tall escarpment known as the *barre* and neither the wide hairpin road up from Cénac nor the twisting minor road in from the wooded south lead one to expect what lies within the wholly walled town. It can only be reached by one of these two roads which lead into the town by the Porte del Bos (des Bois) and the Porte des Tours respectively.

The fact that Domme is a true *bastide* is not immediately evident since it is built in a trapezoid shape on a steep hill and the one-way system for motorists snakes and turns, but within the configuration of the contours it too has its parallel and right-angled streets. Now built entirely of golden sandstone, and scrupulously cared for, it has preserved its medieval atmosphere rather self-consciously. A château had been built before 1214 for when Simon de Montfort arrived to make his base there in his campaign against the Albigensians, a local chronicler, Pierre de Vaux Cernai recorded that he found Domme 'empty and defenceless; it was in an imposing position, on an agreeable site overlooking the Dordogne. Our Count immediately set about demolishing the tall and beautiful fortified tower.' But like so much else hereabouts, the château is being restored.

The site for the new town, higher up the hill and independent of the château, was acquired by Simon de Melun, Philippe le Hardi's seneschal de Limousin, Périgord, Quercy and Agenais, in 1281 at a cost of 500 *livres* from Guillaume de Gourdon, seigneur de Domme. It became important because, with the consent of the abbot of Sarlat, its jurisdiction encompassed a large number of villages in the surrounding countryside. They stretched from Grolejac to Berbiguières and Montfort to Campagnac les Quercy. It was also a seat of royal justice, hence the fleur-de-lys in its coat-of-arms.

The terrain, rocky and difficult of access, was hard to work and the first settlers found it so intractable that in 1301 they were fined 4000 *livres* for being so dilatory, particularly over the construction of the gates and ramparts – along which one can still walk. The fine was eight times the purchase price of the site! In 1308 it was decided that the fine could be paid off over a number of years and would be used partially to build a bridge over the river. Despite complaints by the Dommois of their inability to find this sum they were ordered by the king to do so, but in 1310 they set out their arguments for his representatives at Calviac.

The list of their complaints is interesting: *one*, in the Mont de Dome they were all foreigners who had come from the surrounding countryside, possessing little of their own; *two*, they were all agricultural labourers and earned only what they could gain from working the land; *three*, they could barely support their wives and families on their earnings; *four*, many of them had to work elsewhere to earn enough for the necessities of life; *five*, they could certainly not find the money for the fine, and if the king persisted in its imposition they, like others, would leave the town and, like some who had already done so, become beggars; *six*, the cost of the wooden bridge across the Dordogne had crippled them and to repair it would increase their poverty; *seven*, the stony terrain of the Mont de Dome made it exceedingly difficult to work and to bring supplies over; *eight*, the roads needed repairing virtually every year and the consuls had to take precautions against the local seigneurs who were jealous of the *bastide*; *nine*, their extreme poverty prevented cloth merchants from settling there and they had to go abroad in search of material, and, finally, *ten*, no public road of any use to the inhabitants serviced the Mont de Dome. Ten fairly comprehensive reasons for not paying the fine.

The right to mint their own money – of black leather, called the *obsidionale* – was one of the privileges granted to Domme in its original charter of 1285 and confirmed in 1348, but the Dommois abused it and were renowned for coining false money in the pretty Hôtel du Batteur de Monnaies at the corner of the lower square. Perhaps the Dommois were forced to such practices by the conditions of misery under which they lived during the Hundred Years War.

Certainly the defensive works did not prevent the English troops from taking the town in 1346 and the French from retaking it a year later. In 1393 it was back in English hands; in 1438 it was given by negotiation back to the French: a century of constant attack and intermittent warfare. It is no wonder that many of the inhabitants left the town to find employment elsewhere. In 1415 Guillaume de Marle, the lieutenant seneschal de Périgord announced that if any inhabitant were to leave, all his goods would be confiscated, and that anyone buying the property of a defaulter would have that property confiscated too.

Towards the end of the century, to stop the economic rot, the Dommois applied to the king for permission to hold markets and fairs in their town, and in a charter of 1495 Charles VIII permitted them to hold a weekly market on Fridays and four fairs a year – on 9 November, 17 January, the first Thursday in Lent, and 3 June.

The mint at Domme

But the troubles of the Dommois, as of their neighbours, were far from over. The Wars of Religion were fought with extreme ferocity in the region, led as they were by such as Geoffroy de Vivans, one of the great Huguenot captains. Born at Castelnaud in 1543 he quickly rose by a combination of energy, cunning and ruthlessness. His name crops up again and again throughout the department at this time, but his exploits at Domme remain those most frequently cited. He died at the siege of Vallandrant in Bazadais in 1592.

Geoffroy was anxious to take Domme, which remained a Catholic stronghold but was foiled in his first attempts despite bribing one of the soldiers of the garrison to admit him by the Porte des Tours. He waited another sixteen years before his next attempt; he was successful but resorted to trickery yet again. At four in the morning of 25 October 1588 two of his officers, Captain Bordes and Captain Bramarigues, with thirty men, climbed up the undefended cliff face from the river – undefended because it was thought to be impossible to climb. Guided across the Barre and through the fortifications by a traitor, François Manir, they made their silent way to the market place and there set up such a racket that the citizens and garrison tumbled sleepily out of bed to discover its cause. The confusion gave the storming party time to open the gates to Vivans and his troops. Vivans later managed to capture the château too but the Catholics recaptured it in 1590 by a ruse of their own. Internal dissent between the two Catholic parties, the Royalists and the Leaguers, prevented them from pressing their advantage and capturing the town of Domme too. Indeed, as the Leaguers, who now had possession of the château, set out for Sarlat later in the year, they were fallen upon by Thémines, a Royalist, and the ensuing massacre, as they attempted to cross the river, made the Dordogne run red with blood from

Domme to Castelnaud for two days. Vivans actually regained the château but the country was wearying of religious strife and civil war and, since most of Quercy was by now loyal to the king, Vivans sold Domme – for 40,000 *livres* – to the king's representative, Thémines, in 1592.

Living conditions continued to be hard for a time and, like their compatriots, the Dommois took part in the Croquant uprisings of 1594 and 1597 but after their repression they settled down to cultivate their gardens, at least until the Revolution. Desmarets, a visitor to the area in 1764 found the inhabitants well favoured: 'the fair sex is fair indeed; their healthy looks are doubtless caused by the favourable situation of the town. They make a striking contrast to the ghastly pallor of the Sarladais who look as if they have been buried alive.'

Eugène Le Roy (1836-1907), who lived at Domme for a time and used the town as a setting for his novel *La Belle Coutelière*, found the women attractive for another reason. Water had to be fetched into the town from the Vieilles Fontaines beyond the Porte de la Combe and he thought that 'the women of Domme have the best legs in the region because of their daily exercise.' Today there is a street in Domme called La Belle Coutelière, as there is one named after Geoffroy de Vivans. But Henry Miller, who spent six months there, has not yet been accorded similar recognition, though it was in Domme that he wrote *The Colossi of Maroussi*:

It was a stroke of genius on my part to make the tour of the Dordogne region before plunging into the bright and hoary world of Greece. Just to glimpse the black, mysterious river at Domme from the beautiful bluff at the edge of the town is something to be grateful for all one's life. To me this river, this country, belong to the poet, Rainer Maria Rilke. It is not French, not Austrian, not European even: it is the country of enchantment which the poets have staked out and which they alone may lay claim to. It is the nearest thing to Paradise this side of Greece. Let us call it the Frenchman's paradise, by way of making a concession. Actually it must have been a paradise for many thousands of years. I believe it must have been so for the Cro-Magnon man, despite the fossilized evidences of the great caves which point to a condition of life rather bewildering and terrifying. I believe that the Cro-Magnon man settled here because he was extremely intelligent and had a highly developed sense of beauty. I believe that in him the religious sense was already highly developed and that it flourished here even if he lived like an animal in the depths of the caves. I believe that this great peaceful region of France will always be a sacred spot for man and that when the cities have killed off the poets this will be the refuge and the cradle of the poets to come. I repeat, it was most important for me to have seen the

Dordogne: it gives me hope for the future of the race, for the future of the earth itself. France may one day exist no more, but the Dordogne will live on just as dreams live on and nourish the souls of men.

There is plenty to see in this seductive town. Medieval houses, with their later grey cement rendering unpicked, shine golden in the sun, with sturdy doors and iron knockers made in the local foundries; the remains of an Augustinian convent, which changed hands frequently during the Wars of Religion, is now a private house but has kept its fine gateway; a splendid renaissance mullioned window (on the corner of the Grand'rue) displays a woman clutching a goose; the Maison Communale (now the Hôtel de Ville) has a high flat watch tower and the gendarmerie houses one of the biggest chimney places in the region – with room for a whole ox to be roasted; and there are the Maison du Gouverneur and the *Halle* which date from the sixteenth century. The *Halle* is now the entrance to the Jubilé caves, which display striking natural concretions. The Musée des Arts et Traditions Populaires, in one of the houses in the top square, has a good collection of furniture and memorabilia and local crafts.

The church, destroyed by Vivans in 1588, is now of little architectural value but the view, just beyond, from the cliff top is, as Miller said, one of the most spectacular in the department. There could be no finer combination of all the delights the department has to offer than to sit on the terrace of the Hotel Esplanade, run by the Gilards, eating one of their delicious though undeniably expensive meals and drinking in the smiling valley.

Domme is also unique in containing valuable and little known evidence about the Templars after their arrest in the early years of the fourteenth century. The Knights Templar, a religious and military order, was founded about 1118 to protect the pilgrim roads to the Holy Land and they rapidly became a rich and powerful body within the crusading movement. They acquired property all over Europe on the pilgrim routes and set up commanderies (nineteen of which were in Périgord) to house travellers and ease their journey. A tower of one of their preceptories still stands, bedded into a farmhouse at Sergeac. They, and their rivals, the Knights of the Hospital of St John, were, after the Church itself, the largest land-owning body in Europe. It was a short step for them to become purveyors of 'travellers' cheques' and their banking activities substantially increased their wealth. Their riches enabled them to lend money for crusading activities and, despite fulminations by the Church against usury, their interest rates were high. Their military function as shock troops virtually ceased with the expulsion of the Crusaders from the Holy Land in 1291 and their independence from secular rule as well as their wealth provoked hostility, in particular from King Philippe IV of France.

The Porte des Tours, Domme

By a stroke of incredible co-ordination and efficiency all 5000 French Templar Knights and their servants were arrested simultaneously on 13 October 1307 – the order to do so having been signed on 14 September – and it seems that only about forty knights escaped being taken into custody on that day. The king then mounted an extremely successful propaganda campaign and brought sufficient pressure to bear on both lay and ecclesiastical courts to condemn them. Confessions about irregular and indecent practices were wrung from them by torture and all save three Knights Templar confessed in some degree. Philippe finally persuaded the pope, Clement V (the Frenchman Bertrand de Got), to suppress the order, and it was disbanded in April 1312.

There has been much speculation about Philippe's motives and about the nature of the charges brought against the Templars but that they were trumped up seems more than likely and the touching graffiti in the Porte des Tours at Domme examined by the late Chanoine P-M Tonnellier in 1970 go far to exonerate them.

The Porte des Tours is only open by arrangement. The modern tourist has unfortunately added his more frivolous graffiti to those of the past. The early graffiti bear resemblances to those in the prison of Coudray at Chinon and have perhaps been little studied, because until the roof of the towers collapsed and let daylight in, their full extent and importance could not be seen.

The larger tower, to the left facing the gateway inside Domme, contains a number of drawings and inscriptions. On either side of and above the big chimney are incised crucifixes of different sizes, a crude and agonized Christ on the cross with *Mater Dei ora pro me* scratched under his outstretched arms and the word *Ergastule* repeated several times. This reference to imprisonment in what the author supposed

3. Cave paintings at Lascaux

<< *1. Detail from the porch of St Martin at Besse*

< *2. View of the Dordogne from the Barre at Domme*   *4. The Dordogne from La Roque Gageac*

5. Church at Cénac et St Julien

6. The square at Monpazier

7. The cloister at Cadouin abbey

9. *Château des Bories, Antonne et Trigonant*

< *8. St Jean de Côle*

10. Detail of stonework, Château des Bories, Antonne et Trigonant

12. The cathedral of St Front, Périgueux

14. Doorway in St Léon sur Vézère

15. Market in Monpazier

< 13. Etienne de la Boëtie's house in Sarlat

16. Hautefort

17. La Roque Gageac

19. House near Besse

to be a death cell, together with a number of marks which make up the date 1307, confirm the belief that it was Templars who were here. There are two seated Virgins with the Child in their arms, and more crucifixes with the sun and the moon beside them. Like all graffiti they seem on the whole to be random and amateur: no artist was at work, only perplexed and desperate men whiling away long hours of imprisonment unable to believe that their faith had betrayed them. There are more crucifixes in the corridor leading to the latrines, this time accompanied by figures which might be St John and Joseph of Arimathaea, for one of the objects drawn is almost certainly the Grail. Above the central archway is to be found the only large composition – a view of paradise with angels, seraphim and cherubim in the upper register and St Michael, the Virgin, Christ and St John in the lower. Above both is a battle scene, showing Templar knights fighting the Turks and carrying at the foot of it the inscription *Esca est Deus* (God is my nourishment). Below it, on the right, is a crucifixion surmounted by a huge crown and underneath all these panels is a continuous back drop of little bobbly heads representing the faithful. On one of the benches the words *Destructor Templi Clemens V* is the first of many such overt references to the part played by the pope in the downfall of the Templar order, and at one point the pope himself is represented as a fearful monster, as well as appearing *in propria persona* with the beast of the apocalypse at his feet. There are also references to Clement as Antichrist.

Templar inscriptions in the Porte des Tours

The smaller tower (to the right) contains fewer specifically Templar inscriptions and among them there are several squares with small solid circles inside; these are thought now to be some form of games board – a device invented to pass the weary hours away.

Since so little written evidence supporting the Templars has survived Philippe's campaign of vilification, the graffiti at Domme are of paramount interest and importance. They refute virtually all the more extreme charges brought to discredit the soldier knights. The Templars clearly did believe in the crucifixion as the central dogma of belief; they were devoted to the Virgin; they participated in the Eucharist; they were loyal believers of the Church, not perverted heretics; and they maintained their faith in God – if not his twin representatives on earth, the pope and the French king – to the end.

But the tower prison at Domme has other witness to bear than the refutation of heresy. Both towers contain graffiti of a later date referring to the fighting between the English and the French during the Hundred Years War. Escutcheons of the seigneurs of Beynac and the Beauforts of Turenne are identifiable, and there is a fighting leopard ready to spring from his bed of English roses. There is also a lengthy bilingual inscription commemorating the feat of eight French knights who re-took Domme from the English in 1400, and a vivid, cheeky caricature of Louis XI which must have been scratched some fifty years later. Little of this reaches the books on Domme whose authors seem more anxious to concentrate on Geoffroy de Vivans's exploits, but no visitor to this beautiful and historic town should remain ignorant of the existence of these poignant illustrations of the passions, politics and prisoners of 600 years ago.

Châteaux and Bourgs

The passions, politics and prisoners persisted in Périgord, but the mental energy and physical effort which had gone into the building of so many churches, châteaux and towns from the eleventh to thirteenth centuries could not be sustained over the next hundred years.

Although the provisions of the Treaty of Paris in 1259 had been confirmed, peace between the two emerging nations was uneasy. Edward I did his best to play down complaints that the French were interfering with the lucrative trade plied between the Gascons and England but Philippe IV used an incident in 1294 as an excuse for confiscating Gascony, and alternate fighting and treaty-making continued until 1337 when Philippe declared the English king's land confiscate yet again and sent an army into the Garonne valley. The cannon shots fired from the château of Puyguilhem (in the commune of Thénac, not to be confused with the château of the same name near Villars) are generally claimed to be the first in what has come to be called the Hundred Years War. The site derived its importance from being at the juncture between Périgord and Agenais but only a few remnants of the defensive works of the castle are extant. Edward III replied to French provocation by seizing French property in England and laying claim to the French throne; in 1340 he went further still and assumed the title of King of England and of France – to be borne by his successors for nearly five centuries.

English military superiority was confirmed by their victories at the battles of Crécy in 1346 and Poitiers in 1356 when the Black Prince took the French king Jean II prisoner and Edward elevated the duchy of Aquitaine into a principality for his son – an attractive and cultivated man whose memory lives on in the region even to the point where an apartment block on the road to the east of Bordeaux was called 'Lotissements Prince Noir', and there is a publisher trading under the name of Princi Negri (his name in occitan).

The fighting in and around Périgord continued and the province became a sort of musical parcel; having been bandied about by the two kings, once it reverted to the French crown it was passed on to members of the royal family. Nevertheless it continue to be the centre of conflict. By the mid fifteenth century the tide was turning against the English throughout Aquitaine, and in 1451 even Bordeaux fell to

Charles VII. But he had misjudged the strength of the economic and commercial ties between Gascony and England. His taxation policy, less lenient than that of the English, drove its merchants to revolt.

Sir John Talbot, Earl of Shrewsbury, addressed, according to Shakespeare, by the general in charge of Bordeaux as 'thou ominous and fearful owl of death, our nation's terror and their bloody scourge', was sent out from England with a small force to support the revolt of the Bordelais. Although now eighty-six years old, his reputation and the region's devotion to the English crown ensured that the gates of Libourne, St Emilion and Castillon were opened to him during the autumn of 1452. But Charles was collecting his troops for a confrontation with Talbot and his armies met just to the east of Castillon where, knowing Talbot's reputation, they made good use of their time to entrench their position. Acting on the incorrect information that the French were in disarray, Talbot attacked on 17 July. His cavalry and his infantry were massacred by the fire-power of the French cannon. The French had at last learned the lessons of Crécy and Agincourt; Talbot's confidence in his English and Gascon archers, once England's pride, cost him his life, and the English all their Plantagenet possessions, save Calais and the Channel Isles.

The town of *Castillon*, just in the department of Gironde, has some buildings of architectural merit, including a medieval gateway, the Porte de Fer, and an eighteenth-century church, but its main interest to us is that it was the site of the battle which effectively ended the Hundred Years War. In 1888 the Union Patriotique de France erected a memorial obelisk to the defeat of the English on the battlefield which reads:

Dans Cette Plaine
le 17 Juillet 1453
Fut Remportée la Victoire
où delivra de joug d'Angleterre
les Provinces Méridionales de la France
et termina la Guerre de Cent Ans.

Périgord was free of the English – at least until the invasion of recent years – and on the death of Jean de Bretagne in 1454 went by marriage and descent to the d'Albret family, and on Henri IV's accession finally to the French crown.

Not only had the countryside been ravaged by constant warfare during the fourteenth and fifteenth centuries but the population had suffered from the Black Death and repeated plagues; the widespread depopulation affected towns even as prosperous as Sarlat. It is little wonder therefore that there is virtually no gothic architecture in Périgord. The churches at Villars, Trélissac and Champagnac de Belair are some of the very few that might be called gothic in style rather than romanesque and there are fragments of fifteenth- and sixteenth-century frescos in

Château de Mareuil (19th-century engraving)

the churches of Cheylard, St Geniès and St Julien de Lampon. A tiny wooden pietà in the church at Coubjours has to speak for its century. It is not until after 1500 that we see a new spate of economic activity and building.

One of the most typical châteaux of the time is that of *Mareuil sur Belle*. The original château built for the Mareuil family – one of the four baronies of Périgord – which so distinguished itself at the battle of Bouvines, was sited at Vieux Mareuil, but that is now in ruins. It was the home of another of the department's troubadours, Arnaut de Mareuil. The present château, virtually on the border between Périgord and Angoumois, was built in the fifteenth and sixteenth centuries on the twelfth-century foundations and has a beautiful chapel with elaborate decorations of a kind rarely seen in the department, and – equally rare – a fireplace in it. In the late sixteenth century the château came into the possession of the Talleyrand Périgord family, who although they made some additions did not maintain it after 1770. In 1883 the Prince de Talleyrand Périgord gave it to the Hospice de Chalais in return for three quintals of wheat a year, and it rapidly deteriorated even further into a complete ruin used only as a barn. It was not until 1964, when it was acquired by the Duke and Duchess of Montebello that the work of salvaging it began and with some state aid their descendants have restored it to something of its former glory.

It also houses souvenirs of Maréchal Berthier, and Maréchal Lannes, from whom the present duke is descended and some interesting furniture, amongst which is to be found a copy of an armchair which belonged to Mme de Maintenon, Louis XIV's last mistress and morganatic wife. Among the more touching reminiscences of an imperial past is a letter from Napoleon himself to the Maréchale Lannes announcing her husband's death on the battlefield of Essling. It opens starkly, '*Ce Maréchal est mort ce matin*', but softens slightly as it progresses. There is also an autograph letter from the Empress Marie Louise to the Maréchale who was governess to her son, the Duc de Reichstadt, instructing her on his upbringing. Other exhibits include a collection of lead soldiers and dolls.

The château of *Puyguilhem*, near Villars, on the other hand, is virtually bereft of any furniture or furnishings, but it is a wonderfully homogeneous ensemble restored with their usual care by the Beaux Arts to whom it has belonged since 1939. The building was erected by Mondot de la Marthonie, the eldest son of Etienne de la Marthonie and Isabeau de Pompadour. Born in 1466, Mondot (a diminutive of Raymond) was *premier président* of the *parlement* in Paris in 1514 and was one of Louise de Savoie's chief ministers when her son François I set off for Italy and left her as regent. But Mondot died (of poison?) at Blois in 1517 and construction was continued by his son Geoffroy, who was also responsible for enlarging the château at St Jean de Côle. There is virtually no contemporary documentation about the building, so reminiscent of those being erected at the same time in the Loire valley, and certainly none to explain the enigmatic set of letters above a window in the south-west turret. It may well be one of those cryptograms so loved by the men of the Renaissance or simply an anagram of the initials of various members of the family which add up to MARTHONIE. Be that as it may, the delicate tracery of the letters and the decorative stonework above the three *lucarnes* on the terrace façade and on the roofs and chimney-pieces of the interior display the refinement brought back from Italy by the French after their abortive invasions of that country. The Marthonies were immensely wealthy and part of their income, as well as the wood used in the elaborate roof structure of the château, must have come from the huge forest of Berroneuche given to Geoffroy by the king in 1530.

The château de la Marthonie at *St Jean de Côle* stands in the middle of a medieval village where time seems to have stopped still amidst an ensemble that is miraculously spared the artificiality of a film location. The calm main square, with its covered market, château and church, still has a restaurant called the Hôtel des Templiers, spruced up, but even so a building hardly reminiscent of the days when that knightly order was so rich and powerful that a king of France and a pope conspired together to rob and suppress it.

The church is of particular interest. It is thought to have been founded by Raymond de Thiviers, Bishop of Périgueux, some time before he set out for the Holy Land in 1101. It would seem that it was created, with a lavish endowment, to

Château de Puyguilhem

house sixteen regular resident canons of the Augustinian order. Now the parish church, it is a delicate blending of grey and yellow sandstone cut from two local quarries. It is unusual in the district in that it has no nave and consists of a single square bay flanked by three radiating chapels, a plan thought to have been inspired by the clover-shape used at Tourtoirac, Neuvic, Léguillac de l'Auche and Montagrier. It is probable that it would have been extended had the money not run out; as it was, by about 1241, its revenues were so depleted that it was placed under the protection of the pope, Celestin III. The dome, with a diameter of 12 metres (over 50 feet), making it the second largest in Périgord, collapsed in 1787 and was then restored; it collapsed again in 1860 and the aperture now has a flat wooden ceiling. Eleven rather good capitals surmount the pillars of the three chapels and the sculpture inside is echoed outside by the seventy-five corbels which represent birds, animals and humans fighting.

Of the conventual buildings only a sixteenth-century cloister remains. There is little documentary evidence about the power and influence of the priory during the Middle Ages but it suffered from the see-saw conditions engendered by the wars with the English, passing from bloody hand to bloody hand and back again, though there never seems to have been a period when there was no prior. By the early

Château de Jumilhac

fifteenth century the priory could no longer sustain the canons and Eugene IV was persuaded to grant indulgences to those giving alms for its restoration; but such work as was undertaken was frequently interrupted, and by 1510 the priory was once again unoccupied. It never really recovered and became the subject of arguments and depredations by the Marthonies, to the point where the servants of the seigneur replaced the seats set out by the monks by his own, an incident followed by fisticuffs. These difficulties persisted during the eighteenth century; by 1789 only three monks were in residence.

Beyond the church the village houses run the length of a wide street reminiscent of a Cotswold market town and end at a gothic hog-backed bridge. This crosses the Côle and leads to the *fontaine de l'amour* which guarantees a wedding the following year if a pin, thrown by an optimistic girl, falls on its point.

After the battle of Castillon, Périgord, impoverished and depopulated as it was, slowly recuperated but no sooner had it partially recovered economically than its inhabitants found the even greater savagery of a civil war upon them. In 1517 Luther nailed his ninety-five theses to the door of Wittenberg Palace Church: by 1525 François I, who had originally been sympathetic to the new religious movement, had reverted to orthodoxy. Twenty years later he sanctioned the burning of twenty-four 'heretic' villages. His successor, Henri II, found Lutheranism even more disturbing politically for he had to contend with a general discontent fanned by rising prices and the adherence of powerful members of both the aristocracy and the bourgeoisie to the Huguenots, the new Protestant party. On his death in 1559 he left his son, a minor, a fearful legacy: a deficit, an increasingly powerful 'heretical' movement, and a country split between three contending parties. The 'Massacre of Vassy' in 1562 was the spark for the outbreak of the civil wars, or as they were known until fairly recently, the Wars of Religion. They were marked by the savagery that so often characterizes civil war and culminated in the Massacre of St Bartholomew's Eve. Most of the influential Huguenots were gathered together in Paris for the marriage of Henri de Navarre and Marguerite de Valois in August 1572 and on the night of the 24th over 2000 of them were killed by the Catholics in Paris alone. Eventually Henri succeeded in putting half a century's fighting to an end, but it is hardly surprising that during this period more buildings in Périgord were destroyed than created.

Typical of the period but very unlike any other Dordogne château is that of *Jumilhac*, in the far north-eastern corner, a perfect monument to the rise of capitalism. There is known to have been a building on the site in the second half of the thirteenth century but the forbidding pile that stands here today, softened by two lateral seventeenth-century wings, was a completely new creation built for Antoine Chapelle, an ironmaster who made his fortune selling arms and lending money to

*An angel pinnacle on the roof
of the château de Jumilhac*

Henri IV. Since it is made from the local schist, and not the softer, more luminous, stone used in the south of the department, it was particularly hard to work, and the masons could allow themselves few embellishments on the façades. Consequently it is rather grim, a pale grey cliff rising monolithically, pierced by a few small windows and an unassuming front door which leads to surprisingly small rooms. But, although the stone was intractable and permitted little decoration, when the architect reached the roof he allowed his flights of fantasy to exceed even those of the creator of Chambord. Gustave Doré, no mean fantasist himself, called this roofscape the most romantic in France. It is a forest of innumerable turrets and towers, pepperpots and pinnacles, of different shapes and sizes, unified only by their glistening grey-blue slates. Their peaks are garnished with filigree crests which, though made of lead, seem as light as the air into which they reach. They too are fantastic: birds, angels, one complete with its sword of justice and weighing scales, cabbages and men pirouette above the massive pile like surrealist ballet dancers.

Inside, sobriety reigns. There is nothing fantastic about the austere elegance of the rooms, approached by a circular stone stairway. They seem the very thing for a man who wanted outward ostentation combined with comfortable living. Antoine Chapelle, the epitome of a successful businessman of his time, not content with the property he already possessed and the huge fortune he had made at his foundry at La Vallade, took in 1579 as his second wife Marguerite de Vars Coignac, an heiress to local property. In 1581 he bought up another local *seigneurie* but the acquisition of land belonging to the nobility by a commoner did not bestow the title of nobility and it was nearly another twenty years until he acquired one from Henri IV.

Within the château, the 'Spinner's Room', a tiny closet with the remains of naïve frescos depicting flowers and animals, is a reminder that moral standards remained unchanged. Louise de Hautefort, married to Antoine II of Jumilhac, was suspected of infidelity by her husband and imprisoned in the room. She spent her days spinning, painting the walls and sending messages to her lover who visited her disguised as a shepherd. There are various equally novelettish endings to the story and a nice portrait of Louise with the spindle and distaff, and a skirt with a lacy pinafore ample enough to hide a lover.

Antoine II's descendants, by his marriage in 1609 to Marguerite de Douhet, were responsible for building the two side wings. That on the right houses a magnificent *escalier d'honneur* which leads to a vast salon on the first floor. The walls are panelled and the marquetry floor is modelled on one at Versailles. They, and the elaborately carved Louis XIII chimney-piece, were the work of Limousin craftsmen. Period furniture and paintings by Oudry complete the ensemble. The left-hand wing leads to the romanesque parish church which also has fine seventeenth-century woodwork.

During the eighteenth century two of Antoine Chapelle's descendants became lieutenants general in the armies of Louis XV and Louis XVI. The château was sequestrated during the Revolution but was neither destroyed nor looted, perhaps because the municipality and Société Populaire installed themselves in it. Moreover, in 1794, at the height of the campaign of enforced sale of landowners' property, the Comité de Sûreté suspended the sale of Jumilhac, and it remained in the family.

Louise de Hautefort, the Jumilhac spinner

Antoine Pierre Joseph Charles, Marquis de Jumilhac, was equally lucky; though arrested, he was released and joined the emigrés. He rallied to Bonaparte and returned to enjoy his estates until his death in 1826 on active service. The property, open for visits, was sold in the nineteenth century but was repurchased in 1964 by a collateral descendant, the Comte Odil de Jumilhac.

Périgord owed much of its early prosperity to the presence of iron in the department, and the enormous number of foundries its forests and waterways supported. The area was renowned for the quality of ironwork it produced in the Gallo-Roman period, as Strabo noted, and there is archaeological evidence for many foundry sites, commemorated in village names such as La Ferrière, La Ferronie and La Farge. The industry flourished during the Middle Ages, iron from Périgord was exported via Bordeaux to England under Edward I, and in the fifteenth century it was exempt from French taxes. The constantly increasing demands of the crown for more armaments was the cause for its expansion, despite a setback during the Wars of Religion, and Antoine Chapelle was not alone in having made a fortune fast enough to make him acceptable as a husband for a daughter of the nobility.

The creation of a navy by Richelieu was an additional bonus for the ironmasters of France, not least in Dordogne, and during the early part of the seventeenth century improvements in agricultural tools as well as in cannons and munitions kept the foundries well occupied. At this period they were able to keep pace with more sophisticated means of production by enlarging their furnaces and mastering the new techniques of hydraulic pressure. In 1679 Périgordin ironmasters like the Hauteforts at Ans and the Segonzacs were under contract to supply 100 cannons a year for five years for delivery to the *intendant* of the Marine at Rochefort, even though cheaper iron was by this time being imported from Spain and Sweden, again via Bordeaux – and Périgord began to feel the chill wind of competition. The Périgordin foundries remained in business during the eighteenth century, their ironmasters constantly encouraged to increase their productivity as France became more and more involved in wars, and in 1756 Maritz, the inspector general of the Royal Artillery, toured Périgord on a public relations trip necessitated by the outbreak of the Seven Years War. Between 1760 and 1765 Blanchard de Ste Catherine, a Nontronnais, supplied 835 cannons, of which 592 were of big calibre and by 1765 he was owed the huge sum of 119,000 *livres* by the state.

Towards the end of the century even wood was getting expensive and coke was found to be a more effective smelting agent. By now the Périgordins seemed reluctant or unable to keep pace with developments in technology. Although the 1804 Annuaire for Dordogne lists iron founding as the first industry of the department, it was already in decline. Twenty years later, when Lorraine, Burgundy, Brittany and Berry had adopted more advanced English methods of production, and the state was importing large quantities of iron from England, Périgord could barely compete, and its miners were resolutely opposed to innovation – pig-headed, one might say. Inevitably Périgordin foundries were forced to close, though those at Fayolle, Sarrazac, Taizé, Forge Neuve, La Rigaudie and Ans continued working until 1870; that at Savignac Lédrier continued until 1930; that at Ruelle was taken over by the state; and that at St Médard d'Excideuil was replaced by a foundry smelting works. Remains may be seen at Combiers on the Lizonne near La Rochebeaucourt, La Mothe, La Chapelle St Robert, Forge Neuve, Jomelières, Savignac Lédrier and Les Eyzies.

Not all the products of the foundries were objects of death; domestic as well as agricultural tools were made from both cast and wrought iron, and brass. Many of them may be seen in the museum at Périgueux or *in situ* like a thirteenth-century door knocker in Domme. Bells, chimney backs, firedogs, waffle irons and warming pans were amongst their products as was every kind of cooking utensil from the *marmite* that hung over the fire to the pans for roasting chestnuts. The foundries also specialized in making stamps for decorating and lettering bookbindings and the little badges, rather like Robertson's golliwogs, worn by pilgrims.

That the nobility was not short of money at this time either is shown by the erection of a new château at *Bourdeilles*. The town is dominated by its great double château which rises on the cliff above the river. The shell of the medieval château, built between 1283 and 1298, stands in ruins with an imposing octagonal keep 35 metres high, a reminder that Bourdeilles was, with Beynac, Biron and Mareuil, one of the four baronies of Périgord. A large room, with five chimney-pieces and wooden roof vaulting, may be visited.

The second château, which stands by the side of the first, was built to designs by Jacquette de Montbrun, the wife of André de Bourdeilles, in the style she thought would be suitable to receive a visit from the queen, Catherine de Medici, who, disappointingly, never turned up, so the building was never completed. A sober renaissance pile, it houses a *salle dorée*, with woodwork, ceilings, chimney-pieces and paintings of 1561-70 by Ambroise Le Noble of the Fontainebleau school; a *salle marbrée* and the so-called *chambre de la reine*. The paintings include one by Van Loo of the Duchesse de Chevreuse, an anachronistic history painting of the exploits of Simon de Montfort commissioned by Cardinal Richelieu from Simon Vouet, and Flore and Pomone, two classical nudes which were subsequently over-painted with clothes to render them decent.

During the Revolution the outbuildings served as a magazine and the château was used during the Second World War to store the national treasures. Both châteaux were bought in 1967 by the Santiards who had previously owned the attractive château of La Treyne (Lot) and, when they died, it, and their collection of Italian

117

Pierre de Bourdeilles, Seigneur de Brantôme (engraving by Desroches)

and Spanish furniture, was left to the department. It is, however, a rather sad monument touched by disappointment and dust.

The town of Bourdeilles itself is situated on both banks of the Dronne which is spanned by a fine gothic bridge. Its church has been heavily restored but the medieval mill, in the shape of a boat, has been put back into working order more recently and with rather better taste. The chapel in the former hospital has a good stone renaissance retable and pietà. Bourdeilles has other claims to fame in that it was the birthplace and home of the witty chronicler of François I's racy court.

Pierre de Bourdeilles, Abbot and seigneur de Brantôme (*c.* 1540-1614) was brother to André de Bourdeilles and nephew of Pierre de Mareuil, whom he succeeded as a commendatory abbot of Brantôme. Brantôme was educated at Poitiers and joined the Valois court as a young man intent on a military career. He accompanied Mary Queen of Scots home in 1561 and saw service in Portugal, Spain, Italy and Africa, but retired from the court after the Catholic victory at the battle of Jarnac in 1569. He was later instrumental in preventing Huguenot troops under Coligny from sacking his abbey. He returned to take up an appointment as chamberlain to Charles IX but a fall from his horse round about 1584 crippled him and he retired permanently. He spent the next four years in bed (some say rendered impotent) and the rest of his life dictating his memoirs to his secretary Mathaud. He died in 1614 and was buried in the chapel of the nearby château of St Crépin de Richemont, a privately owned sixteenth-century château now open to visitors.

These wide-ranging travels, and a far-reaching circle of acquaintances, who numbered kings, poets and royal mistresses, gave Brantôme material for his risqué portraits of *Dames galantes*, *Dames illustres* and *Grands capitaines étrangers et français* that are extremely entertaining, if too full of uncritical anecdote. His political disinterestedness, his amoral attitude and his easy, lively style allowed him to write freely about the affairs of the men and women of his time, though he did take the precaution of not having his work published in his lifetime.

The small town of *Brantôme* was eulogized by André Maurois (who for a time lived at Eyssendiéras near Excideuil) as 'the pearl of Périgord – one of the jewels of France ... where sometimes nature and man combine to create a masterpiece. This has happened at Brantôme – the most ravishing, the most fairy-like of all the small towns of Périgord.' Raymond Poincaré, during his presidential visit in 1913 called it 'the Venice of Périgord'.

The river Dronne runs through the town and is flanked on one side by the abbey church and conventual buildings. The Benedictine abbey is reputed to have been founded by Charlemagne in 769 when he gave the relics of St Sicaire (one of the Innocents) to the abbot, but it was certainly consecrated by Pope Leo III in 804. It was sacked by the Normans, who found access easy up the river in about 849, rebuilt in the eleventh century, and subsequently radically rebuilt again and again right up to the nineteenth. The earliest extant building is the bell tower; dating from the eleventh century, it stands isolated from the abbey on a rocky promontory and is remarkable for its gables, which were copied over a wide area in the locality .

The abbey buildings were deconsecrated in 1791 and were restored between 1846 and 1860 by Abadie, to be used, as they are now, for municipal purposes. A seventeenth-century staircase leading to the refectory and dorter remains and the eighteenth-century building by Bertin, rather disfigured, now houses the Fernand Desmoulin Museum containing prehistoric objects and the work of the painter after whom it is named. He lived from 1853-1914 and the works of his on exhibition were painted while under the influence of a medium. The cloister is of little interest. The caves behind the buildings contain curious fifteenth-century sculptures in their walls of the Last Judgement and the Crucifixion. The church, embellished by the bourgeois made rich by the river traffic, has some romanesque and gothic remains but is in general unremarkable though it contains a few items of interest. There is a thirteenth-century relief, the Massacre of the Innocents, in the porch above the font; a fourteenth-century stone relief of the Baptism of Christ in the baptistery; two sculpted panels in wood on either side of the choir – one depicting the Massacre of the Innocents, a copy of a tapestry made in Arras for the Vatican after the Raphael cartoon in the V&A, the other representing Charlemagne's gift of St Sicaire's relics; and a sixteenth-century wooden statue, Notre Dame de Reclus. There is also a small museum, 'Rêve et Miniatures', devoted to dolls' houses and room boxes filled with furniture, and household goods, all to a 1:12 scale.

The monks' garden, now well tended for public enjoyment, is reached by crossing a curious bridge over the Dronne and contains a charming renaissance pavilion and two small shelters thoughtfully erected to protect the clergy by Pierre de Mareuil, abbot in 1538. A good restaurant, wonderfully sited on the millstream, faces the garden: an enchanted spot for a summer gastronomic and visual feast. There is a twelfth-century chapel in the hospital; and there are many fine renaissance houses to make a walk round this seductive place a pleasure. Also to be noted nearby are the monument to the hostages shot by the Germans in 1944, the dolmen of Pierre Levée, and the renaissance *manoir* of Hierce.

Michel Eyquem de Montaigne, greater by far than Brantôme, also happens to be Périgordin – just. He was born in the château of *St Michel de Montaigne* at the far western edge of the department and lived there for the better part of his life. The building was destroyed by fire in 1885, save for the one wing which contained his private room:

> It is placed on the third storie of a tower. The lowermost is my Chapell; the second a chamber with other lodgings, where I often lie, because I would be alone. Above it is a great ward-robe. It was in times past the most unprofitable place of all my house. There I [pass] the greatest part of my lives dayes, and weare out most houres of the day. I am never there a nights. Next unto it is a handsome neat cabinet, able and large enough to receive fire in winter, and very pleasantly windowen. The forme of it is round, and hath no flat side, but what serveth for my table and chaire: In which bending or circling manner, at one looke it offreth me the full sight of all my books, set round about upon shelves or desks, five rancks one upon another. It hath three bay-windowes, of a farre-extending, rich and unresisted prospect, and is in diameter sixteene paces void. In winter I am lesse continually there: for my house (as the name of it importeth) is pearched upon an over-pearing hillocke; and hath no part more subject to all wethers then this: which pleaseth me the more, both because the accesse unto it is somewhat troublesome and remote, and for the benefit of the exercise which is to be respected; and that I may the better seclude my selfe from companie, and keepe incrochers from me: There is my seat, there is my throne. In endevour to make my rule therein absolute, and to sequester that only corner from the communitie of wife, of children and of acquaintance. Elsewhere I have but a verball authoritie, of confused essence. Miserable, in my minde is he,

Montaigne's tower

who in his owne home, hath no where to be to himselfe; where hee
may particularly court, and at his pleasure hide or with-draw himself.

The far-extending views, blessedly, are still there. To the west he could see the
plains of Castillon and to the north the forest of Brétenord, where in 1584, he organized a staghunt for the pleasure of his guest, Henri de Navarre, and the château of
Gurson for whose *châtelaine* he wrote his famous essay on the education of children. But his books are no longer there and the library is an echoing chamber, only
the inscribed beams recalling his love of classical literature and his learning.

Montaigne was born in 1533, put out to wet-nurse in the nearby village of
Papessus, and subjected to a most rigorous education at home:

Before the first loosing of my tongue, I was delivered to a Germane,
he being then altogether ignorant of the French tongue, but
exquisitely readie and skilfull in the Latine. As for others of [my
father's] household, it was an inviolable rule, that neither himselfe,
nor my mother, nor any man, nor maid-servant, were suffered to
speake one word in my companie, except such Latine words, as
everyone had learned to chat and prattle with me. It were strange to
tell how every one in the house profited therein. My Father and my

121

Michel de Montaigne (engraving)

Mother learned so much Latine, that for a need they could understand it, when they heard it spoken, even so did all the household servants, namely such as were neerest and most about me. To be short, we were all so Latinized, that the townes round about us had their share of it; insomuch as even at this day, many Latine names both of workmen and of their tooles, are yet in use among them. And as for my selfe, I was about six yeares old, and could understand no more French or Perigordine, than Arabike, and that without art, without bookes, rules, or grammer, without whipping or whining.

Montaigne was sent to the Collège de Guyenne and went on at sixteen from the university of Bordeaux to that of Toulouse. He had a legal post in Périgueux when he was twenty-one and his father was made mayor of that city, and transferred to Bordeaux in 1557. It was in the following year that he met the friend who inspired the rest of his life which he wrote of in a way that has given rise to one of his most often quoted sentences:

And the greatest I ever knew living (I meane of naturall parts of the minde, and the best borne) was Etienne de la Boëtie: Verily it was a compleat minde, and who set a good face, and shewed a faire countenance upon all matters: A minde after the old stampe, and which, had fortune therewith beene pleased, would no doubt have brought forth wondrous effects; having by skil and study added very much to his rich naturall gifts.

In the amitie I speak of, they entermixe and confound themselves one in the other, with so universall a commixture, that they weare out, and can no more finde the seame that hath conjoyned them together. If a man urge me to tell wherefore I loved him, I feele it cannot be expressed, but by answering: Because it was he, because it was my selfe. There is beyond all my discourse, and besides what I can particularly report of it, I know not what inexplicable and fatall power, a meane and Mediatrix of this, indissoluble union. We sought one another, before we had seene one another, and by the reports we heard of one another; which wrought a greater violence in us, than the reason of reports may well beare: I thinke by some secret ordinance of the heavens, we embraced one another by our names. And at our first meeting, which was by chance at a great feast, and solemne meeting of a whole towneship, we found ourselves so surprized, so known, so acquainted, and so combinedly bound together, that from thence forward, nothing was so neere unto us, as one unto another.

Montaigne went to court in 1561 and returned to Bordeaux in 1563; six months later Etienne de la Boëtie died. Montaigne's father died in 1568, leaving him his estates. By now Montaigne was publishing his writings, which were interrupted by the Wars of Religion. Montaigne was a good Catholic and a royalist – he was given the Order of Saint Michel by Charles IX but he was devoted also to Henri de Navarre to whose entourage he was attached in 1577, and who honoured him with two visits. From 1571 onwards Montaigne spent most of his time in Périgord, either at his château or in Bordeaux – of which he, like his father, became mayor – except when he journeyed to spas in Italy and Germany in search of a cure for his kidney troubles. He died in 1592. Montaigne's fame rests on his *Essais*, a remarkable work of wisdom and perception, full of humanity, learning and humour. The passages above come from an almost contemporary translation by John Florio, Elizabeth I's Italian master, which according to Florio's modern successor is 'one of the greatest Elizabethan translations – [though] its virtues lie in the vigour of its English rather than in the truth of its rendering'.

Vineyards, Montaigne's *bien principale du pays*, are the characteristic feature of the adjoining region, Bergeracois. The château of *Monbazillac* is another of the department's fairy castles; whether in the brilliant sunshine of summer or the more romantic haze of a winter hoar-frost, its elegant silhouette shimmers above its impeccably barbered and world-famous vineyards. It is one of the few châteaux that

The château de Monbazillac

was not only constructed *de novo* at one time but it has also miraculously escaped later alteration, restoration and mutilation. Built by Charles d'Aydie from 1550 onwards, it is a judicious mixture of medieval and renaissance styles. Never a fortress, its moat is dry, its drawbridge fixed and its machicolations purely decorative; it was built as a country gentleman's home, and so it remains. It has changed hands many times since the sixteenth century but now belongs to the Cave Coopérative de Monbazillac which looks after it with the same scrupulous care it devotes to its vineyards.

The rooms in the interior have been arranged to display a series of permanent and specialist exhibitions. One is devoted to popular crafts: there is a complete set of tools used by coopers and sabot-makers, and many for rope-makers and cartwrights; there is a model of a *gabarrot* (a full size *gabarre* would be too big), and examples of oars, rigging and so on. Another displays some very fine Périgordin furniture and makes it look as if it had always been there. There is also a sixteenth-century Italian dining-room suite of particular nastiness that belonged to Jean Mounet Sully (1841-1910), a classical actor, born in Bergerac, who worked for the Comédie Française. It is good to know that the actor famed for playing Orestes organized with three friends in Paris *cassoulet* competitions and ate that delectable local dish once a week for all his adult life. There is a fine collection of maps and engravings of subjects pertaining to the region – one of the most interesting is the plan, never executed, that Vauban drew up to transform Bergerac into a fortified town. Yet another room is devoted to the history of Protestantism in the area, for the owners of the château were staunch Huguenots and many consistories were held there. There are portraits of the most famous European Protestant luminaries – Luther, Calvin, Hus, Zwingli and Cranmer – and many Bibles and prayer books, a good proportion of which were printed in Holland. The Dutch connection with Monbazillac started in the thirteenth century when wine was the principal link but it was strengthened during the Wars of Religion and intensified even further when the Edict of Nantes was revoked and many Huguenots from the district found refuge in the Low Countries. During the eighteenth century it seems that the entire wine production of Bergeracois was exported to Holland. One supposes that the Dutch at least knew where Bergerac was, unlike the pope who asked a party of pilgrims from that town where it was, and knew exactly when told that it was near Monbazillac. The wine, that honey-coloured and honey-tasting nectar, was world famous then as now. The cellars of the château, which run the full length and breadth of the building are laid out as a museum containing ancient bottles and wine-making equipment, and one can taste, and buy, the golden liquor in one of the outhouses.

Another fine golden château of Bergeracois worth visiting is *Lanquais*, near Monbazillac. Built over a number of years from the fourteenth century to the Renaissance, it presents a harmonious if seedy appearance. The renaissance wing is reputed to have been constructed by the builders of the Louvre, and there is some good Louis XIII furniture inside, as well as two impressive chimney-pieces and some fine decoration. Not far from Lanquais is the small village of *Urval,* which has a pretty, small, fortified church with a square eleventh-century chancel and a nave of the same date. But it is worth a visit if only to see the curious communal oven preserved by the old presbytery. It is a relic of that seigneurial right obliging the villagers to use the *four banal* for all their baking, which gave rise to many complaints.

Although the Wars of Religion had officially ceased, the miseries they left behind them in the Dordogne countryside prompted a peasants' revolt and the rising in 1594 came to be known as that of the Croquants (from the word *cros* – the bent pitchfork that was their major weapon). It lasted spasmodically for a period of three years, during which the châteaux of Grignols, Excideuil and l'Evêque were fired, but it was suppressed by the action of the gentry, who in the face of a common enemy sank their religious differences. By 1610 an uneasy peace returned, but not for long. The increase in taxes in the 1630's necessitated by the expenses of the Thirty Years War, prompted more uprisings and in 1637 an army of about 10,000 peasants took Bergerac. No sooner had this wave of discontent subsided than renewed fighting generated by the Fronde – a rebellion by the aristocracy against the increasing centralization of power by the monarch – was upon them. A few decades of relative peace and quiet descended, with one-third of the population dying of plague in 1692-93, until Louis XIV' s great blunder, the Revocation of the Edict of Nantes, led to a mass exodus of some of the most hardworking and prosperous of the province's inhabitants. In 1700 the *intendant,* Bazins, wrote to Fénelon's pupil, the Duc de Bourgogne, saying:

> Bergerac is a town which was recently very considerable. It housed a large number of rich merchants who did a good trade; they sold a variety of merchandise from Périgord and the Limousin to outsiders, and had a good entrepreneurial trade and commercial links with Lyon, the Auvergne and Bordeaux. All were of the reformed religion – there were more than 40,000 of them in the province. Now they have deserted in large numbers and fled the country.

Complaints leading to endless litigation also characterized the sixteenth and early seventeenth centuries, and the history of the Abzac family of La Douze exemplifies this, as well as showing the emergence of a new class of *nouveaux riches* – the lawyers. *La Douze* itself is a small village with a romantic history and a charming twelfth-century church on its outskirts. The house of Abzac was connected with the village from that date; a Pierre d'Abzac was Archbishop of Narbonne and in general the family was distinguished throughout the province. Its history followed that of other similar families until, at the beginning of the sixteenth century, Jean II d'Abzac La Douze changed the laws of inheritance so that not the eldest, but the most worthy, son should be heir. In the mid-seventeenth century Gabriel II decided that his eldest son (by his first marriage to Jeanne de Lastoux) was 'unsatisfactory', perhaps because he had married a Protestant, and designated another son, Charles, his heir. The eldest son, justifiably angry, continued to call himself the Marquis de La Douze, and violently attacked his parents, killing some servants in the process. Arraigned before the court at Bordeaux, Gabriel III was sentenced to death by decapitation. However he escaped, and on the death of his father proclaimed himself rightful heir. The authorities remained lax in prosecuting Gabriel III and eventually he and Charles worked out an arrangement over the property and money. A year later Gabriel was found dead in the forest of Orléans and his widow accused Charles of the dastardly deed. Charles was tried, but, in 1627, acquitted. This did not satisfy Gabriel's widow who pursued the matter in the Paris courts and eventually succeeded in getting Charles condemned to death. Louis XIII in 1639 rescinded the death sentence and freed Charles, but although Gabriel's widow had subsequently died, her daughter, Marie d'Abzac, pursued the matter and the feud persisted until 1656 when Charles, exhausted, agreed to pay his niece 50,000 *livres*.

Charles had one son, Pierre, born in 1633, by his second wife, Charlotte de Thinon, to whom he left the life tenancy of La Douze and a handsome dowry. Pierre married Magdeleine de Chaumont de Clermont and on his father's death threw his mother and one of his sisters out of the house. His mother promptly sued him. The *parlement* of Bordeaux, under the direction of Président Pichon, eventually in 1664 found in Pierre's favour – a decision Pierre's mother reckoned to have been influenced by the fact that Pichon was a cousin of Pierre's wife.

Bernard Pichon was a typical new man of his time – a rich lawyer with political pretensions whose house in Bordeaux typified the wealth and intellectual standing of the *noblesse de robe,* those ambitious bourgois lawyers and office-holders who aspired to and achieved ennoblement. Widowed early, he had, by his first marriage, a daughter known as Finette. Pierre d'Abzac naturally, on account of the litigation he was involved in, found himself frequently in Pichon's house and he fell for Finette. According to the lurid reminiscences of Bussy Rabutin, Pierre and Finette set about murdering Magdeleine, and Pierre, who protested his innocence to the scaffold, was duly executed. It seems more likely that Pierre was executed because he had fought a duel with his wife's brother and Cardinal Richelieu was determined to make an example at the flouting of his ban on duels. Pierre's son never lived at La Douze; the fortifications were dismantled and the proud house fell into ruins. Only in the church, a small and sturdy masterpiece, can we see a calmer monument to this turbulent family, the peaceful statues of an earlier Pierre d'Abzac and his wife Jeanne de Bourdeilles, and a sculpted altar.

Tourist brochures publicize *Sarlat* as the epitome of a medieval town but, although in the Hôtel Plamon it boasts a fine example of fourteenth-century architecture, it is rather a conglomeration of renaissance buildings overlaid on the earlier medieval base. As such its general configuration is astonishingly well preserved and even though it was brutally sliced through the middle in 1837, has survived virtually intact, largely because its site has no natural advantages and the town lies away from the main roads and railways. Tucked away in an unsalubrious valley nine kilometres from the Dordogne, its withdrawn position saved it from the depredations of the Normans and the nineteenth-century restorers alike.

Despite some evidence of a Gallo-Roman settlement it seems to have been of little importance under the Romans, and the hermitages of the sixth and seventh centuries remained modest. There is thought to have been a Benedictine monastery by the eighth century which fell into disrepute until Cluniac reforms, and the gift of a Holy Thorn and a piece of the True Cross by Charlemagne on his visit to Sarlat in 778 did much to raise its prestige and attract settlers, as did the transfer of the relics of St Sacerdos at much the same time. St Sacerdos, born in 450 at Calvac, became renowned as bishop of Limoges. In 940 Bernard, Count of Périgord, gave the town of Sarlat to the abbey, under whose protection it remained relatively untroubled by the surrounding strife and Viking incursions. The abbey slowly acquired great riches and its jurisdiction extended over a wide area. Its reputation was even further enhanced when in 1147 Sarlat was on the itinerary of St Bernard of Clairvaux as he travelled France to preach the Second Crusade. He seems to have met with a cool response in the neighbourhood although, according to Chanoine Tarde, he worked a miracle while he was in the town:

> One day, when he had finished preaching, he was presented with a large number of loaves, and was asked to bless them as he had done elsewhere. He lifted his hands and blessed them in the name of the Lord, making the sign of the cross and said 'this will be a sign to you of the truths I have preached and of the errors put about by the heretics, for those amongst you who are ill shall, after they have eaten of this bread blessed by us, recover.' The bishop of Chartres who was also present, added 'if you eat with perfect faith', to which St Bernard without hesitation replied, 'I do not say that, but whosoever shall eat of it shall be cured of no matter what illness so that they may recognise us as the true and only messengers of God.' No sooner said than done; and so huge a multitude was cured by eating the bread that news of it spread throughout the province, and St Bernard found so many people thronging the roads and places that he passed on his return that he had to take to the byways to continue his journeys.

St Bernard (Cathedral of St Front, Périgueux)

It has been said that the beehive structure, now known as the Lanterne des Morts, was erected, in 1180, to commemorate his curing the sick with bread he had blessed, and that it was only later that it was used as a sepulchral chamber (350 coins bearing the effigy of the Black Prince were excavated there in 1970).

Sarlat continued to expand and flourish in the twelfth century, proud of its two indigenous troubadours, Elias Cairels and Aimeric de Sarlat, a carpenter's son. In 1204 the burghers, restless with their subservience to the abbey, started their campaign to achieve independence, or at least self-government, but they did not finally succeed until 1298 when they were granted a charter by the French king and proceeded to elect four consuls and twenty-five *jurats*. When Jacques Duèze, a native of Cahors, became Pope John XXII, he was particularly attentive to the affairs of the church in Périgord, and in 1317 elevated Sarlat to a bishopric (which it remained until 1818), thereby considerably increasing its importance and influence, and the monastic buildings were transformed into the bishop's palace.

Despite being on the French-English border, Sarlat was less severely troubled during the Hundred Years War than many of the surrounding châteaux and villages. It was ceded to the English after the Treaty of Brétigny and accepted for the English crown by Sir John Chandos in 1360, but ten years later it was back in the capable French hands of Bertrand du Guesclin. The aftermath of war, compounded by a series of poor harvests, and aggravated by the low-lying position of the town, made it particularly susceptible to the plagues that infected Europe during the fourteenth and early fifteenth centuries. In 1440 there were not enough men to furnish a garrison and, in 1521, 3000 people, that is half the population, died. The following year the town was completely deserted for the better part of twelve months. Nevertheless it recovered economically and its population began to increase again, encouraging the merchants and artisans, whose wealth came from the cloth woven from hemp, a staple local crop, to build new and renovate old houses.

A good deal of our information about Sarlat of this period comes from the chronicles of Jean Tarde. He was a distinguished mathematician and astronomer who met Galileo on his visit to Italy and returned to draw his maps and record his history at La Roque Gageac where he was born in 1561 or 1562. One of his nineteenth-century descendants, Gabriel Tarde, was a noted sociologist who lived in the family château there. La Roque Gageac is one of the most beautiful of Dordogne villages, happily not disfigured by the re-building necessitated when in the winter of 1956-7 a cliff fall destroyed many of the houses, plunging them and their inhabitants into the river below.

General Fournier-Sarlovèze by Gros (Louvre)

Sarlat suffered, as did everywhere else, during the Wars of Religion, when on the whole it remained staunchly Catholic. Captured for the Protestants by the tireless Geoffroy de Vivans, helped yet again by treachery, it was quickly back in Catholic hands and is still proud to recall that it withstood a siege by so doughty a commander as the father of the great Turenne in 1587. But these troubles over, the Sarladais went on with their building and embellishments, helped by the establishment of the royal seat of justice there in 1552, in the building known as the Présidial, with the consequent expansion of legal business throughout the seventeenth century. The Hôtel Maleville was erected by Jean de Vienne who was Henri IV's Superintendent of Finance, and the Hôtel de Ville by Henri Bouissou in 1615.

François de Salignac, Bishop of Sarlat and a member of the family that occupied the see from 1567 to 1688 with a break of only twenty years, asked his nephew Fénelon to commission Louis XIV's renowned landscape gardener, Le Nôtre, to design a garden for the town. Vestiges of work by one of his pupils are still to be seen in Le Plantier, the Jardin Publique, once the remains of the kitchen garden of the abbey, and recently replanted.

The Revolution took place with many of the usual excesses but caused little structural damage, and Sarlat suffered more from Napoleon's policy of centralizing all government, which prevented the town from expanding further. Both the Revolution and Bonaparte provided the opportunities for the flowering of the career of one of Sarlat's heroes. François Fournier-Sarlovèze was born there in 1773. The son of a rather shady speculator who ran a bar called the Tapis Vert, a bright child educated by the monks of Gourdon, he was destined for a legal career, but the army was a quicker route to promotion in those days. His Jacobin sympathies led him to change his name from François to Réséda (a yellow dye-plant) in keeping with the fashion for adopting botanical forenames in a flush of revolutionary enthusiasm, to serve with General Augereau, and consequently to share his disgrace in 1798. He distinguished himself on the field of Marengo with, according to Berthier, rare bravery, but turned violently against Bonaparte and was exiled to Sarlat for four years for his part in an abortive assassination plot but rejoined the Grande Armée and fought at the battle of Friedland. Opportunist as ever, he was made a Baron of the Empire in 1808 and was one of the heroes at the crossing of the Beresina. He continued his life of double-dealing and survived to be invited by Charles X to his *sacre*. He died in his bed in Paris in 1827. His house in the rue Montaigne was furnished with spoils looted during the Spanish campaign.

A deathly calm, and renewed economic stagnation, descended upon Sarlat during the nineteenth century, when its main economic activity was in the production of walnut oil and truffles, and photographs of the town at the turn of the century make depressing viewing. Sarlat however was lucky; it was amongst the first towns in France to benefit from the law brought in by André Malraux in 1962 to safeguard historic monuments. Work has been going on ever since. It is being carried out with

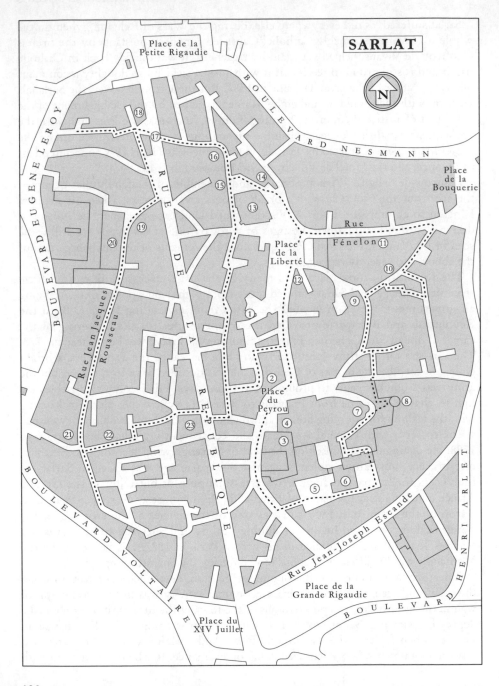

SARLAT

great sensitivity as the façades and roofs have to be restored to their original state while modern conveniences such as electricity, water and sewerage have to be installed to make the houses habitable. Since 1966, it has hardly looked back, and the trebling of its population during July and August makes it impossible either to park or walk unjostled through its narrow streets.

Careful restoration of its beautiful honey-coloured stone and its wide curving expanses of *lauze*-topped roofs have made it the tourist trap of Périgord. But out of season, or even during these crowded summer months, it remains *vaut le voyage*, in the Guide Michelin's three-star terms. Every steep road and alley leads to some delight; the plethora of carved doorways, the profusion of its commercial and eccle-siastical monuments, its markets, its restaurants and now its boutiques, are entrancing in their homogeneity and evocation of the past.

All the most interesting sights can be seen in a good half day's walk. Start at the *Hôtel de Maleville* (1), one of the fine bourgeois mansions of the sixteenth century, also known as the Hôtel de Vienne, after its original owner, Jean de Vienne. He was born in Sarlat in 1557, of humble parents and rose to become a member of the par-lements of both Bordeaux and Paris, and Henri IV's Surintendant des Finances et Premier Président à la Cour des Comptes. The house later passed into the hands of the Maleville family (to whom it still belongs) and whose best known members are Jacques de Maleville (1741-1824) and Lucien de Maleville (1881-1964). The former was a jurist who became vice-president of the departmental Directory and who was instrumental in drawing up the Code Civil. The latter, who lived at the château de Fénelon (see page 144), was an artist of some talent whose illustrations are to be found in a number of books published locally.

The hôtel is an elegant stone building consisting of two wings. The one on the right (with the Tourist Office) is in the French renaissance style, with a narrow gabled front, of three storeys, with finely decorated windows rising above the ground floor with its basket-handle-shaped doorways. The other wing, set back to the left, has a more Italianate façade. The classical portico, somewhat crumbling, supporting a small terrace above, has on either side two delicate small pillars on high stylobates and a frieze on which there are three stone medallions in shallow relief; round portraits of Henri IV and his mistress Gabrielle d'Estrées on either side of the Maleville M in the centre. There are four storeys above and a small round turret rising in the corner.

Sarlat   (1) Hôtel de Maleville; (2) Hôtel de La Boëtie; (3) Bishop's Palace; (4) Cathedral of St Sacerdos; (5) Cour des Fontaines; (6) Cour des Chanoines; (7) Jardin de Enfeus; (8) Lanterne des Morts; (9) No. 1 rue de la Salamandre; (10) Présidial ; (11) rue Fénelon; (12) Place de la Liberté; (13) Ste Marie; (14) Hôtel de Magnanat ; (15) rue des Consuls ; (16) Fontaine Ste Marie; (17) rue de la République; (18) rue des Armes; (19) rue Jean-Jacques Rousseau; (20) Penitents Blancs ; (21) rue de Turenne; (22) No. 7 rue Rousset; (23) rue de Cordil.

Hôtel des Consuls

The former *Hôtel de Dautrery*, in the rue de la Liberté, belonged to Anne de Dautrery and her husband Jean de Cerm, who lived in it during the Wars of Religion and who are both buried in the Jardin des Enfeus. It has a beautiful stone staircase inside, and there is another one worth seeing in the small courtyard at the end of the adjoining passage way. The doorway to the left of the Hôtel de la Mothe has a decorated, leafy frieze with two fluted pilasters on either side.

The *Hôtel de La Boëtie* (2) is one of the finest renaissance houses in the city. It was built between 1520 and 1525 by Antoine de la Boëtie, and it was here that his son Etienne was born on 1 November 1530. His writings include a translation of Xenophon's *Oeconomicus* and a political diatribe *Contr'un ou Discours de la servitude volontaire*, but he died at the age of only thirty-three much to the distress of his friend Montaigne, who immortalized him in his writings on friendship. A less well known writer of much the same time, Gautier de Costes de La Calprenède (1610-63), also lived in Sarlat. He wrote heavy tragedies, of which *Cassandre*, *Cléopatre* and *Faramond* were performed at Louis XIII's court.

It is double-fronted; the ground floor pierced by two bays of unequal size, one of which is a window and one a door, and a series of richly carved mullion windows rising above – an overt display of the conspicuous taste and wealth of its owner. A steeply pointed gable with ornamentation along its sides surmounts the building on the right hand side, whereas that on the left hand wing has not been preserved. It has been replaced by a stone lucarne piercing the *lauze*-covered roof, decorated with an exuberant fantasy that recalls the ornate armour of the sixteenth century.

The *Bishop's Palace* (3), by the side of the cathedral, also shows an Italian influence, this time the legacy of Nicolas Gaddi, a Florentine cardinal who was a cousin and friend of Catherine de Medici, and bishop of Sarlat, although he never actually lived in the diocese. Its size and its style of decoration are reminders that in the sixteenth century the see of Sarlat was as important as those of Cahors and Périgueux. The windows on each of the two storeys have sculpted surrounds with a delicate frieze above them. There is a small turret at the corner of the building which neatly rounds off the top balconied storey.

The entrance to the *Cathedral of St Sacerdos* (4) is through an imposing porch which was added in the seventeenth century. On either side of the architrave supported by pilasters, are pairs of badly mutilated stone figures (there is a fifth to the left) thought to be of a very much earlier date, though it is difficult to place them with any accuracy. The bell-tower, which rises above the porch, is the dominating feature not only of the cathedral but of the city itself, for it can be seen from many vantage points. The lower twelfth-century part is built of stone and consists of an elongated first storey of blind arcades above which rise two smaller storeys, the second with two open and two blind arcades on each face, each surrounded by a narrow column, and the third with two louvred windows each. There is then a sloping slate roof surmounted by a curious bulb-shaped edifice topped by an openwork lantern and crowned with a pointed conical cap, which was added in the eighteenth century. It was known to the Sarladais as *casso graulo* – 'rout rook' – and glistens in sun and rain alike like a Christmas sparkler.

The interior of the church is full of light and is calmly impressive, with few remains of the former Benedictine abbey, for it was rebuilt by bishop Armand de Genteuil under the direction of Pierre Esclanche at the beginning of the sixteenth century. There is a wide nave and two aisles consisting of four bays with ogee vaulting supported on sturdy round pillars. The pentagonal chancel, with openings of unequal size, leads to the chevet behind. The choir stalls, with misericords, date from the seventeenth century, and the organ casing from the eighteenth. The organ was built by Cliquot and it has recently been restored to be played with something like its original tonality. The sacristy is the only remains of the fourteenth-century part of the building, when it was the chapter house.

The *Cour des Fontaines* (5) is a quiet square made pleasant by the sound of the running water of its single fountain and leads to the only remains of the cloister, and the beautiful chapel of St Benoît. This tiny romanesque edifice has been lovingly restored, both in the seventeenth century and more recently in our own times, and retains its purity of line. It was formerly used as a chapel by the Penitents Bleus, who were a confrerie of the bourgeois and master craftsmen whose industry and wealth made Sarlat the treasure house it is today.

On the other side of the Cour des Fontaines (there is a small house with a beautiful mansard roof in the south-east corner) an alleyway leads into the *Cour des Chanoines* (6), an elegant ensemble of buildings, including one which belonged to the dean of the chapter, and a charming, cluttered fifteenth-century house in the corner. A small arched gateway leads out of the courtyard along a cobbled path down into the *Jardin des Enfeus* (7) at the back of the cathedral. There are rows of early sarcophagi buried in grassy plots in three successive terraces. Originally a cemetery, hence its name (*feu* = late), it later became the garden of the Peninents Bleus. At the top of the steps there is a mutilated stone calvary from which there is the most wonderful view of the exterior of the cathedral, glowing a rich golden colour in morning and afternoon sun alike. The great mass of the nave is lightened by its flying buttresses as it soars up to a huge *lauze*-covered expanse of roof.

To the right is the most curious building in the whole of Sarlat - the *Lanterne des Morts* (8) whose conical roof with slit-shaped openings rises from a circular base which houses a vaulted chamber. These stone towers, looking for all the world like light houses, and of which ninety exist, seem mostly to have been built in central and south-western France, roughly between the Loire and the Dordogne and are common in the Limousin, though there are a few in Provence, Burgundy and Paris. They probably began to be built in the twelfth century but went out of fashion by the fourteenth, by which time lights for the dead were burning *inside* churches.

The street from the tower leads into the rue Montaigne, passing the Impasse de la Vieille Poste, which formerly housed the royal post and the post-horse stables and, until a few years ago, a foundry.

Fournier-Sarlovèze lived in the narrow rue d'Albusse in a house with a fine decorated portico clad with terracotta tiles and the poet Gabriel Cousino (1891-1953) lived in the one on the corner where the rue de la Salamandre turns to the left and the rue du Présidial.

Rue de la Salamandre, No. 1 (9) has an exceptional door surround. It is the entrance to the Hôtel de Grézel (or St Aulaire) built for a magistrate in the fifteenth century, who took the salamander so beloved of François I as his device. The next house is a fine example of medieval half-timbering and on the opposite side of the road is to be seen one of the most striking expanses of *lauze*-covered roofs.

The *Présidial* (10) is at no. 6 rue du Présidial. Originally built as the seat of justice in 1552 on Henri II's orders, by 1687 it housed a whole army of lawyers and no doubt innumerable clerks as well. It remained the headquarters of both civil and criminal justice until the Revolution. The building is an unusual structure, with two contiguous sections, each pierced with large bays on the ground and first floors, and

Doorway in the rue de la Salamandre

it has an extraordinary polygonal lantern tower roofed in slate and supported on stilts.

On the corner of the rue Fénelon is the house in which Fénelon's aunts lived. The Hôtel de Salignac (at no. 16) was built in the fifteenth century and remodelled in the eighteenth when the iron balustrades were added to the three-light windows. Note the gargoyle on the corner of the house.

There is a fine range of houses all along *rue Fénelon* (11); on the right hand side of the road: the Hôtel d'Aillac, at no. 13, was the convent of the Mirepoises, occupied by the Dames de Foi; no. 15 has a sixteenth-century façade, mullioned windows and two small turrets. On the opposite side of the road there are a number of well preserved fifteenth-century houses (nos 14, 12, 10 and 8). There is an attractive balustrade above a good seventeenth-century doorway, with carved fleur-de-lys at no. 6, and facing it, at no. 3, the Hôtel Gérard du Barry, which retains some of its fourteenth-century features, though it is mainly an eighteenth-century building. It belonged to one of the most distinguished families of Sarlat. A small passage leads through a gothic porch to the courtyard of a fifteenth-century house by the side of the seventeenth-century house (no. 1) at the corner of the street.

The *Place de la Liberté* (formerly the Place Royale) (12) in which many royal and civic functions took place, and where film designers erect a frighteningly realistic guillotine from time to time, becomes a lively market centre on Saturdays. The row of arcades, which shelters some of these market stalls, is part of the Hôtel de Ville, which was built in 1615 by Henri Boissou, an architect and mason from Monpazier. It is in a simple classical style with balustraded windows on the first floor over which are carved stone Greek friezes.

During the drama festival the main square becomes the auditorium for the plays which are performed in front of the magnificent natural back drop of the buildings on the north side. To the left is all that remains of the parish church of the trade guild of *Ste Marie* (13). The building was started in 1368 and took well over a hundred years to complete. It was secularised at the time of the Revolution, sold in 1815 after the chevet was demolished and used until fairly recently as the post office. Now all that remains of a vast edifice is the two transepts, the side chapels which are occupied by shops, a large incomplete stone tower and the side wall with its huge gothic window.

Behind it is the *Hôtel de Magnanat* (14), a sixteenth-century building with two wings joined by the hexagonal staircase tower. The right hand building has double mullion windows, and is gabled. The ramp passes the Hôtel Chassaing with a seventeenth-century decorated doorway and leads back down to the place du Marché aux Oies, which now has a fine group of bronze geese by the talented sculptors Claude and François-Xavier Lalanne. The Hôtel de Vassal (no. 9), on the corner, has an impressive fifteenth-century façade, with a charming double tower embedded in the corner of its two buildings. It belonged to the Vassals, a prolific family who also owned the now ruined château of La Tourette at St Julien de Lampon.

The *rue des Consuls* (15), sensitively if extensively restored, presents perhaps a perfect example of urban medieval architecture. Pride of place to this epitome of bourgeois wealth goes to the Hôtel Selve de Plamon (nos 8 and 10) often erroneously referred to as the Maison des Consuls. The two ogival openings on the ground floor and three windows on the first floor date from the fourteenth century whereas the mullioned ones on the second storey are of the fifteenth. It is a wonderful ensemble, and it would not be difficult to imagine the building gaily decorated with banners and tapestries hung out of those elaborate traceried windows during processions in the Middle Ages. The classical portico (at no. 12) was added in the seventeenth century but has the armorial bearings of Guillaume de Plamon embedded in the stone; he was a consul in 1330.

Next door is the Hôtel de Labrusse at no. 14. Dating from the seventeenth century, it belonged to a president of the Présidial who was killed at his window during the Fronde. No. 6, along to the right, is the Hôtel Tapinois de Betou, remarkable for both its façades, the one on the street and the other on the inner courtyard. They are fifteenth-century and the monumental wooden staircase, with its barley sugar twists of balustrades, was added a hundred or so years later.

The *Fontaine Ste Marie* (16) is on the other side of the road. It was for a long time the town's only water supply and has a grotto-like appearance set back under a high gothic arch. By its side is the Hôtel de Mirandol and another range of attractive dwellings. At the corner of the street is a curious recessed shell-shaped enclave, known as the *coquille de Montpellier*, an architectural fantasy which serves to support the balconied terrace above.

The rue des Consuls now leads in to the *rue de la République* (17), known locally as the Traverse. To the far side of it lies the western part of the city, less extensively restored than that of the eastern part and to that extent even more picturesque and redolent of the past. There are also fewer shops, and so it has retained more of its air of authentic medieval domesticity. The *rue des Armes* (18) is so called because it leads straight from the north gate of the city to the ancient guard room, still extant, which adjoins on the left the house in which the money-changers had their boutique. The Hôtel de Ravilhon (no. 2) and the houses at no. 5 and no. 7 are all of the fifteenth century and were clearly shops in those days, keeping their arcaded ground floor windows intact.

The small alley to the right leads to the line of the ancient ramparts (now the boulevard Eugène Le Roy) through the brèche de Turenne where the stone steps – the *escalier du guetteur* – which led to the watch tower are now embedded in the side of the wall. The *rue Jean-Jacques Rousseau* (19), which was the main street of the town before the Traverse was cut through in the nineteenth century climbs quite steeply and leads to the huge chapel of the *Penitents Blancs* (20). It is all that remains of the building erected by the Récollet fathers who arrived in Sarlat in June 1612.

A group of bronze geese in the Marché aux Oies by Claude and François-Xavier Lalanne

The monks demolished the former Hôtel de Tustal and the smaller houses surrounding it to put up their convent and cloister, and the chapel itself was erected between 1615 and 1628. Although the building was reworked in later centuries, the doorway retains the purity of its baroque inspiration. Two pairs of fluted columns standing on deep stylobates rise to support, on doric capitals, a pair of broken volutes. The chapel, a fine open space with a beautiful barrel vault, was taken over by the Pénitents Blancs, a confraternity of aristocrats, in 1805.

The Hôtel de Monmeja, at no. 9, rue Jean-Jacques Rousseau has an elegant seventeenth-century façade and the long wall on the left surrounds the courtyard of the former convent of Ste Claire, a huge ensemble with the remains of a cloister adjoining the chapel. The 'Clarisses' who lived there settled in Sarlat in 1621 and like the Récollets down the road were part of the revival of religious communities brought about by the Counter-Reformation. The building has been converted into flats and only the exterior can be seen.

A number of other fine houses, at present undergoing restoration with the skill and taste that has made Sarlat so remarkable over recent years, line the rest of the street which becomes the rue de Siège as it gently descends to the remains of the city wall supported by a flying buttress. Those that merit attention are no. 5, of the fifteenth century; no. 8, at the corner of the *rue de Turenne* (21), of the fourteenth century with gothic windows and no. 13, the Hôtel de Cerval, a Louis XIII-style house, with a grand staircase made of walnut. *No. 7 rue Rousset* (22) is the Hôtel de Marzac and the Hôtel St Clar, with a fifteenth-century tower embedded in its walls and another fine wooden staircase, on the corner of the *rue de Cordil* (23). The Hôtel de Meynard also has a noteworthy wooden balustraded stone staircase.

Plans are afoot to open two museums – one devoted to religious art – but until then Sarlat has to be content with its own living attractions and its annual theatrical festival, which takes place during the last weeks of July and the first of August. Even if one doesn't understand French or find the hard wooden benches uncomfortable, it is worth seeing one of the plays for the setting alone. As the daylight fades and the artificial lights illuminate the old buildings, the effect is magical. So too is the annual *nuit du patrimoine*, which takes place towards the end of September. Selected streets are lit only by flickering nightlights and if it is a fine evening the city turns golden under a dark, velvety sky.

Street in Sarlat at the turn of the century

From Classical to Modern Times

The grander bourgeois buildings of the sixteenth and seventeenth centuries in Sarlat are the last interesting architectural fling in the area. Thereafter the region, like the town, settled into economic stagnation and became one of the poorest parts of France, at least until the middle of the nineteenth century, when the railways were built. Consequently there are few classical and virtually no neo-classical monuments, although the exception – that of the magnificent château of *Hautefort* – is so impressive that it would hardly matter if it were the only one.

Stupendously situated, the great silhouette of a yellow château with a dark slate roof terminating at the corners in classical domes dominates the surrounding countryside. The complex we see today was built in the seventeenth century on foundations of a much earlier date. There is mention of a castle on the site before 1000 AD which in view of the area it commands is hardly surprising. Its most famous occupant in the mid-twelfth century was the troubadour Bertrand de Born (*c.*1140- *c.*1215), born at Salagnac, who was deeply involved in his own family quarrels and those of the Plantagenets. He was a deeply quarrelsome fellow, dispossessing his brother Constantine and stirring up trouble all around. For a time he sided with the Young King, against his father, Henry II, but on his death was not too proud to receive the castle back from his overlord, though he lost it again to his brother and co-seigneur Constantin and retired in about 1195 to the Cistercian abbey of Le Dalon, where he died. It is said that one reason Henry II forgave his treachery was because of the matchless elegy he composed for the Young King.

Bertrand was one of the most individual of the troubadours who frequented Eleanor of Aquitaine's court, and in the manner of his time reconciled chivalrous love with the practice of warfare. Dante, however, thought his behaviour was lamentable and put him in the eighth circle in hell; in *Inferno* xxviii, 134, he makes him say:

> know that I am Bertrand de Born, he who to the Young King gave evil counsels. I made the father and the son rebels to each other; Achitophel did not do more with Absalom and David by his malicious instigations.

Ezra Pound was deeply interested in the troubadours and was fluent in the *langue d'oc*. He wrote a long poem *Near Périgord* which celebrates Bertrand de Born's love for the lady Maent and includes references to the Plantagenets.

And our En Bertrans was in Altafort,
Hub of the wheel, the stirrer-up of strife,
As caught by Dante in the last wallow of hell –
The headless trunk 'that made its head a lamp',
For separation wrought out separation,
And he who set the strife between brother and brother
And had his way with the old English king,
Viced in such torture for the 'counterpass'.

The four round towers, four brothers – mostly fools:
What could he do but play the desperate chess,
And stir old grudges?

The property passed out of the hands of the Born family by marriage towards the end of the fourteenth century and became indissolubly linked with that of the Hauteforts in the mid-fifteenth. Jean de Hautefort became chamberlain to both Charles VIII and Louis XII, and it was he who started to transform the feudal building. The royal connection continued and Marie de Hautefort, successively lady-in-waiting to Catherine de Medici and Anne of Austria, excited Louis XIII's interest. Her brother Jacques François employed a local architect, Nicolas Rambourg, and a Parisian, Jacques Maigret, to re-design and rebuild the château which, with some eighteenth-century additions, is substantially unchanged. Though two of its subsequent owners went to the guillotine and the building itself was used as a prison during the Revolution, it miraculously escaped destruction, at least until a fire in 1968. A lighted cigarette thrown carelessly from a window caused an immense amount of damage especially to the roof, which had to be entirely replaced. The château is surrounded by fine gardens and a park, and at its foot is the former hospital, now the parish church. This strictly classical cruciform building was also founded by Jacques François for thirty-three inmates (thirty-three because that was the age at which Christ died).

In these later centuries our interest inevitably tends to shift from buildings of interest for their own sake to those in which individuals lived, for during the late seventeenth and eighteenth centuries Périgord produced some figures of genuine national importance. The most famous and the greatest of these was Fénelon.

François de Salignac, one of eleven children, was born in the château of Fénelon at

Marie de Hautefort with Louis XIII

the south-eastern extremity of the province on 6 August 1651. He was put out to a wet-nurse who lived in a small cottage outside the castle walls. François's mother is said to have waved her kerchief daily from the ramparts to enquire if all was well with the child; she seems not to have seen him until he was about two. A great cedar of Lebanon, said to have been planted at his birth, stands in one of the courtyards – a mark of prescience considering that he was his father's eleventh child. Fénelon was well educated, went into the church and rose rapidly, becoming a disciple of the great Bossuet. In 1681 he became prior of Carennac (see page 23) and four years later was sent to convert the Huguenots of Poitou back to Catholicism. His gentle methods and partial success brought him to the notice of Louis XIV who appointed him in 1689 tutor to his grandson, the young Duc de Bourgogne. He was preferred to the see of Cambrai in 1695.

Fénelon's subsequent career however did not run so smoothly because he became involved with a group of Quietists, led by Mme Guyon, and, although he did not share her extremist views, he felt bound to defend some of them against Bossuet and the King. Indeed he wrote *Explication des Maximes des Saints* in her defence, but it was condemned by the pope. In great disfavour already, aggravated by the publication of *Télémaque*, written for his pupil, and in which he propounded his disaffection with monarchical government, he was banished from court to spend the rest of his life in Cambrai, dying there in 1715. He was greatly loved and kept the friendship of the Duc de Bourgogne with whom he maintained a clandestine correspondence. He wrote many spiritual treatises, in a simple and lucid style, showing a mixture of learning and compassion, wisdom and poetry. He was extremely critical of the King's attitude and behaviour in the later years of his reign but had the wisdom not to publish his famous diatribe against him:

> Sire, He who takes upon himself the liberty of thus addressing you has not interests to serve in this world ... if he speaks to you bluntly, be not dismayed, for truth at all times is strong and free, for all that it is seldom that you hear it ... You were born, Sire, with a heart that knows the meaning of justice and honesty. It was those who were responsible for your upbringing that taught you, in order to govern ... you should show favour only to men of servile dispositions and that your own selfish interests should ever be held to be paramount ... Reference is no longer made to the State or the laws of the State, but only to the King and the King's good pleasure ... You have yourself been raised to a pinnacle of glory, far surpassing, so they aver, the accumulated lustre of all your predecessors, which, in other words, means that they have reduced France to destitution in order to maintain a state of prodigal and incurable luxury at Court.
>
> Your people, whom you should love as your own children and who have hitherto so passionately loved you, are now dying of hunger. Cultivation is almost at a standstill, population in town and country is falling, trades of all kinds are dying out and producing ever fewer workmen: commerce is non-existent ... Instead of extracting even more money from your poor people, you ought to be giving it to them to buy food.
>
> Because you have always been fortunate you are unable to conceive of yourself as ever ceasing to be so; you are afraid to open your eyes; you are afraid that someone will open them for you; you are afraid that you might be obliged to diminish some of your glory.

Strong words – but his description of the life of the peasants of his day ring only too true for Périgord.

The château de *Fénelon* in which Fénelon was born stands high on the hills to the south of the river Dordogne and is one of the best preserved châteaux in the department, having been scrupulously restored by the Maleville family who owned it until 1927. The most renowned members of that family were Jacques de Maleville, a lawyer who was responsible for writing *Réflexions sur les interêts et les prétensions des trois ordres* at Domme in 1789, a member of the Directory and one of the editors of the French Civil Code; and Lucien de Maleville, who illustrated many of the books on local history between the wars.

The road up to the château through Ste Mondane winds through the woods and it is a surprise when you reach it to find that the castle has disappeared behind its huge outer wall. When it reappears, standing proudly on a rocky escarpment behind its triple enclosure, still roofed in *lauzes*, it demonstrates a certain elegance with its great mass. It was built during the fourteenth and fifteenth centuries when it was the most important château in a defensive line between Périgord and Quercy which included the châteaux of Rocanadel and La Tourette. The rooms are furnished with objects dating from the fifteenth to the eighteenth centuries, and there is a good collection of arms and armour. The great Fénelon's bed, his chasuble and other personal belongings are preserved there in the room in which he spent much of his youth. Unfortunately the mementoes which belonged to his ancestor Bertrand de Salignac, who was for a time ambassador to England in the sixteenth century, and which included a ring belonging to Mary Queen of Scots and a gold chain presented to him by Elizabeth I, seem no longer to exist.

Another Salignac possession in the neighbourhood is the château in the attractive large village from which they took their family name. The château de *Salignac* was built on twelfth-century foundations and still has its thirteenth-century chapel, though most of the building is of the fifteenth to seventeenth centuries. It is in good condition and contains a fair number of Fénelon's relics, including a sword reputed to have belonged to his young charge, the Duc de Bourgogne, and some provincial

Château de Fénelon

Louis XIV period furniture. (The peasants of the surrounding district retained their *droits de puisage* – their rights to draw water from the well – until as recently as 1940.)

The Salignac family, who re-purchased the château after the Revolution and to whom it belonged until 1959, also had connections with another building of interest, the bishop's palace at *Issigeac*. Fine and even elegant, it was erected by François de Salignac, Fénelon's uncle, in the second half of the seventeenth century. The church, one of the few Périgordin ecclesiastical monuments not of monastic foundation, was built by Armand de Gontaut Biron, Bishop of Sarlat, but was badly damaged during the Revolution and has been restored. Issigeac is an agreeable small town, which was once wholly walled, with some half-timbered houses and attractive winding streets.

It is a short step – about 20 kilometres – albeit just beyond the departmental boundary, to the birthplace of one of Fénelon's rather less saintly contemporaries, the Duc de Lauzun (1632-1723). The château de *Lauzun* is a fine sixteenth-century building, well worth a visit for its own sake as well as for the sake of its owner – a rake who dallied monstrously with the affections of Louis XIV's first cousin, the Grande Mademoiselle, and who spent some years in the Bastille before returning to favour. Barbey d'Aurevilly in a famous work on dandyism – a mannerism he thought to be specifically English – called him a dandy before the advent of dandyism and an English Frenchman, but as usual it is the Duc de St Simon who in his inimitable manner conjures him up best:

> M. de Lauzun was small and fair, extremely well built, with a noble air, a countenance that sparkled with intelligence and inspired respect, but was without charm – at least, so I was told by his contemporaries.
>
> Overflowing with ambition, whims, and fancies, he was covetous of everything, always wanting more, never content with what he possessed. He had no education, no culture, no intellectual graces or refinement. By nature he was melancholy, unsociable, violent; lordly in all his ways, essentially spiteful and malicious, and made more so by jealousy and ambition; yet when he made a friend, which was rare, he himself was a good one, and a good kinsman also.
>
> Quick in making enemies, even with persons of no importance, he was cruel to their defects and in discovering and mocking their absurdities. He was courageous in the extreme and most dangerously rash. As a courtier, he was insolent, mocking, and servile to the point of cringing, ready to use any mean trick, plotting and labouring with infinite care in order to gain his ends, therefore dangerous to ministers, feared by everyone at the court, uttering biting remarks with a wit that spared no one.

M. de Lauzun

The opening years of the eighteenth century saw no amelioration in the lot of the peasants in Périgord: indeed it was aggravated by a series of disastrous winters, such as that of 1709, and the failure of harvests, although the introduction of *blé d'Espagne* – maize – made their diet a little more varied, solid and nutritious. There was little change throughout the century; industry and commerce stagnated, and its backwardness on the eve of the Revolution was noted by Arthur Young:

> Cross the Dordonne by a ferry; the boat well-contrived for driving in at one end, and out at the other, without the abominable operation, common in England, of beating horses till they leap into them; the price is as great a contrast as the excellence; we paid for an English whisky [a light carriage], a French cabriolet, one saddle-horse and six persons, no more than 50 sous (2s. 1d.); I have paid half-a-crown a wheel in England for execrable ferries. This river runs in a very deep valley between two ridges of high hills; extensive views, all scattered with villages and single houses; an appearance of great population of chestnuts on a calcareous soil, contrary to the Limousin maxim.
>
> Pass Payrac, and meet many beggars, which we had not done before. All the country girls and women are without shoes or stockings; and the ploughmen at their work have neither sabots or stockings to their feet. This is a poverty that strikes at the root of national prosperity; a large consumption among the poor being of

The Marquis de Cardaillac being ferried across the Dordogne at Pinsac

more consequence than among the rich. The wealth of a nation lies in its circulation and consumption; and the case of poor people abstaining from the use of manufactures of leather and wool ought to be considered as an evil of the first magnitude. It reminded me of the misery of Ireland.

As might be expected, when the communes were asked to prepare their *cahiers de doléances* in 1789, the burden of complaints in them related to the heavy taxation and the increasingly strictly applied hunting privileges of the aristocracy. A curious incident marked the beginning of the Revolution in the district. The Bastille fell on 14 July and, though the news of its fall and of subsequent events travelled fast, it is none the less strange that two weeks later, on 29, 30 and 31 July, there was a seemingly spontaneous outbreak of panic throughout Périgord, when rumours flew about that thousands of English or Spanish or Moors or just simply nameless brigands were on the rampage. The consuls of Périgueux were alerted as the parish registers of both Grand Brassac and Condat sur Trincou record, but nothing seems actually to have happened, and no Russians with snow on their boots were actually seen.

Périgord did not play much part in the Revolution nor contribute any great men to the various governments; relatively few nobles were executed though many emigrated, and the Terror was less terrible than elsewhere. Some châteaux were fired by the peasants, but that after all was nothing new in the area, and even the feared Lakanal boasted to Maine de Biran, admittedly in 1814, that he had the satisfaction that no one could say he had spilt a single drop of blood. Joseph Lakanal (1762-1845) had been sent to Bergerac to govern the province and, though he was held responsible for the destruction of the châteaux of Laforce, Montferrand and Badefols, his administrative and educational reforms were beneficial. Similarly the Restoration was achieved without the excess found further south despite the behaviour of the Ultras (the die-hard monarchist party) in Périgueux.

The one figure of international standing that the department claims as its own who emerged at this period was Talleyrand, the cynical priest turned cynical politician, the man 'who betrayed Napoleon to save France', the ringmaster of Europe at the Congress of Vienna, and the ambassador to London who stunned the capital with the table kept for him by Carême. In his memoirs, perhaps written while wearing rose-coloured spectacles, he recalled the Périgordin nobility of the *ancien régime*:

> In the provinces far from the capital, special attention was paid to dignity and position by the higher ranks who still lived in their ancient châteaux with those of lesser degree and their tenants. The leading aristocrat would have considered it beneath him not to have behaved with impeccable manners and kindness. His more distinguished neighbours would have felt a lack of self-respect in failing to display the regard due to their superiors in the form of love. The seigneur

Talleyrand

only visited his peasants in order to give them assistance and address them in kind and comforting words; which set an example of correct behaviour.

The manners of the Périgordin nobility resembled the architecture of their houses – they were unchanging and solid – there was little light but what penetrated was gentle. Progress towards enlightenment was slow but steady. There was no petty tyranny – it had been destroyed by the spirit of chivalry which followed, in these people of the south, from a sentiment of gallantry and above all from the growth of royal power which was based on the liberation of the people.

The Talleyrand Périgord family had deep roots in the province and owned a good deal of property there. The most famous member of the family in the early Middle Ages, was Hélie, Archdeacon of Périgueux, Abbot of Chancelade and Bishop of Limoges. He was raised to the cardinalate, and became known at Avignon as 'le faiseur des papes'. His sister was married to the nephew of Pope John XXII, through whom the truffle is reputed to have come into the department from the Rhône; and his brother was a friend of Edward III and the Black Prince, and a protector of Petrarch. Their family power and influence continued, and in 1700 one of their descendants was chosen to accompany the Duc d'Anjou when he succeeded to the throne of Spain. The family died out at the end of the nineteenth century, when two of Talleyrand's own great nephews were involved in a scandal by both marrying the same American heiress, whose only son committed suicide.

Their châteaux included those of Montignac, Chalais, Neuvic sur l'Isle, a fine example of Périgordin renaissance building, and Excideuil. That of Excideuil now has only two fourteenth-century keeps and two renaissance wings standing, and a fine entry portal. It stands at the edge of a busy small town whose church is also worth a visit, for its gothic doorway, pietà and seventeenth-century retable.

The largest and most elegant early nineteenth-century building in Dordogne is the château of *Rastignac*, near La Bachellerie on the road from Terrasson to Périgueux. The château was built some time between 1789 and 1815 when it was completed by a local architect, Mathurin Blanchard, for Jean Gabriel de Chapt de Rastignac or his son, and bears a surprising resemblance to the White House in Washington.

It is uncertain how the similarity came about but it is thought that the Marquis de Rastignac may have met in Paris the architects employed by Thomas Jefferson when he was ambassador to France from 1785-89. The plans were perhaps drawn up by Charles Louis Clérisseau, a pupil of Claude Nicolas Ledoux, or possibly by James Hoban, the Irish architect of the White House. The house was largely destroyed by

Eugène Le Roy, woodcut by Maurice Albe

the Germans in 1944, except for the façades, vestibule and main staircase. It has been empty since, and is now up for sale. Nevertheless, it is worth driving up the magnificent poplar-lined avenue to take a closer look at the exterior.

Lacking genuine nineteenth-century sages or heroes – save for Fournier-Sarlovèze, Daumesnil and Bugeaud – the Périgordins were fortunate in their novelists. *Pontcarral*, written by Albéric Cahuet, is a bitter story of a Napoleonic colonel exiled to Fondaumier at the Restoration and the trouble he had in being accepted into the society of the provincial nobility. While it unquestionably has a whiff of historical reality about it, finding out whether or not Colonel Pontcarral actually existed proved surprisingly difficult, so deeply is he now embedded in local culture. He turns out to be a work of pure fiction, though based on a number of oral traditions. A man by the name of Vergnolles certainly lived at Fondaumier, near Cénac, where much of the action of the novel takes place and where Cahuet's house was – indeed still is. Vergnolles fought at Austerlitz and survived the retreat from Moscow. He lived to an advanced age, as did his daughter, Mariette who died, nearly 100, only just before the Second World War. Cahuet's novel, if of indifferent quality, has the merit of some verisimilitude in describing provincial rural society just after the Napoleonic wars.

Similarly, the hero of *Jacquou le Croquant*, a justly more famous novel by Eugène Le Roy, was modelled on a Pierre Grelety who led a peasant's revolt in the early seventeenth century. He and a band of disaffected men lived in the Forêt Vergt from

Illustration for Jacquou le Croquant *by Julien Saraben*

1637-41, but he was pardoned in 1643 and later served honourably in the Italian campaigns.

Le Roy's works, which run to ten volums, include *Le Moulin du Frau, Nicette et Milou, Les Gens d'Auberoque* and *La Damnation de St Guignefort*, but *Jacquou le Croquant*, published in 1899, is the best known. It is a minor masterpiece of its genre, full of evocative descriptive writing about a countryside the author loved and portrayed faithfully. Part of the action takes place at the château de l'Herm, a dramatically ruined building in the heart of the forêt Barade which is now, quite wrongly, linked indissolubly with Jacquou's exploits. In fact it was built in 1512 by Jean III de Calvimont, witnessed a series of particularly atrocious and violent crimes – so common in the sixteenth century – and was a ruin by the early nineteenth-century, which is when Le Roy's novel is set.

Le Roy was born in Hautefort in 1836, the son of the château bailiff, and he grew up knowing the habits and life-style of the gentry. After army service which took him all over Europe, he became a tax collector and was based both in Domme and Montignac, where he died. His *cabinet de travail* there, over which he presided in a Tolstoy-like fashion, has now been made into a small exhibition room. His work brought him into daily contact with the peasants and gave him a deep understanding of their problems. It was this experience and his concern which were the basis of the series of historical novels, all of which are set in Périgord.

The attempts at land reform during the middle of the century have been discussed on page 46 but that they did not alleviate the grinding poverty of the local peasantry is clear. Deeply distressed by what he still saw as social evils in his own day, Le Roy used his tales, set fifty years earlier, to draw attention to contemporary conditions. Certainly he tends to idealize the peasant and his life tied to the soil, and he portrays both the old and the new aristocracy as the villains. He makes no reference to the tentative commercialization of agriculture and urban growth that resulted from the building of the railways, but this hardly invalidates what he has to say.

By 1840 the economic life of the province was improving at least within its urban communities, and not least in Périgueux which began to install mansions and boulevards and display the acquisitive tastes of the bourgeoisie so accurately evoked in the *Comédie Humaine*. It was a fine day when a Gourdon draper could advertise his clothes as being *à la mode de Sarlat*.

One might well be forgiven for confusing the picaresque figure of Antoine Tounens with one of Le Roy's creations or even one of Balzac's. Of obscure origin, by 1858 Tounens was practising as a lawyer in Périgueux when he conceived the desire to capture a South American tribe, become its king and earn untold riches. To this end, he borrowed money, set out for Chile, raised an army and proclaimed himself King of Auracania in 1862. The Chilean government had him repatriated, but he collected

Antoine Tounens·

more money and set out again, going this time to Patagonia and repeating his previous behaviour. He was repatriated yet again and managed two more equally unsuccessful forays, acknowledging defeat at last and retiring to Tourtoirac, where he died in 1878.

Tourtoirac itself a small town of about 650 inhabitants lies on the Auvézère. It shelters the remains of a Benedictine abbey. Alas, remains is the right word, for what is left is in a sorry state and even the restoration is itself crumbling under damp and decay. Part of the monastic buildings are still extant and are grouped round a charming little garden made from the remnants of the cloister which encloses the parish priest's house. There is a small romanesque chapel which has amphorae bedded into the roof to improve the acoustics (although they do not appear to work very efficiently) and an abbey building, the crypt of which contains a chapter house with romanesque pillars surmounted by amusing capitals of monks pulling at their beards.

Cyrano de Bergerac is best known as the hero of Edmond Rostand's play, but, unlike Jacquou and Pontcarral, is based far more directly on a genuine figure whose life gave Rostand (1868-1918) the main facts for his play. Savinien de Cyrano was born in Paris and the registers of the parish of St Sauveur record his baptism there in 1619. He was at the Collège de Beauvais until 1637 and served under Captain Carbon de Casteljaloux (who figures in Rostand's play) at the siege of Mouzon where he was wounded. His military career ended when he was wounded again, in the throat, at Arras in 1649. Back in Paris, he studied under the astronomer Gassendi and worked in the household of the Duc d'Arpajon, in whose hôtel he lived in the Marais. He died in 1655.

Although Savinien's association was with his family's estate at the Bergerac in the Chevreuse valley near Paris, and nowhere near Gascony, Bergerac in Périgord took him over as a local hero long before Rostand's day and it is possible that Rostand got the idea from the long and learned article that appeared in 1854 in *Le Chroniqueur*, a monthly magazine founded in Périgueux the previous year. What however is certain is that Rostand's play, such an evocative piece of seventeenth-century pastiche, did not have its first appearance until 1897. Performed at the Théâtre de la Porte St Martin in Paris, it was an immediate success. Appropriately enough it is now often staged at the Sarlat summer festival where it touches a chord in the native audience, for Rostand displays a genuine knowledge of and feeling for the region:

> *Du double étui de cuir tire l'un des fifres,*
> *Souffle, et joue à ce tas de goinfres et de piffres*
> *Ces vieux airs du pays, au doux rythme obsesseur,*
> *Dont chaque note est comme une petite soeur,*
> *Dan lesquels restent pris des sons de voix aimées*
> *Ces airs dont le lenteur est celle des fumées*
> *Que le hameau natal exhale de ses toits,*
> *Ces airs dont la musique a l'air d'être un patois.*
>
> *Ecoutez, les Gascons, ce n'est plus, sous ses doigts*
> *Le fifre aigu des camps, c'est la flute des bois!*
> *Ce n'est plus le sifflet du combat, sur ses lèvres.*
> *C'est le lent galoubet de nos meneurs de chèvres!*
> *Ecoutez ... c'est le val, la lande, la fôret*
> *Le petit pâtre brun sous son rouge beret,*
> *C'est la verte douceur des soirs sur la Dordogne,*
> *Ecoutez, les Gascons: c'est toute la Gascogne!*
>
> (ACT IV, ii)

Ach, ye think of naethin but food!
– C'moan, Bertrandou, auld shepherd, gie's yer flute;
Take wan a yer fifes oot of its leather case,
Gie it a blaw, shame thae greedy-guts tae their face,
Pley the auld folk-tunes wae their repetitions,
Ivry note a little sister's visions,
– Listen, Gascons! His fingers'll no pley
The sherp fife a the camps, but the flute's wey

A the foarests; nae whusslin up the clans
But dreamy goatherds pipin slaw pavanes …
– Listen … This is the glen, the wids, the hill-tap,
The sunburnt herd-laddie wae'z rid cap,
The gloamin ower Dordogne, its dear green mastery …
Listen, Gascons: it's here, it's yours, it's Gascony!

(trans. Edwin Morgan)

A street was named after Cyrano in Bergerac in 1857, forty years before the play was first performed and the town is still proud of him, as it is of another and more genuine of its distinguished natives, Marie François Pierre Gonthier (1766-1824), who after 1790 called himself Maine de Biran, the name by which he is now always known. He was the son of a doctor and spent the better part of his life in Bergerac. His philosophical writings, in which the humanity of Montaigne and the spirituality of Fénelon meet, were important in their time for their emphasis on psychology. He was led by a difficult path to a belief in the existence of God by his insistence on man as a reflective being. His *Journal Intime*, published posthumously as late as 1927, remains his most important work.

Of the town of *Bergerac* itself, despite its obvious strategic importance, little is known of the origins of a château or a *seigneurie* before the twelfth century, and it seems always to have been more of an economic than a military centre. Until the fourteenth century Bragairac (with variations on the spelling) was English and French by turns until the end of the Hundred Years War. Bergerac has always

Maine de Biran

*Cloister of the
Récollets, Bergerac*

been the centre of the wine industry in the department and, being only 30 miles from St Emilion and about 55 from Bordeaux, has inevitably suffered from the proximity, for even its best wines are, in the words of E. Penning Rowsell, 'no rivals to the fine growths of the neighbouring Gironde'. The growers of Bergeracois tried to ship their own produce direct via Bergerac or Libourne so as to avoid the necessity of passing down the Garonne through Bordeaux itself. In the Middle Ages the Bordelais appealed to the king of France to impose restrictions on the navigation of the Dordogne so as to hinder this, and when that failed they attempted to get the regulations about the size of the barrels changed. Since taxes were levied on the number of barrels, the Bordelais hoped to get the size of the barrels originating in Bergerac made smaller. But they were no more successful in this either.

The town was a Protestant stronghold and became a hotbed for printing Reformist propaganda; it suffered badly from the Revocation of the Edict of Nantes and the subsequent emigration of at least half its population, and has few memorials to its medieval past. But, although many people are inclined to dismiss the town as nothing other than busy and commercialized, the old quarters down by the river have some charm, as does the former Convent of the Récollets, where there is a Maison du Vin, kept by the producers of Monbazillac and where many of the local wines may be tasted in the pleasant fifteenth-century surroundings.

Despite the importance of the river Dordogne and the need to cross it frequently, ferries and fords were the only means of doing so upstream as far as Beaulieu and Bort les Orgues until the nineteenth century. The bridge at Argentat was built in

1829 and others followed slowly. There had however been a bridge at Bergerac since the twelfth century but that had been destroyed in the floods of 1444-45 and it was not rebuilt until 1502. This one was a sight sung both by Rabelais, who marvelled at the enormous size of its supporting beams, and by Montaigne. There was a small shrine in the middle of it where women would light two candles, one for the saint and one to guard them against snakes, but it was destroyed yet again by floods of unprecedented severity in 1783.

The church of Notre Dame, rather flamboyantly called the cathedral, is a neo-gothic pastiche with a spire 80 metres tall, and the church of St Jacques, restored in 1868, houses two pictures of some merit: an Adoration of the Shepherds by Gaudenzio Ferrari and an Adoration of the Magi by Pordenone. There is a small municipal museum devoted to local history attached to the Tobacco Museum, and there is now also a small private museum containing a collection of religious objects.

The twentieth century has failed to produce any local painters of note but there are at least two writers of whom the department may be proud. Léon Bloy (1846-1917), who was certainly the most recent writer of any note. He was born and brought up in Périgueux. His writing is violent and embittered and has a frenetic power. His two best known works, out of a large and varied œuvre, are *Le Désesperé*, an early novel and *Le Mendiant ingrat*, the journal of his later years.

A contemporary of his, whose name is frequently mentioned in the department, was 'Rachilde', Marguerite Eymery, born in Cros in 1860. She was married to Alfred Vallette, the director of the *Mercure de France*, wrote essays and kept a fashionable literary salon. She died in 1953.

Dordogne was largely insulated from the First World War, except in so far as she sent her sons to be killed in the trenches, but suffered to a much greater degree in the Second. At first in the unoccupied zone, her inhabitants plied a brisk black market trade in tobacco and food, but once the Germans moved in and discovered what good *'maquis'* country the limestone caves and forests afforded, reprisals and deportations were frequent. Oradour sur Glane – the village where the Germans, moving reinforcements up to the Normandy coast to counter the Allied invasion in 1944, shot the men and burned the church into which they had herded the women and children – is only just outside the confines of the department, and Mouleydier, in the department, was also destroyed. However the department, which sheltered refugees from Strasbourg during the Vichy regime, recovered rapidly and life returned to normal fairly quickly after the end of the war.

The arrival of Josephine Baker, who bought the château of *Les Milandes* in 1948 was a considerable surprise. It was there that she raised her adopted polyglot family and installed her 'village of the world'. But her dream faded, leaving behind only art nouveau bathrooms and the hatred of the villagers. The château was originally built in the fifteenth century and belonged to the Caumont La Force family until the Revolution. It was added to and restored in the nineteenth century and now, set in a large park, offers many popular attractions including demonstrations of falconry.

The influx of wealthy buyers for the grand houses and châteaux in the department in the nineteenth and twentieth centuries can be explained by the coincidence of the increasing wealth of the bourgeoisie and the installation of an extensive railway system. One of the most beautiful small houses in the region, the manoir of Cipières, nestling in a secret valley at St Crépin and Carlucet, is a case in point. Owned by a prosperous stonemason and now by an architect, it has been lovingly restored, and lies behind a low yellow stone wall flanked by leafy trees and backing on to the hillside. With a square tower at one end, and a hexagonal one at the other, a *lauze*-roof pierced by a solitary window and one chimney pot, it is the epitome of the domestic architecture of the region.

Apart from the grand bourgeois mansions in some of the towns, most of the

The manoir of Cipières

country buildings were simple dwellings for man and beast, and virtually all are built of stone. Eugène Le Roy says in *Nicette et Milou*: 'Hereabouts there is stone everywhere and it comes from all over the place. The inhabitants reckon that it is born in the earth, for the ground is covered as if it had rained stone. The hedges are walls of stone, the paths are quarries and the roofs are sloping sheets of stone rising obliquely on the roof-trees of all the houses and barns.'

The lower storey, only occasionally sunk below ground level, housed at night the cattle whose steamy heat helped to keep the sleepers above warm. Many of the houses therefore have a flight of stone steps, sometimes with grand iron banisters leading to a shallow balustraded terrace, sometimes roofed, giving access to the living quarters. All had attics, with small air inlets known as *lucarnes*, or in some parts of the departments as *sourcils* (eyebrows), used in the past for drying tobacco or beans, onions and garlic. Some have dovecotes, though these are not as common as in neighbouring Quercy where the poverty of the soil on the upland *causses* greatly benefitted from the birds' droppings. *Lauze*-covered roofs were common and many are still to be seen, but their incredible weight – a ton per square yard – and the need for the special flat stones to be laid by skilled craftsmen means that they are no longer used except in cases of expensive restoration. One of the finest expanses of such roofing is to be seen on the church at St Geniès, which occupies, together with its adjacent château, an island site in the centre of the town. The old presbytery with its tower has recently been renovated with its *lauze* roof, and there is talk of a museum dedicated to stone roofing.

A fine expanse of a lauze *roof in Sarlat*

Most of the houses, simple though they are, have great charm and beauty, derived from a harmonious use of local materials which blend with the landscape in an entirely satisfying way. They are well proportioned, and quite large – space being no problem. Neither the inside nor the outside of the stone walls are rendered, at least as a general rule, and the only living room will have an open hearth, with a flight of stairs often leading up behind it to the sleeping quarters. The thick stone walls keep the houses cool in hot summers though they are liable to retain the damp in the winter. One of the most noticeable changes over the last twenty years is the high proportion of houses that now have central heating installed.

Most, if not all, the houses have at least one barn, sometimes set at right angles to the house, sometimes facing it across a courtyard – and many have a whole series of outhouses to accommodate cattle, pigs, fowl and nowadays farm machinery. The barns, with their characteristic basket-handle-shaped arched doorways to allow for the entry of a hay-wagon, are as beautiful as the houses, though they may be slate roofed, whereas the houses are likely to have terracotta tiles. However humble and simple the small complex, and however higgledy-piggledy it appears, the whole farm ensemble is one of the delights of the region. As stone was less easy to come by in the area of Double, the houses there are more likely to be built from daub and wattle, and timbered; some are even of brick.

The poverty of the region has on the whole meant that there is very little fine furniture though there are some fruit-wood, especially walnut, cupboards and chests of pleasing solidity in a simple provincial style; even these are now fetching high prices. The absence of regional painting or sculpture or even of idiosyncratic styles in pottery or textiles may be accounted for by the rigours of extracting a livelihood from the soil which left little time or energy for such leisure or moneyed activities. There were potteries in the eighteenth century at Thiviers, Bergerac, Le Bugue, Montpeyroux, Ste Foy la Grande and Le Fleix. 'Art' has gone into the requirements of everyday living and it is the artisans serving the needs of the community – the masons, the carpenters, the tilers, the roof-coverers and metal-workers – who have been and still are the artists of the region. These skills happily persist. But 'art for art's sake' is now being imported. The department is alive with signs sending you to some painter on silk, some sculptor in metal, some potter or wood carver. The young, no longer wishing to be apprenticed, have taken to a uniformly boring series of craft works and the simple life, hoping thereby to make a living with their poker-work belts, spindly jewellery, lampshades from sheepskin and wooden knick-knacks. There are also seasonal courses in arts and crafts for summer visitors and the substantial number of people who have holiday homes in the region.

How is one to explain the atttractions of the area, and in partiular of Périgord noir, for people seeking *maisons secondaires*? Some thirty years ago there were a number of British buyers. Petrol was still cheap, the roads relatively uncrowded; the houses or barns, especially if they needed restoration, were cheaper than those in Provence and it was less far to drive. The absence of large conurbations and any sign of industrial activity together with the lush greenness, relatively mild winters and hot summers made it seem like a vision of a long-departed rural England. Perhaps too there were some deep atavistic memories of the long-standing connection with Gascony and of the excitement of rediscovery at the end of the nineteenth century when the first archaeological explorations of the decorated caves brought Cro Magnon man and his artefacts to the atttention of the British, always intrepid travellers.

Perhaps the reasons the Dutch like it too are similar, compounded by nostalgic historical recollections of the time when so many of the local Huguenots fled to Holland after the Revocation of the Edict of Nantes. If it is true that they took with them their taste for the sweet wines of Monbazillac, perhaps today their descendants believe that the wine tastes still sweeter on its native soil.

Because some foreign families who bought houses for children's summer holidays started to sell them as the children grew older and the value of sterling fell, for a short time property lost its value. Today however there is a new boom fuelled by the ease of access either by Eurostar and faster trains, or by the improved though far from perfect motorways, and especially by the increasing numbers of French who choose to retire here. There are some 27,740 secondary residences in the department, housing an estimated 104,000 people.

The days in the 1970's when 'Oc' was scratched and painted on walls throughout the department and local magazines were liable to publish articles under headings such as 'France, ton patrimoine fout le camp!' have passed, and the acquisition of property by outsiders is no longer news in either the English or the French press, although the former continues to publish articles, some nowadays a bit snide, on the area or at least on the expatriates.

Opposition to this silent invasion which in 1976 led to two explosions in estate agents' offices in Sarlat has faded and farmers, who once objected to the price of land being forced up because of foreign buying and profiteering, have more pragmatically turned to cashing in themselves. Today's boom in property prices is also partly due to the increasing number of French who choose to retire here.

Last year I met an ancient Frenchman who lives by himself in a tiny house set in a small plot of land. He is a healthy 94-year-old and moved into the department some years ago. He was born in Cambrai and worked in commerce all his life, spending six years after the Second World War in the City of London. He loved it and developed such an enduring passion for things British that on his return to France he took out a subscription to the Sunday Times to keep in touch. There he repeatedly read that Britons were flocking to buy houses here and he decided to find out why. He came, he saw, he moved in.

The inflow of millions of francs (3.5 milliards a year) earned from tourists each season (of whom there were 2 million in 1998, accounting for 22% of the department's income), while a joy to the hearts of the tourist offices and a just reward for the deliberate policy of the departmental administrators, cannot disguise the fact that a swarm of holiday-makers who come for two months a year will not till the soil nor compensate for the flight from the land by the young.

Many of the farmers own several houses, so there are plenty to be let in the summer months and the welcome you will receive in them is warm. It is symptomatic of the area, and the natives' changing attitudes, that the number of *gîtes ruraux* has more than doubled in the last twenty years.

You can now buy local produce from over 450 farms, and over 500 offer bed-and-breakfast accommodation. Camp sites with good amenities, 75% of which are in Périgord noir, are springing up like mushrooms, and new attractions, like the 'living village' of Bournat at Le Bugue, provide education as well as popular amusement, and there are even various courses in regional cooking on offer. Much more exciting, the French have at last discovered sharing the joys of gardening. 'New' gardens are opened to visitors almost every year. Some of the most impressive are highly formal, like Marqueyssac and Eyrignac. The latter, some thirteen kilometres northeast of Sarlat, was created in the eighteenth century by the Marquis de Coste de la Calprenède to the designs of an Italian architect, and lovingly restored by the Sermadiras family. The main feature is the topiary: rows of immaculate box, yews, hornbeams and cypresses punctuate lawns (mowed every five days) that would not disgrace an Oxford quad.

Some are small like that at Cadiot just outside Carlux, some more ambitious and *outré*, like the Jardin de l'Imaginaire at Terrasson which consists of a series of linked gardens, landscaped by Kathryn Gustafson, on a terraced hillside each of which has a somewhat nebulous and trendy theme such as: *bois sacré, fil d'or, théâtre de verdure, axe des vents, tracé éphémère*. The plants and shrubs are chosen for their mystical or medicinal significance and there are attractive water stairs and a stone terrace from which jets of water gently sussurate above a large rose garden. 'Concepts' seem to have taken precedence over the desire to create beautiful vistas or enclaves but perhaps this is unfair as the garden has only been open for three years and nature may yet get the upper hand. The café and shop were designed by Ian Ritchie (also responsible for the new Jubilee line station at Bermondsey).

The hoteliers and shopkeepers too find the trade brought by these temporarily resident and visiting foreign and French campers lucrative. The number of hotels and restaurants has doubled over the past ten years. Local artisans and craftsmen earn a third of their income from restoring property bought by foreigners, and the producers of local food claim that a quarter of their tinned preserves is bought by visitors. It is not for them, as *Le Monde* so elegantly put it, 'to spit in the faces of their clients'.

Foreign residents and tourists will find life very pleasant and everyone almost without exception polite and above all friendly. Restaurateurs are always pleased to see one, market stall owners are always willing to give tastes or discuss their wares, masons and plumbers and electricians are always ready to help in a crisis, and to share a glass of red wine when the work is done.

For the immediate future, therefore, it would seem that tourism will be the most profitable industry, and strenuous efforts are being made to extend the area visited beyond the valleys of the Vézère and the Dordogne and the immediate vicinity of Sarlat, and the season from the overcrowded months of July and August.

The department is however undergoing change in other directions; whereas in 1982 21.7% of the population earned its living from the land only 15.7% are now engaged in agriculture, forestry and fishing. Industry accounts for some 17.8% and, a recent development, building and civil engineering, takes up another 9.1%. Although it is official departmental policy to promote 'artisanat' and small businesses, and every effort is being made to sustain and encourage agriculture, the real growth is in the service industries.

John Ardagh is surely right in concluding in his recent *France in the new century: Portrait of a Changing Society* that, after some years in an uneasy state of transition, France has done better than it thinks in adapting to modern change while keeping the best of its traditions. Indeed in adjusting to new lifestyles while keeping a French flavour, the return to rural roots, the revival of interest in cuisine, the renewal of folk culture, and the eager new concern for local history all contribute to ensuring that this land of beauty continues to offer an unparalleled *douceur de vie*.

Life in Périgord

The rhythm of daily life in Dordogne is governed as absolutely by the year's cycle today, both in the market towns and the countryside, as in the past and, although there has been a decline in religious observance, the nomenclature used by the church to denote its feast and saint's days persists. One will be told that the wheat must be sown by All Saints' Day and to beware of the three *terribles chevaliers* – St George on 23 April, St Mark on 25 April and St Eutropius on 30 April – for these are the days when late frosts will ruin the harvest. (St Eutropius was a first-century martyr who had reputedly evangelized the region.) The Feast of the Assumption of the Virgin on 15 August – the summer holiday equalled only in importance by Christmas – brings life in the department, as in the rest of France, to a complete standstill.

One may reasonably start the agricultural year in January for that is when the vines, on which so much of the department's income depends, are pruned to remove the old wood. The plant will weep if it is cut after the first growth appears. Temperatures during the winter months from November to February are rarely lower than zero, though the lowest reached in recent years was in January 1985 with minus 22 to minus 28 degrees. This is the time too when the middle leaves of the tobacco are taken to SEITA and when the family pig may well be killed. Bought in the previous March, it will have reached its optimum weight of 120-130 kilos. In the past killing the pig was a great occasion and it required the presence of a considerable number of people to deal with it. The blood had to be collected while it was still fresh and, before refrigerators and deep freezes were common, the sausages had to be made and eaten quickly. The women would spend these short winter days preparing their *confits* after cooking them in pots large enough to take the whole animal and preserving them in the *toupines*, the great stoneware jars, which are still to be seen, in which they would be stored in the cool of the cellar.

In February, when the evenings are still dark and the days liable to be wet – the mean annual rainfall in 1997 was 975.6 mm – amusements such as the *fête des cornes* would enliven the week before Lent. Philip Oyler saw one such *fête* on Ash Wednesday in Domme (where it still took place as late as 1971):

167

On that morning there are sudden blasts from horns, not in harmony or any attempt at it! It sounds like a number of bullocks at play. This is the signal for those who were married in the preceding year – the period between the Carnival of Horns – to assemble, disguised and masked, on the Place de la Rode. The last of those who were married in that year carries a hayfork decorated in the following way: slipped over the points of the fork, one over each, are two ox horns, the largest that can be found. Sprays of ivy and laurel are wound round the lower part of the prongs and the handle of the fork as well and tied with golden ribbons. It may represent a trophy of some old image dedicated to the great Pan or other rural divinity.

When the inhabitants have all collected, the troop of masqueraders betake themselves, with musical instruments leading, to the house of the first man married during the preceding carnival year. They arrange themselves in front of his house and give him a morning serenade of sorts! When the music stops, the oldest married masquerader steps forth and calls out three times *le saffre*; that is, the surname of the owner. There is no *monsieur*, no *politesse* in the address. He is not reticent to hear. He knows that everyone is outside and that any show of objection or resistance would 'add fuel to the fire' of amusement and exuberance and that enough of that is to follow anyway. So he comes out on to the steps at his front door and the music greets him with fury!

When that stops again, the man steps forward, teased on all sides and conducted by the master of the ceremonies. Firstly, he is made to curtsey very humbly to the decorated hayfork, which is held in the centre of the circle. If his bow does not satisfy the audience, he has to repeat it till it does! After that he is made to kneel on a large rough stone, where he is asked a number of farcical questions put in similar form to a catechism at marriage. When he has answered as best he can these impudent, ludicrous, and (I may say) embarrassing queries as to his relations with his wife during his first year of marriage, he is made to recite word for word a profession of faith! In this he promises to be deaf and blind and die of laughter! And to finish, he has to swear on the sacred horns that he will never believe that 'it is, even if he should see it'! What 'it' is, is left to the imagination.

When he has made this avowal, the great garlanded horns are made to do obeisance to him and indeed are laid across his head for a moment; and he has to embrace them. Then the master of ceremonies pronounces in a burlesque formula that the wretched victim has now been received into the illustrious fellowship! He is then honoured, dubbed like a knight, and the music acclaims him in no uncertain manner.

During these proceedings the man's wife watches from the background, laughing or blushing according to the nature of the questions and answers.

When this farce is finished, the novice takes the hayfork and leads the procession to the second man married in the preceding year and the fun begins again.

On a sharp March morning in the relatively recent past, you might have seen the arrival of the itinerant distiller. An antique still – known as an *alambic* – a machine of beauty and of copper, with pipes and tubes like any Heath Robinson contraption, was drawn by a tractor and parked conveniently for the use of the greatest number of outlying farmers to save them having to make the burdensome trek to the permanent still. The remains of the grapes and their stalks were carted along, with wood and water to fuel the machine, and the distillation began. (Plums were –

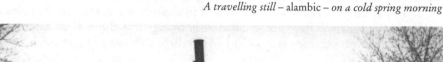

A travelling still – alambic *– on a cold spring morning*

and still are – distilled in November.) Apart from the fact that it took place in the open air it was reminiscent of nothing so much as one's schooldays when principles would joyfully be put into practice in the lab – but the taste of the end product was very different. This pleasurable activity has ceased, for the same reason that private indoor stills are fast vanishing. In the past licences were automatically granted to the sons of previous licence-holders, and only to them, but in 1960 this jealously guarded right was abolished in an attempt to reduce alcoholism. In any case the *eau de vie* distilled by these *bouilleurs de cru* was not for sale, though it tasted better than the commercially produced variety now freely – though expensively – available in the shops. You can see the occasional still displayed at local fêtes, and one is frequently parked in the Place de la Liberté in Sarlat.

By early March the valleys are breaking into new life as the leaves of the thin poplars lining the streams turn pale green and the branches of oak and chestnut on the hills above acquire their soft pink haze. The hedgerows will be showing their violets, called hereabouts the 'March flower'; the hawthorn and wild roses are bursting into flower and the fields are alive with yellow and white and pink and purple and the first dandelions put up their tender leaves for a spring salad. The last of the tobacco has gone away, the maize is sown and, if Easter is late, there will be clusters of mauve and white lilac to decorate the altars and, until not so long ago, the doorways of girls whom admirers wished to impress. By Easter too the yolks of the free-range eggs will have become that deep orange that those of us who live in towns have almost forgotten exists. On 1 May village children still go from house to

Tour de la Vermondie

house begging an egg and then disappear to some quiet spot to consume omelettes made over a wood fire or goodies bought with the money that is sometimes offered in place of eggs.

Edith Simon, in *The Piebald Standard*, says that in fourteenth-century Périgueux, a woman wishing to marry for the fifth time could only do so on the production of a small tub of excrement of a white hen. While this custom is no longer practised, that of *charivari* was common until very recently. A widower (or a widow) who announced his intention of re-marrying would be subjected to nightly ordeals, sometimes lasting for as long as a fortnight, when the most appalling cacophony (to represent the return of the dead spouse) would be let loose outside his house. The men of the village, with musical instruments, saucepan lids and bottles jangled together, even cats tied into baskets and pinched until they squealed, would gather before his door and continue until he invited them in for liberal helpings of wine. Only engagement to a widow gave exemption. *Charivari* was a cruel practice and one employed on other occasions too. Sixty years ago a curé, seen too often at a woman's house, was driven from his village by this means.

There is no longer a special fair on 25 January at Villars to which young people would make the journey to find a spouse, though economic conditions were such that the young men did not do so until they were at least twenty-five. It is a sad comment on the harsh reality of peasant life in this area in the past that local folk-lore can only provide one tale of young love. The Tour de Vermondie, between Montignac and St Léon sur Vézère, like the leaning tower of Pisa, is inclined, and has been so for many years. It is said that once upon a time a young prince was imprisoned in it, and he looked sadly at his fiancée as she passed to see him each day. One day the tower took pity on the young lovers and leaned over to allow them to exchange a kiss.

The performance of the marriage ceremony was frowned upon, if not forbidden, during Advent (from the Sunday nearest to 30 November and Epiphany – 6 January) and during Lent. Most ceremonies in fact took place during February – a dead season in the agricultural year. Nowadays with no such restrictions, and the arrival of the summer in May, the wedding season is in full flood. The doorway of the bride's house, and those of the church and the *mairie*, will be flanked by sawn-off juniper trees decorated with pink and white paper flowers, and the paths leading to and from them strewn with box leaves.

The old custom of presenting the *tourain des mariés* has not died out though it is less common than it was, say, twenty years ago. A *tourain* (see page 182) was sprinkled with a large amount of pepper, and offered to the young couple, either the night before the wedding or on their return from its celebration, preferably in a chamber pot. The groom would be forced to drink as much of it as his companions could contrive. To avoid this it was therefore customary for the married pair to arrange to sleep their wedding night away from home, but some young relation could always be bribed to reveal the secret of their whereabouts and the merry-makers would remorselessly track them down.

A juniper tree, or a pine branch, was also used in the past to indicate to travellers the availability of an inn with beds (as against a café for refreshments). Today whole pine trees, shorn of all but their uppermost branches and rubbed down until they are shiny, surmounted with a placard and perhaps two flags – are erected outside the house of the groom about a week before the marriage ceremony to signal the end of his bachelor days (a custom known as the *plantage du mai*). They are also commonly used to honour a newly elected councillor, a whole village council or a newly installed shopkeeper – a custom not practised for example in the neighbouring department of Lot.

The origin of this custom, like so many others, remains obscure and subject to various theories – perhaps connected with fertility rites or poor men's substitutes for a status symbol such as the nobles' right to build a tower adjacent to his house. What is certain is that their erection, for whatever purpose, gives rise to an occasion to drink a *vin d'honneur*.

Vestiges of the high summer fête of St Jean also persist; traditionally the bonfire – midsummer fire – was lit on 24 June. The great pile of faggots would be topped with pine and juniper, crowned with a bunch of lilies, roses and sweet-smelling herbs, blessed and sprinkled with holy water by the curé, and lit by one of the altar candles. The young men would compete and show off by seeing who could jump it at its roaring height, to be rewarded by a kiss from their girl. Glyn Daniel saw one such at Tayac in the 1960's when he was told that it would be the last in the immediate neighbourhood, but it still takes place in a modified form on some river banks in the department to this day. It was traditional too for the revellers to carry a burning ember home; if it was still glowing by the time it reached their hearth, they were certain to have a good year.

The hay is brought in in early June; harvesting the wheat follows and methods have certainly changed since before the First World War when, without even reaper-binders, the women and children had to follow the men as they reaped and tied first the sheafs and then neatly stacked the stooks in the criss-cross pattern used in these parts. The combine-harvesters will go from field to field, at it night and day unless some mechanical fault halts the work. A broken fan belt one midday left the men lying, spread-eagled like the figures in a Breughel painting, in the shade of the new hay rick, bottles of red wine by their side. Since a group of farmers will usually share a combine-harvester and their wheat will ripen at the same time, speed is of the essence and the men will work late into the night, headlamps ablaze, until they all roll back exhausted but happy to a communal meal prepared by their women-folk who wait on them much as they used to in the days of *métayage* when man and master would celebrate together the feast of *beau blé* or *gerbe baude*, such as Marcel Boulestin remembered from his childhood:

The whole family sharing the work of threshing

The touring threshing machine has been booked (in remote parts the Biblical flail was still in use), and while it does its dusty work, while the chaff is carried away by the wind, the wife of the *métayer* cooks.

In the barn a table is prepared, covered with a sheet, and there sit together the family of the master and the family of the servant. The dinner begins at about half-past three, when the work is finished, and lasts till eight o'clock.

There is soup, a *pot-au-feu* so thick with bread that the ladle stands upright in it, and after that they drink a little red wine in the soup plate. Then comes a fowl, marvellously stuffed, which has been cooked in the soup, served with vegetable; then roast mutton or veal served with a salad, cheese, a *crème* of sorts, home-made cakes (usually rather heavy), fruit, coffee and brandy (brought by my father).

At the end of the feast, friendly and dignified, the sacks of corn are divided, the share of the master piled up in a cart – and we used to like going home, perched on the sacks next to chickens and ducks tied together by pairs, driven by two slow-moving cows.

With the disappearance of *métayage* such feasts have vanished, though those held at country weddings display gastronomic excesses on a gargantuan scale. Incredible amounts of time and money are still spent on preparing an enormous meal, laid out and eaten on trestle tables set out in a shady corner of the farm or a cool barn. They

173

are liable to go on until the early hours of the next morning, if not for several days, since relatives may have travelled some considerable distance to attend the jollifications. Private parties for no specific social reason given by the younger, more affluent farmers with barbecues and canned music are a relatively new development.

Genuine public fêtes, which have been in existence since the fourteenth century, when some would last a fortnight, still take place in a minor way all over the department. (In 1803 Fayolle listed 122 communes with the right to a fair.) They vary a good deal in attractions, and attendance.

That of *Caminel*, takes place on 11 August each year. Caminel is a grove near Masclat, a village with a lime tree said to have been planted in the time of Henri IV and Sully, and measuring 4.55 metres round its girth. At this *fête champêtre*, the stallholders spread their wares out under spacious avenues of huge old chestnut trees, affording a pleasing shade. All the stall holders have been allotted their places for the day by the *plantier*, who takes over from the ground landlord and is responsible for the good conduct of the fair, to which, says the euphoric local press, 5000 people come.

Although melons and peaches dominate the fruit stalls – it is after all the *foire aux melons* – there is a wide variety of vegetables, flowers, cheese and charcuterie as well as the inevitable travelling shoe shops and novelty stalls. Plaits of new garlic hang in tresses or lie in great roseate piles on the ground; the aroma of nuts crushed in chocolate or cocoa powder and warmed in copper basins mingles with that of the inevitable spitted chicken and the spice stalls tempt with all the herbs of the east. But not all is food. There is a fine selection of basket-work and white china; plastic – *le vrai* – objects for kitchen and garden; sun hats and *casquettes*, and fishing waders and *bleus de travail*; shoes and sandals and gum boots; music on cheap discs which increasingly include folk music; bales of material, including ticking for mattresses; tools and agricultural machinery. One year we bought some delicious chestnut honey from an old peasant couple. They told us that they had recently applied it to a wound which was slow to heal, with the most beneficial results. Even the local doctor was impressed.

Fifty years ago Caminel was still a fair for selling livestock as it had been for over a hundred years; horses and donkeys changed hands all morning, but now one is regaled with the brilliant colours of Massey Ferguson or Poclain tractors, combine-harvesters, watering machines and other sophisticated mechanical devices There is little at Caminel that cannot be bought elsewhere (and probably cheaper), but the holiday feeling and the absence of licensing hours at the *buvettes* – bars run up overnight and serving oysters and ice-cold drinks – induce a reckless spending mood. The rhythm of the morning slows down towards noon when the shopping is over; large, competent, white-aproned matrons emerge from their ramshackle bivouac kitchens to produce the midday meal under the communal awning.

By the early evening the fruit and vegetable vendors have packed up and the *dancing*, fortune-tellers and dodgems scream into action as the *jeunesse* arrives. The gendarmes flail their arms frantically like windmills, shouting genially and totally ineffectually, *'par là pour Lyons, par ici pour Marseille.'* Sometime between two and three in the morning, the merrymakers extricate themselves and their cars for the drive home, and by dawn next morning all evidence of a twenty-four hours' revel is over. The trees look majestically down on the earth that has been swept and cleared of human debris as if nothing had happened – and they had been alone these hundreds of years.

If perhaps the prime reason for holding the fair at Caminel these days is no longer the economic one that it was in the past, when it was truly, as advertised, *le centre du monde* – for it was where the donkey breeders of Poitou sold them to the Spaniards – it is clear that its continued existence is not simply as a bait for the tourist. It still fulfils that vitally important function of all fairs – the exchange of information and gossip. It is interesting as a sociological fact to note that, as roads and railways improved in the mid-nineteenth century, fairs, far from declining, increased in popularity and any pretext served, as it still does for going to them.

The *quinze août*, though such an important holiday, seems to have no special fêtes attached to it in Périgord, but the fair at Carlux, which takes place about this time is also worth a visit different though it is from that of Caminel. Here pancakes, rather than melons are the central feature and it is not basically a trading fair – just a good day out for sporting events, like climbing the pole, and racing aged and recalcitrant donkeys, and above all as an excuse for eating, drinking and dancing. It is more ordered than Caminel, more fabricated in a sense, more of a determined effort at jollity than an organic event of the annual calendar, where groups of local folk-dancers have been imported as a rather self-conscious side show.

Regional dancing has become one of the few repositories of past customs and may be seen throughout the department during the summer. The dancers wear their traditional costume, which is not now worn on any other occasion. The women wear white lace caps and blouses, with pinafores over mid-length flowery skirts; the men black hats, short smocks and waistcoats, a coloured kerchief at their neck. The instruments, almost always played by the men, are hurdy-gurdies, bagpipes, accordions and double-reeded oboes, and make a suitably *folkloristique* sound The dancers themselves, with charming names such as the Abeilles Bergeracois or Les Pastoureux Sarladais, travel from fair to fair.

A striking feature of the fête at Carlux is the active participation of the young people of the village who support and encourage the day's activities as much as their elders. The festivities come to a climax at about midnight with a fireworks display, greatly enlivened by the intrepid man who carries a harness shaped like a bull's head, which is alive with more fireworks charging through the crowd.

There are of course many other fairs all over the department, each with its own speciality or local flavour. That at Cénac mixes community singing, walking the plank and political propaganda rather uneasily; those at La Roque Gageac and Beynac have little boats with lanterns and fireworks on the river; all offer simple entertainment and a good time for people of all ages.

Another annual event, while not strictly speaking a fair, which takes place in a different commune each year, is the Félibrée or 'Lou Bournat'. The women of the communes in which it is to be held spend cosy winter evenings together making thousands of flowers from crepe paper which are then strung together across the streets. It is an offshoot from the Félibrige – a literary group founded in 1864 by provençal poets led by Mistral with the specific aim of keeping the language of occitan alive. It is organized by an association of the same name in Périgueux (the *bournat* is the beehive which symbolizes a group of busy like-minded people) and is a rather elaborate and expensive way of preserving the songs and dancing and recreating the genuine gastronomic delights of the past. Other attempts to keep occitan alive are made by the Comité du Périgord de la Langue Occitane, who fear that the patois spoken by Périgordins over seventy is dying out.

'Save on feast days,' said Lorca, 'the days slough their skins like snakes.' But in Périgord the autumn days seem reluctant to part with their summer warmth. September brings blackberries and mushrooms; the former left for the birds and the foreigners – bramble jelly seems unheard of – the latter culled before dawn by the gypsies and the energetic. Sloes, too, abound, but like blackberries seem not to be much used, although Henri Philippon at least gives a recipe for making sloe *eau de vie* identical to that for making sloe gin. The lovely mushrooms in the fields in which the crickets sing in the warm evenings are there for the picking, their pale pink caps barely open in the misty chilly dawn. The dun-coloured cèpes sprout indistinguishable from the dry leaves that cover them in the coppices and thickets, the difficulty of finding them doubtless the reason for their enormous price in the markets and restaurants. The last of the tobacco is brought in to be hung in the *séchoirs* to dry in the autumnal winds and dying heat, and the toads clamour for the last remaining insects.

But the working year is far from over; the fields are rapidly ploughed once the tobacco has been cut and above all there is the *vendange* to bring in and celebrate before the walnuts and the chestnuts are gathered. The *vendange*, like the harvesting, is a communal affair, with neighbour helping neighbour and students and townsfolk coming to share the joyful work. In the east of the department at least, wine is now produced mainly for domestic consumption, and usually on a co-operative basis. Most of the farmers grow grapes but only a minority own wine-making machinery; at the vintage everyone's grapes are fed into the communal press indiscriminately. After it has fermented in barrel, each participant carries off a quantity of wine, generally in barrel, proportionate to his original contribution of grapes.

Part of the procession during a félibrée

This makes it pointless for any small individual grower to cultivate superior strains of grape unless all his neighbours can be prevailed upon to do the same, and even then all efforts can be frustrated by lackadaisical and unhygienic methods of vinification. But there is nothing lackadaisical about the parties connected with the *vendange*.

By the end of October the nights have truly drawn in and the long winter evenings, before television came to while away the hours, were occasions for minor social occasions when entertainment had to be provided by oneself or one's immediate neighbours, who would gather together in each other's houses for the *grande* or *petite veillée*, to sit round the fire in which maize cones stripped of their grains – the *cocoricots* – would shoot off their glittering sparks. (The maize hereabouts is grown only for poultry food, and it is stacked in tall, narrow cages at the edges of fields by the farmhouses.) It was on occasions such as these that the elderly would tell their dark tales of *léberous* and *sorciers*.

For so long a wild and afforested land, with ill-kept roads and tracks (in 1789 Verneheuil said the roads of hell could not be worse than those in Périgord), it is not surprising that tales of fear and evil prevailed. No crossroads in Double was free from its demons; these *cafourches* frightened man and maid alike as the devil himself flitted across the stagnant ponds. Elderly women, bent double with rheumatism, prematurely aged and frequently toothless, would be taken for witches with the evil eye, but though they inspired terror, they were never persecuted. A man who would not look you straight in the eye or who shook your hand palm down, might be, albeit unknowingly, a *léberou* (a *loup garou*) – a haunted creature who would leave his bed at night to don a hare skin and destroy the dogs. He carried evil with him and, like his namesake, the wolf who roamed these parts, stole sheep and frightened the peasants. They carried with them too sexual threats and made improper suggestions to young women, though woe betide their hunters. With the dawn, they reverted to their normal selves.

Sorciers were of a different order: they were, in a manner of speaking, the witch-doctors of the community, who competed with the surgeon-barbers and itinerant quacks eager to make a dishonest penny from a credulous and ailing population. Superstition was rife and even now it is difficult for a sociologist to acquire accurate evidence about the *sorciers*, for the populace, perhaps still half ashamed of its beliefs in the sometimes ludicrous recipes for cures, is secretive and silent on the subject. Certainly there were ills to be cured, whether by herbal remedies, *sorciers* or by saints; an ill-fed and impoverished peasantry living in highly insanitary conditions and exhausted by the rigours of the working life suffered as much from rickets, rheumatism, epilepsy, scabies, malaria and all manner of skin diseases as from infectious diseases against which there was no protection. In 1853 *Le Chroniqueur* published, with some scorn, the recipe for curing a child of epilepsy, but publish it it did: 'The mother should obtain the head of a corpse from the cemetery and put it in the oven until it is quite dry, and completely calcified – then it should be pulverised and the powder mixed into the child's daily food.'

Fifty years later, Pipète, the *sorcière* from Domme, made her clients spit into a handkerchief or box which she then took into the open air to be picked up by a *cupide* who would acquire the disease and free the sufferer from it. The *sorcier* from Boisseuilh sold magic amulets with dire warnings for them not to be opened; one literate sceptic who did so was amazed to discover the inscription rolled up within it was simply, '*In te Domine speravit non, confundar in aeternum*' with the punctuation making a nonsense of it. Blanche, the *dévinaire*, the finder of lost objects, was still alive and practising in Grolejac in 1927. One of the more bizarre forms of birth control noted by Georges Rocal relates to a practice in St Julien de Lampon. The women there gave their husbands a soup made from the small grey lizards (*rapiettes*) which live in the dry stone walls to 'dry them up' – a phenomenon observed in the cats who ate them.

Whether or not the saints were more efficacious is uncertain but there were any number of pilgrimages to their shrines in search of a miraculous cure. St Fiacre at St Martin de Freyssingeas and St Astier at Boulazac cured rickets; Ste Mondane at Ste

Mondane cured headaches; and St Hilaire at Sarrazac set straight malformed bones. Each village claimed some speciality and was particularly fortunate if it possessed a spring or fountain for, despite the seven large rivers, 600 named streams and countless rivulets in the department, fresh water at any distance from their banks was at a premium. It is no wonder that it was felt to have miraculous powers. Not that any excuses for outings were wanting, for above all the Périgordins love a good reason for conviviality, and drinking.

And so to the goose fairs in November. Sarlat, impossibly crowded on Saturdays in summer, has changed tone and colour. Instead of the great bunches of gaudy flowers gaily arranged under the arches of the Hôtel de Ville, instead of the peppers and courgettes, peaches and melons, olives and *cacahuétes*, the market square has turned grey and brown, lit only by the pale flesh of the plucked fowl and the white napkins holding the roseate goose and duck livers. In December and January, Baudelaire's *maladie savoureuse*, the truffle – the glistening black diamond – is to be found there and in the other market towns such as Périgueux, Thiviers, Ste Alvère and Excideuil.

The fish stall with its oysters and mussels still stands in the shadow of the cathedral next to one where bales of raw wool are sold for stuffing mattresses; old men and women sidle up to you as if offering black market goods, to tempt you with little white goat cheeses, the local *chabichous*. Itinerant butchers' vans, their sides split open, display orange and brown sausages, the peppery *merguès* of Africa amongst them, *petits salés*, such a delicious winter dish when served with lentils, and an incredible variety of charcuterie and home-made brawns and pâtés.

Preparations for the celebrations of Christmas and the New Year are in the air.

Truffles

Mountains of food are to be made ready for St Sylvester's feast, when alas the children no longer sing in the streets, though the churches are full and Christianity has a field day. In general though the people of Dordogne are not especially pious – one village boasts that it has need neither of a priest nor of a *gendarme* – and the clergy, relatively few in number, are held in little regard. Though they had their uses in exorcising the devil or blessing the crops, they were lumped together with the aristocracy as members of a hated and oppressive establishment.

Even in Eugène Le Roy's day, a time when there was a revival of religious observance, they came in for a good deal of criticism as this extract from *Jacquou le Croquant* shows:

> Behind the two long files of pilgrims came the curés intoning their litanies, some with their surplises billowing like wings, others with embroidered flowers on them. Bringing up the rear was the parish priest in a golden chasuble carrying the closed chalice. It was a sight to see all these well fed men, their red faces glistening and their black or greying hair falling in ringlets about their shoulders beneath their square caps or round hats.
>
> They were not ill, oh no, that was immediately apparent. They were curés of the old school, used to living well, not making difficulties where none need exist and gently nudging their flock towards paradise without bothering about dogmas such as the Sacred Heart, the Immaculate Conception or the Infallibility of the Pope. Doubtless amongst them were some whose parishioners criticised for a predilection for the consecrated wine or for having two servants in their twenties rather than one of fifty or perhaps even a resident niece. Nevertheless they were as good as or better than some today who water their wine and employ elderly domestics but who are bilious, malevolent, hypocritical, intriguing and greedy and who extort from the laity what they do not themselves possess.

Before the 1939 war one village was excommunicated because it treated its priest so roughly, but the occupants were not much disturbed by this, and during the war clerics acquired the reputation for being black marketeers, fornicators and poachers (indeed some still are at least the last). On the whole the priest was only valued in the presence of death. In 1887 the average expectation of life was thirty-seven years and ten months, so they were kept fairly busy. Now they are kept equally busy because they have several parishes to look after and their image is gradually improving, but Christianity and the church between them have done little since the Middle Ages but capitalize on, and overlay with thin veneer, pagan rites and atavistic prehistoric customs, which after all virtually saw their birth in this region.

Sans Beurre et Sans Reproche

Like all regional cookery in the days before nation-wide distribution of identical tinned and deep-frozen foods, that of Périgord is based on its local produce, and we are fortunate that so much of it is still available. Wheat and maize lie chequered in the valleys; and happily for us, their stubble, still shadowed by the majestic walnut trees in their midst, serves as ready-made beds for red-legged partridges.

Eels, lampreys, pike, barbel, salmon, crayfish and endless small fry abound in the many rivers and streams. The forests that clothe the hills yield chestnuts as highly prized as those of the Ardèche and provide beneath them homes for woodcock and quail; at their feet the *cèpes, coucourles, girolles, morilles* and *oronges* that are so difficult to distinguish in the pale light of dawn mysteriously appear after days of heat and soft nights of rain. The high *causses*, deserted and seemingly arid, nourish sheep and keep the secret of the truffle.

But Périgord man and woman think it right to give nature some help; they breed rabbits in hutches to compete with the coney and wild hare; they keep tame herds of boar to compensate for the disappearance of his savage ancestor; they run 'finishing schools' for pigs (how else to translate *élevage de porcs?*), nurseries for trout and – a recent innovation – for sturgeon too; and above all else, they pay attention to their farmyard with its free-ranging maize-fed poultry: geese, duck, hens, turkey, guinea fowl and pigeons.

Of course they cultivate their garden too: peas and beans in neat rows; tomatoes and melons and pumpkins like so many red and orange balloons; sorrel sprouting endlessly in green bunches; scorzonera and salsify poking dark fingers into the rich earth. The soil and the climate are good too for fruit; cherries are for *clafouti*; plums for the sweetmeats of Agen; apricots and peaches for preserving in *eau de vie*; grapes for the table and wine.

There are many specifically regional dishes, although sadly not many of them appear nowadays on restaurant menus, which are depressingly uniform. Both the *menu touristique* and the *menu gastronomique* – which is correspondingly more expensive – will consist of a pâté of goose or duck, an omelette with *cèpes*, a *confit*, (a dish of preserved goose or duck), *pommes sarladaises*, a salad dressed with walnut oil, cheese and fruit. They may be good, but they give no indication of the range and robustness of Périgordin cookery, and are not really dishes well matched with each other, though each in itself is excellent.

The most typical soups, with which the locals all start their meals, are ones we could easily emulate, and to congratulate a cook on her ability to make a good soup is the highest compliment you can pay a Périgordine. A *tourain blanchi* or *tourain périgordin* is a refreshing starter. For eight people, crush 25 grams of garlic and let it brown gently in goose fat or lard. Add one soup-spoonful of flour and stir well. Then add a litre of boiling water, thyme, salt and pepper, and cook for 10 minutes. Sieve the liquid, and put it back on the heat until it boils, then add a lightly beaten white of egg. Add a small amount of the hot soup to an egg yolk mixed with a spoonful of good wine vinegar, stir it well and add back to the soup, which must not now boil again. Serve the soup in bowls lined with thin slices of bread. Just before you finish eating your bowlful, pour in a glass of red wine and stir well with your spoon; then drink the mixture direct from the bowl and you will be behaving like a true Périgordin – *faire chabrol* as it is called.

The *potage au saffran*, known in patois as *mourtairol*, is another local variation. Dissolve one gram of saffron in one and a half litres of good chicken stock and pour the boiling soup on to slices of bread until they will absorb no more. Put the soup into a low oven for 30 minutes adding stock as necessary to keep the top layer of bread moist, and serve when the whole has the appearance of thick cream.

A good summer soup, although expensive, is the *soupe aux écrevisses*. For eight people you should lightly fry the whites of two leeks, three onions and two carrots, all finely diced, until soft. Then add one and a half spoonfuls of flour, stir and moisten with a little hot water. Add a bouquet garni, salt and pepper, and two litres of water. Set to boil. Put sixteen unshelled crayfish to boil in two decilitres of white Monbazillac and add the boiled wine to the soup. Shell the crayfish, and put the pulverized shells into the soup too. Lay the crayfish on thin slices of bread at the bottom of a soup tureen and pour the soup, which has been strained and thickened with a yolk of egg, on to them. There are many other soups, with sorrel, beans, carrots or tomatoes, and a filling one, perfect for a chilly winter day, is made with cabbage and *miques* – maize-flour dumplings.

Hors d'œuvres, though commonly served in restaurants, do not figure much in household cookery, though the local *grillons*, the left-over fatty pieces of goose or pork fried till they are crisp, can be compared with those of Touraine. Omelettes too feature large; omelettes with truffles, omelettes with *cèpes* or *morilles* cooked in goose fat, omelettes with sorrel – even omelettes with *sauce périgordine* or *sauce périgueux*. The local raw ham too is a great speciality; Mme Coudoumié, who lived on her farm at Nabirat for over ninety years, used to preserve two or three handsome legs of pork a year, and the only problem in producing one's own is to get enough fine wood ash. You need a large fresh leg of pork; rub about three handfuls

A flock of geese still at liberty

of coarse salt over it, taking particular care to see that the bone is well covered. After three days throw away the liquid that the salt will have extracted and wipe the ham carefully. Put it in the middle of a clean linen cloth and sprinkle two pounds of coarse salt over it; rub black pepper round the bone and wrap two thicknesses of cloth very tightly round immediately. Stitch the outer layer of cloth so that it is tightly drawn round the ham, put the parcel in a clean linen bag (an old pillowcase is ideal) and lay it in the wood ash in a wooden, not a plastic, container. See that it is well covered with the ash and leave in a dry, cool place for at least 4 months. If you choose a good leg of pork at Christmas time, or shortly afterwards in the best pig-killing time, you will find that the ham is just about ready to eat with melon at the end of July.

Although sea fish can be bought in the larger towns, and travelling vans, now mercifully refrigerated, appear in village squares on Fridays, with spring balances to weigh out the glittering prizes of the Atlantic, most of the regional fish dishes consist of river fish: carp from the Isle, trout from Brantôme, pike, perch from Vergt, eel and lampreys stewed in good red claret, salmon, shrimps and the *friture de la Dordogne* which is made of the small fry.

Périgord is not rich in meat dishes, for unlike Limousin it is not good cattle country and, until about one hundred years ago, the inhabitants did not care much for mutton and lamb. The pig and poultry have sufficed, as well they may. One of the most delicious ways of serving pork, however, for which Elizabeth David gives the recipe in *French Provincial Cooking*, is the *enchaud périgordin*, a boned loin rolled with slivers of garlic and truffle and gently roasted, which, though good hot, is wonderful cold, cut in thin slices and served on a bed of the pale pink jelly its juices make. Not slow to adapt their own methods, the Périgordins have used their age-old techniques to treat lamb in a similar way and *gigot de mouton à la périgordine* is cooked much like the *enchaud*, but with the addition of a little armagnac. The leg of lamb should be larded with finely sliced truffles and small cubes of fat bacon, basted with goose fat, salt and pepper, and roasted in a hot oven. Pour three soup-spoonfuls of armagnac over the joint and burn off the alcohol 15 minutes before it comes to table.

It is difficult to get fresh calves' sweetbreads in England, and indeed, even in Dordogne they have to be ordered from the butcher at least a week in advance so that they are reserved for you when the animal is killed. But you can sometimes find the small frozen New Zealand sweetbreads and, although at home sorrel is not easy to come by in greengrocers, it grows so readily that it is worth attempting in one's own kitchen the delicate dish of *ris de veau à l'oseille* so often served in the region. Lightly fry the blanched and cleaned sweetbreads in goose fat with tiny whole onions and thin slices of carrot; add skinned and de-pipped tomatoes, salt, pepper, a bouquet garni, one decilitre of white wine and one decilitre of water. Cover and leave to simmer gently. Meanwhile clean and blanch a kilo of sorrel, drain it well and let it simmer in a little goose fat for twenty minutes. Serve the sweetbreads surrounded by their vegetable garnish, with the seasoned sorrel and pour over the reduced pan juices.

There is plenty of beef to be had nowadays – nearly always firmly labelled 'produce of France' – and a plain grilled entrecôte served with a périgordin sauce makes it a dish fit for the gods. It is not a sauce one can make with ease at home, though the good housewives of course, with the ingredients to hand, do, and keep little jars and tins of it to produce throughout the year, like their *confits d'oie*, to delight and surprise out of season. But because onions and shallots sautéed with goose fat and simmered with white wine and a little flour, to which truffles are added at the last moment, keep very well in airtight or sterilized containers, sauce périgordine is one of the local products that is worth buying, however expensive.

Poultry and game figure large in the regional cooking. Truffled goose, duck and turkey; casseroled chicken with potatoes, salsify and garlic, drained, cut up and turned into a flaky pastry case to make a golden pie; stewed pigeons and chicken in verjuice: all are frequently eaten. Verjuice is the liquid obtained from pressing by hand through a strainer slightly unripe grapes. Obviously the genuine juice can only be obtained for a short time during the year and its use was far more common in the past when grapes were actually grown specifically for this purpose – the *Encyclopédie* refers to them. There is some difficulty in keeping verjuice though you can bottle it, strained, topped with a little oil and stored in a cool dark cellar; restaurateurs now cheat by using tartaric acid bought at the chemist's instead.

The countryside is rich too in wild fowl, and *la chasse*, which opens in mid-September, is a universal and rather dangerous sport, though with excellent practical results. As late holiday-makers start drifting home, the fishing nets, espadrilles and rubber swimming rings are replaced in the shop windows by row upon row of gaily coloured cartridges, and it is a wise mother who keeps her children indoors during the opening weeks of the season; guns are fired at any moving object.

Hare is teamed with maize dumplings, rabbit stuffed with bacon and onions, pheasant and partridge roasted with truffles or verjuice. Lark (which are netted not shot) are stuffed with their own livers and truffles or chestnuts and fried in goose fat. This way of serving lark is reputed to have been invented for Talleyrand by Carême. Quail and fig-peckers escape neither the hunter nor the gastronome; how little of the true nature of Périgord do tourists who only visit in the summer months know.

Vegetables abound – the choice is endless, but perhaps the most renowned dish served is *pommes sarladaises*, a rich confection of potatoes, garlic and parsley fried in the ubiquitous goose fat. Whilst sorrel has been used in many dishes over the years, an interesting novelty is the ease with which one can now buy pots of basil. Not an indigenous herb, it has taken to the soil with pleasure and, as in Italy, is used on a fresh tomato salad.

There are four locally known cheeses, all of which are difficult to find, except one. La Trappe, fairly easily available, is a cheese made from cow's milk by the nuns at Notre Dame de Bonne Espérance at Echourgnac, near Montpon. There is a small goat cheese made at and known as Thiviers; Cubjac or Cujasson, a form of goat *chabichou* best eaten with a glass of Monbazillac, and a blue cheese, rather like the bleu d'Auvergne, made at Bassillac.

Apart from fruit, puddings are nearly all farinaceous, either made from wheat or maize flour, and, though heavy, are comforting. The *miques de maïs* are dumplings made from a mixture of wheat and maize flour, and are often eaten hot in soup or instead of bread, and although they can be sprinkled with sugar and eaten for dessert they should not be confused with puddings of similar names. *Le millassou* is a cake made from maize flour with raisins and is eaten warm; *les millasses du Périgord* are little pastry cases filled with a light spongy mixture and *le millas* is a pudding which is a cross between crème caramel and a soufflé. Though *clafouti*, a wonderfully light sweet toad-in-the hole made with cherries, and eaten warm, is of Limousin origin, it is frequently to be found in this area; and Périgordin pancakes rival those of Brittany. There are any number of walnut cakes, tarts and biscuits.

Of course it is possible to find many of these less obvious local specialities in the restaurants but to do so it is best to visit out of season. It was a great delight to arrive one wet November day, unannounced and late, at a small restaurant at Marquay to be offered the remains of the family's own luncheon which ended with a *millassou*, tasting better than anything one is likely to make oneself. By the same token sublime preparations such as *lièvre à la royale* and stuffed carp are best left to the restaurateurs and *traiteurs* (suppliers of ready-prepared provisions) as they involve long preparation on a scale that is impracticable in a small household.

Cooking in French restaurants has come in for a lot of criticism recently, and that of Dordogne is no exception; indeed Mirabel Osler in *A Spoon with Every Course* (1995) quotes an anonymous source as saying that nowhere is it more relevant than in Périgord or Quercy that '*si on ne sait pas, on fait le coulis*'; and Paul Bocuse as having said '*Le Périgord, de beaux produits, oui, mais de l'année dernière*'. There is of course the usual grain of truth in these malicious *mauvais mots* but to dub *confits*, which by their very nature, are preserved, as being last year's, is unfair. Notwithstanding such complaints, one can still eat well and very well in the department. The travelling gourmet should refer to the current Michelin or Gault-Millau guides, but also be prepared to take risks.

How lovely, though, it would be if some enterprising restaurateur were to offer the meal served by the young Nogaret's mother in Eugène Le Roy's *Moulin du Frau*. It would be as well balanced and as imaginative today as it was in Périgueux in 1844. It started, traditionally, with soup and *bouilli*; then barbel was served with *oronges*; a young hare, larded, chicory salad dressed with walnut oil and garlic followed, to be finished up with small jam tarts and almond cake. *Eau de vie* from Azérat and liqueur-preserved *reines claudes* accompanied the coffee and cigars. What could possibly be more delicious.

This kind of meal typifies the *cuisine bourgeoise* or even *paysanne* of the region. There are no great chefs, no great *maîtres* of either classical or *nouvelle cuisine*; it is cooking which has evolved from the domestic ranges and ovens, presided over by the women of the house. The women tend to look after the poultry yard and it is they who make the conserves and the *confits*, who bottle and can the mushrooms and beans and tomatoes, who dress the pig and pot the charcuterie; more often than not too the women will be found in the kitchens of the restaurants whilst the men do the marketing and run the dining rooms.

Henri Philippon, in *Cuisine du Quercy et Périgord*, gives authentic recipes in an attempt to pass on the genuine rural cooking which he rightly says has disappeared from the country restaurants. He says that the deterioration is due to the fact that the cooks nowadays, despite being the sons of the excellent women who ran the inns of the past, have learned their trade in catering schools or in the kitchens of famous chefs, and come back full of theories which they put into practice; and secondly, to be fair, they were never geared to cope with the number of people they are now faced with. Certainly nearly all the practical books on the regional cookery have so far been written by women, both English and French.

One oddity is that none of the books on local cuisine give a recipe for the delicious walnut soup which first appeared as far as I know in Elizabeth David's *Summer Cooking*, though not as a specifically Périgordin dish. Such dishes are given in her excellent *French Provincial Cooking*, which apart from the *enchaud* already mentioned includes a recipe for *reines claudes* in *eau de vie* – those intoxicating greengages loved by François I's queen, which make such a perfect marriage with a cup of coffee at the end of the meal. They are sold, at vast cost, at all the bars, or can be bought, at even vaster cost, in tall glass jars at the grocers, but it is worth the trouble of making them at home even though it takes three days to do so. *Eau de vie* is now generally available in the shops.

Les Secrets des Fermes en Périgord by Zette Guindeau-Franc is a handsome, large, well-illustrated volume with genuine and attractive old recipes. Unfortunately two of the best books, La Mazille's *La Bonne Cuisine du Périgord* – learned and meticulous, though not for the beginner – and Henri Philippon's book have not been translated into English but nowadays there are many in English to choose from. There is Anne Penton's *Customs and Cookery in the Périgord and Quercy*; it is detailed and the recipes can be followed with confidence since they give accurate descriptions of local food and how to produce it; and more recent and covering a wider area, Jeanne Strang's *Goose Fat and Garlic, Country Recipes from South-West France*. Other works of interest are listed in the bibliography.

The men who have written about the region have tended to take, not surprisingly in view of the domination of women in the kitchen, a less practical and more poetic attitude and devoted themselves rather to its history and reputation outside the province, though some do, of course, include recipes. Marcel Boulestin for example, who spent much of his holiday childhood in his grandmother's house at St Aulaye writes in *Myself, My Two Countries*:

> I lived all the daytime out of doors, and in the evening my favourite place was the kitchen. The ways of cooking were very primitive; that is to say they were perfect, and gave results which I did not appreciate enough then, and which we try now, often in vain, to imitate. The roasting was done on a spit, and the rest of the cooking on charcoal. If a dish had to be braised, it was cooked in a casserole with a hollow lid; in this warm ashes and burning charcoals were put, and the dish cooked slowly, resting on square holes. There were three or four holes in the tiled covered stand, which was a fixture. This was called a *potager*.
>
> If something required baking as opposed to roasting, it was sent to the baker's to be cooked after the bread had been removed.

In the storeroom next to the kitchen were a long table and shelves always covered with all sorts of provisions; large earthenware jars full of *confits* of pork and goose, a small barrel where vinegar slowly matured, a bowl where honey oozed out of the comb, jam, preserves of sorrel and of tomatoes, and odd bottles with grapes and cherries marinating in brandy; next to the table a weighing machine on which I used to stand at regular intervals; sacks of haricot beans, of potatoes; eggs each one carefully dated in pencil.

And there were baskets of fruit, perfect small melons, late plums, under-ripe medlars waiting to soften, peaches, pears hollowed out by a bird or a wasp, figs that had fallen of their own accord, all the fruits of September naturally ripe and sometimes still warm from the sun. Everything in profusion.

Edmond Richardin, the proprietor of a famous restaurant in Nancy, waxed equally poetic about both the province and its capital: 'We arrive in Guyenne. Ah, here too, a hundred hurrahs! Yes, hurrah for Périgord; its black truffles, its barbels, its suckling pigs, its sweetbreads, its pigeons, its pheasants, its partridge pâtés and its foie gras.' His recipe for pheasant tells us to choose a young one, one that has not been hung for too long; then stuff it with a truffled goose liver that has been cooked in champagne; and be sure to bard its 'stomach rounded like the breast of a fifteen-year-old'. Then,

the delectable roast is savoured in silence, in a sort of rapt bliss. Oh Périgueux, fair city, where the truffle spreads its fragrance through your fine avenues with statues of your illustrious sons – Montaigne for wisdom, Fénelon for charity, Daumesnil for patriotism, Bugeaud for martial valour. How right you are, fair town, to be proud of your great men with their immortal names. But your glory does not rest on them alone. How can one over-praise your incomparable sauces whose heady scent perfumes the four corners of the civilized world?'

Georges Rocal and Paul Balard in *Science de Gueule en Périgord* refer to the poor diet of the peasant before the nineteenth century but go on to give a series of delicious local recipes. Though there were few famous restaurants in the department, Périgordin cooking was known about and appreciated in Paris. Edouard Rouzier took it to the capital in the early twenties of this century to the Grill Room St Michel where the *confit d'oie* and *coq en pâte* were 'worth a panegyric' in Robert-Robert's *Guide du Gourmand* of 1925. Rouzier and his brother Albert subsequently opened the Rotisserie Périgourdine in the Place St Michel, which they decorated with furniture brought from a château in Dordogne. It figures as one of the best thirty selected restaurants in Paris in Julian Street's *Where Paris Dines* (1929) and was renowned above all for its *lièvre à la royale* and *gratin périgordin* (a confection of mushrooms, cream and truffles served in flaky pastry) as well as *brochet farci*. Rouzier is also remembered for his publication of the *Livre d'Or de la gastronomie française* which was founded to mark the presentation of dinners composed of the regional dishes of France at the Salon d'Automne in 1931. The Rotisserie Périgourdine was carried on until 1956 by Edouard Rouzier's widow.

It was Curnonsky, the self-elected 'prince of gastronomes', who so brilliantly described the cookery of Périgord as being 'without butter and beyond reproach' and he thought the cooking of the region had been, and still was, amongst the finest in France, with Delsaut's restaurant in St Léon sur Vézère the *apothéose gastronomique*. When he and Marcel Rouff came to write their *France Gastronomique* it was with Périgord that they started. It appeared in 1921 and now strikes us as very much a period piece, full of little jokes (*l'esprit périgordin?*) such as '*voyager en Dordogne ne saurait passer pour une sinécure (même une sinécurenonsky)*'. It starts for some inexplicable reason with a short dissertation on *zakouskis* and includes an extremely entertaining account of the authors' visit to Les Eyzies: they liken their descent into the caves to the interior of a huge gruyère cheese and as they followed the young guide their thoughts were more on her shins than on prehistory. But as they dreamed of the past, so they concocted a suitable and typically whimsical

Curnonsky and Rouff at Les Eyzies:
'Nous sommes guidés par l'éclair
alternatif des deux belles
jambes blanches'

menu for their ancestors; plesiosaurus soup, wing of pterodactyl, helicopter gizzard with pebble sauce and a quarter of moratorium cooked in iguana fat and an omelette made from ornithorinchus eggs.

However, even though Raymond Oliver in his *The French at Table* has more recently been tempted to make these monstrous jokes about prehistoric cookery, Périgordin *restauration* has a long and respectable history. The *traiteurs* of Périgueux were known for the excellence of their pâtés throughout the fifteenth century, although in those days they were made from the red-legged partridge, stuffed with chicken liver and sold in the earthenware terrines in which they were cooked. It was Michel de Montaigne who invented the phrase *science de gueule*, and although the methods employed in Montaigne's own kitchens were primitive – he had never seen a mechanical spit until he visited Switzerland – he kept a table which impressed a connoisseur as demanding as Henri de Navarre. It was perhaps this experience which so struck Henri that, when he became king, he employed Buade de St Cernin, a Périgordin, as his first *maître d'hôtel* and gave him the charge of organizing his menus.

By the eighteenth century, Périgord, like Alsace, had become renowned for its pâté – a confection which requires some definition. There is a certain amount of confusion over what constitutes a pâté and, for that matter, a terrine. Originally a pâté was a pastry crust filled with a meat or game stufffing. The *pâtissier* was the pastry-maker and by extension became the man who made the stuffing too. When the stuffing was put directly into an earthenware pot without pastry it too became known as a pâté or terrine, and now, even if the stuffing is in a tin, it is commonly referred to as a pâté, just as 'to drink a glass' means to drink its contents. Today it is necessary if referring to a pastry-filled dish to describe it as a *pâté en croute*.

Périgordin pâtés in pastry during the eighteenth century were so highly thought of that they inspired Parisian blue stockings to give them to each other and to expatiate on their virtues in verse which they had published in the daily gossip paper, the *Mercure de France*. Later in the century a native of Périgueux, Pierre Villereynier, became *pâtissier du roi* to Louis XV and was ennobled as the seigneur de la Gatine by him. His fame spread throughout France and beyond, while at home his pâtés were thought so highly of that they were used as bribes. Villereynier's pâtés were constantly sent, perhaps in the rustic Thiviers pottery terrines of which the museum at Périgueux preserves some examples, to both Boucher, the *intendant* at Bordeaux, and Dupin, his secretary, in an attempt to soften their hearts and prevent them from billeting troops in Périgueux.

Jean Charbonnier, who kept the Trois Rois in the Limogean quarter in Périgueux, was associated from 1745 with Villereynier and, some fifteen years later, Courtois, from the Franche Comté, settled there to make his name. Courtois was responsible for the pâté for which Frederick of Prussia thanked the Prince of Brunswick in

1764: ' I have kept it in the hope that you will join me in eating it.' Frederick was clearly devoted to Périgordin food. When his Lyonnais master-chef died, he promoted André Noël, born in Périgueux in 1726, to his position, and Noël remained in the king's service until his master died. He was present at Frederick's funeral and remained with his successor, Frederick William III, until 1801. He died in Berlin aged seventy-five. Three years later he was seen to appear, ghost-like, at a masked ball: 'He made his entrance with his customary umbrella, decorated with a piece of mourning crêpe to denote his ethereal state, saying that his nose, as befitted a cook, had led him out of hell to join the present company – 'the scent of pheasants and truffles drags me heavenwards.'

Another noted denizen of Périgueux, who may have left his home town for an equally prestigious post, was Michelet. He produced a meal which cost 620 francs for the authorities to offer to Maréchal Pérignon (1754-1818) when he passed through the town. It was paid for out of the 800 francs voted for the upkeep of the library and a collection of scientific apparatus – a case of matter over mind. Michelet was much patronized by Talleyrand, who, coming himself from the region, knew a good man when he saw one, and later took a Michelet (presumed but not known to be the same fellow) into his service under Carême, rewarding him with a complete *batterie de cuisine* in silver.

An eighteenth-century pâté dish (Musée de Périgueux)

The pâtés made in Périgord during the seventeenth century were as we have seen made mainly from partridge but some included goose liver too. Whilst it may be of academic interest only to try to establish whether the credit for popularizing pure *pâté de foie gras*, whether truffled or not, should go to Jean Pierre Clause (or Close) who is reputed to have invented it in Strasbourg in the late eighteenth century, it is certain that the *Dictionnaire des Aliments* (published in 1750) lists two pounds of truffles and twelve goose livers in the ingredients for a *pâté de Périgueux*; and *Le Cuisinier Gascon* published in Amsterdam two years earlier gives a recipe for *petits pâtés de foyes gras aux truffes*. So Périgord has a high claim to its invention; certainly Didon, a *traiteur* in Périgueux until 1914, advertised his *terrine de perdrix aux foie gras truffé* as being based on the recipes of Villereynier, Lafon and Courtois all of whose pâtés had been sent regularly throughout the eighteenth century to London. However, there seems no doubt that it was Salvetat, the proprietor of the Hôtel du Cheval Blanc in Périgueux, who, in the mid-nineteenth century, was the first to preserve the pâtés by sealing them in tins and sterilizing them.

The French government is very strict about the classification of tinned goose or duck liver: a *foie naturel* must contain 98% liver (2% is salt and pepper); a *bloc de foie* is a reconstituted liver but must also be 98% liver; a *pâté de foie* need only contain 50% whole liver; and a *mousse* also 50%. If the tin advertises that its contents are *foie gras truffé* it must contain 3% truffle and *pâté de foie gras truffé* 2%.

An old-fashioned gaveuse d'oie

The goose liver has always been esteemed. Pliny refers to large fat livers, which when removed from the animal 'will grow even larger if soaked in milk and honey' and Juvenal refers to it: 'The master was served with a huge goose liver, a chicken as large as a goose and a boar worthy of the traits of blond Meleager. Then he would be offered truffles if it was spring time and the hoped for storms had produced this delicious extra.'

It is well known today that the *foie gras* is achieved by forcibly over-feeding the goose or duck so that its liver becomes unnaturally large. This practice, known as *gavage*, the English find particularly distasteful, though they are not averse to eating the end product. Morever it must be said that the geese do not in fact seem to object to this treatment. The House of Commons even went to the lengths of debating the subject in 1976 when a Labour Member felt impelled to say that 'any cruelty to animals in this country is the direct responsibility of the government'.

The technique consists of holding the animal tightly, while slightly warmed maize mixed with a little fat is rammed down the bird's neck through a funnel known as an *embuc* or *entonnoir*. It is not new; Cato in *De re rustica* (c. 160 BC) talks of 'small dumplings made of a paste of flour-dust or barley soaked in water being slipped down the gullet of the goose'.

Until recently the peasants in Périgord used to stuff their own geese, and there are still today elderly men and women who take in flocks like so many paying guests for the fifteen days or so needed to fatten them sufficiently. But because the demand for *foie gras* is increasing and because the rearing of geese is so well suited to the polyculture of Dordogne, large flocks are being raised and new methods of *gavage* are being employed. A typical flock consists of about 400 geese, of whom 150 are kept for breeding at any one time. The geese lay, from the end of January until the beginning of June, on average one egg every two days. They present some problems in rearing for the goose will not hatch her eggs and they have to be artificially incubated. The goslings are either sold as one-day-old chicks or kept on the farm to be sold later. The geese kept for fattening live out of doors, where they rapidly strip the grass, until they are about four months old. They are then taken indoors and penned, three or four to a cage. From then on they are doomed to darkness and death. They are fed three times a day, at intervals of six hours, a total of about one kilo of maize, with a little added fat, through a machine which pushes the grains down their gullets while the *gaveuse* with tender care and great skill eases the food down their long necks and into their crops. After about two to three weeks of this intensive and forced feeding, the geese, which will then weigh between 8 and 12 kilos, of which about 9 per cent will be the enlarged liver, are killed, plucked and eviscerated. They are then sold to the local co-operative, where there are stringent veterinary regulations, or sold direct in the markets or to producers of conserves. Several farms throughout the department hold open days to watch the *gavage* in the early stages of the force-feeding.

A recent development is the increase in the production of duck livers by comparison with goose livers which has declined. In 1996 Périgord was the second largest producer in France of geese and only the eighth for ducks, producing 89 tons and 190 tons of the finished product respectively. Its farmers cannot produce enough of the raw material to satisfy the demand and they have to resort to importing them. Geese from Hungary, Romania and Israel and duck from Hungary, Bulgaria and Israel are flown in in refrigerated containers for processing locally. A high proportion of the end product of both is then exported to Belgium, Great Britain, Holland, Japan and Hong Kong. (Imagine my delight to discover tins of *foie gras* from one of our local shops on sale in the duty free shop at St Petersburg airport in March 1996.)

The price to the consumer has fallen somewhat since 1994 which saw overproduction and imports have also been reduced. One factor in the price fall has been that these *foie gras* products are now to be found on the shelves of supermarkets who drive a hard bargain; in 1998 the price ranged from 300-350 francs a kilo for goose and 200-250 francs a kilo for duck liver.

Cooking the liver is a delicate and worrying process. Some years ago a friend who we had taken to Sarlat market in November bought us, as a surprise, the largest *foie gras* he could find. I read every book I had to discover how it should be cooked. The easiest recipe seemed to be one where you put the *foie gras*, covered with baking paper, into a moderate oven for twenty minutes. Imagine everyone's consternation when fifteen minutes later we found a hard ball of gristle swimming in a bath of golden fat. Two errors: the first, in buying the largest *foie gras*; the second in that the oven should have been as low as possible.

It took me some time to nerve myself to tackle one again but now I buy it vacuum-packed, put it into a pan filled with enough cold water to cover it and bring the heat up very slowly to blood temperature, watching like a hawk to see if the fat runs. Take the packet out, let it cool and then refrigerate for two days. Unpack it carefully, scraping off any fat and removing the nerves, if there are any. Eat with a slightly sweetened, lightly toasted *pain de mie,* and a glass of Monbazillac to the sound of trumpets. Sydney Smith was right.

Apart from their livers, geese are useful birds in that so much of them can be eaten. The flesh is heavy and rich, particularly if served as a *confit*. The breasts, known as *magrets*, have become what one might call designer food, served either smoked or fresh, undercooked and in a variety of sauces. The wings and legs are occasionally served roasted, which allows some of the fat to be drained, but are more often preserved – *confit* – to be reheated and eaten later. They are of course fatty and need lentils or beans as a floury accompaniment. The gizzards (*gessiers*), surprisingly tender, appear nowadays in many salads. The neck can be stuffed with the minced gizzard and small pieces of shredded flesh and offered as a first course, hot or cold, and often truffled. One of the best *cou d'oie farci* I have ever eaten was served with a small green salad and a trickle of raspberry vinegar. The blood is made into a kind of pancake, the *sanguette*, sprinkled with salt, pepper and garlic, left to coagulate, and fried in goose fat, with onions, parsley and verjuice. The carcase, skinned, emptied of the liver and shorn of the breast, legs and wings, is roasted and any remaining shreds of flesh, by now deliciously crisp and known as *grillons*, are considered a tasty snack by hunters out for a cold day's sporting activities, or are popped into soup. The skin and fat by themselves are known as *manteaux*, or if the legs and wings are left attached, as *paletots*. Nothing beats an egg fried in goose fat; and even the beak and feet are eaten, as in China.

The excellence of the geese and duck in the region today is in large part due to their being fed on maize, white from the Landes and yellow from Périgord. Their presence in Dordogne is, however, age-old. A curved horn antler, known as the baton de Teyjat, with engravings which include three birds which are almost certainly wild geese, was found at the Abri Mège, a Magdalenian site dating from between 15,000 and 9000 BC. The head of a goose carved in bone was found at another prehistoric site of the same period at Recourbie, near Brantôme, but since no skeletal remains of these birds have been found in any of the excavations, it is unlikely that early man ate them.

Eating truffles is as much a speciality of the region as the goose and its liver, but it arouses no moral indignation, and it was on this tuber – the *perle noir du Périgord* of J. C. Fulbert Dumonteil (1830-1912), a writer born in Vergt, who did so much to publicize the products of his native province – that the renown of Périgord's gastronomy came to rest. Attempts to describe its magic have led to the most extravagant flights of poetic fantasy; the *pomme féerique* of George Sand becomes Curnonsky's *l'âme parfumée de la cuisine périgordine* and Colette's *diamant noir de la cuisine*. She had clear views about how to deal with them:

> At least I learned […] how to treat the true truffle, the black truffle, the truffle of Périgord. The most capricious, the most revered of all those black princesses. People will pay its weight in gold – for the most part in order to put it to some paltry use. They stuff it into glutinous *foie gras*, they bury it in poultry smeared with fat, they submerge it, they chop it into brown sauce, they combine it with vegetables covered with mayonnaise … Away with all this slicing, this dicing, this grating, this peeling of truffles! Can they not love it for itself? If you do love it, then pay its ransom royally – or keep away from it altogether. But once having bought it, eat it on its own, scented and grainy skinned, eat it like the vegetable it is, hot, and served in generous quantities.
>
> Once scraped, it won't give you much trouble; its sovereign flavour needs no complications, no complicities. Bathed in a good, very dry

white wine – keep the champagne for your banquets, the truffle can do without it – salted without extravagance, peppered with discretion, it can then be cooked in a simple, black, cast-iron casserole with the lid on. For twenty-five minutes, it must dance in the constant flow of bubbles, drawing through the eddies and the foam – like Tritons playing round some darker Amphitrite – a score or so of smallish strips of bacon, fat but not too fat, which will give body to the stock. No other spices! And a pestilence upon your rolled napkin, with its taste and smell of bleach, last resting place of the cooked truffle! Your truffles must come to the table in their own stock. Do not stint when you serve yourself: the truffle is an appetite creator, an aid to digestion. And as you cut into this jewel sprung from a poverty-stricken soil imagine – if you have never visited it – the desolate kingdom where it rules. For it kills the dog rose, drains life from the oak, and ripens beneath an ungrateful bed of pebbles. Imagine too the harsh Périgordin winter, the hard frosts which whiten the fields, and the roseate pig poised for its delicate journey of discovery ...

Although this mysterious fungus which grows on the roots of oak trees has been known and valued since the time of the Greeks, *Tuber melanosporum*, the Périgordin variety, still baffles the scientists. Mushrooms in general, according to Theophrastus writing in the third to fourth century BC, were 'vegetables brought about by the autumn rains when accompanied by a clap of thunder'. It would seem that this is still the only explanation for the appearance of the truffle which, unlike that of the common mushroom, defies the efforts of agronomists to cultivate it.

These *enfants de Dieu* appeared on European tables in the fourteenth century and were clearly considered a delicacy. They were served at the banquet given for the wedding of Charles VI and Isabeau de Bavière in 1385 and they figure large in the accounts of Jean de France, Duc de Berry, in 1370 and 1376 when he was governor of Poitou and Saintonge. However they cannot have been in general use since neither the *Menagier de Paris c.*1393 nor Taillevent (Guillaume Tirel) *c.*1490 refer to them.

Despite the multitude of progeny begotten by Priam being ascribed to the power of the truffle by the Greeks, their aphrodisiac qualities are not mentioned again until the sixteenth century when they were much appreciated on that score at the court of François I at Fontainebleau. Fagon denied them to Louis XIV because they were indigestible, and the young Louis XV hunted for them at La Muette. Mme de Pompadour was reputed to have stuffed herself with them, and chocolate, to maintain her sexual attraction for Louis XV.

The birth of the King of Rome has allegedly been ascribed to the truffle. Napoleon, in conversation with one of Murat's aides-de-camp, asked him how he had achieved his nineteen children. On being told that it was due to eating truffles, Napoleon sent to the *préfet* of Sarlat and ordered a turkey to be entirely stuffed with *le divin tubercle*. Some months later, when the Empress was pregnant, the Périgordin officer received his colonel's commission.

By 1800 serious efforts were being made to find methods of cultivation and Jean de Serville, Châtelain de Beaupuy, hoped that sowing truffle peelings soaked in water would produce results. But their astonishing increase in Périgord in the mid-nineteenth century was due to inexplicable natural causes. They became so rampant that the *vignerons* – whose main source of income came from their vines – had to dig trenches to prevent the truffle from invading their vineyards. Wine was then the biggest single product of the department; in some communes half the cultivatable areas was given over to vines. Consequently their destruction between 1868 and 1885 by phylloxera was a major economic disaster. Périgord was fortunate in having the truffle to fall back on and as usual economic necessity was exploited by an adroit propaganda campaign. Many of the small manor houses on the *causses* were built in the boom that followed. Truffles had taken as long as eight days to reach Paris from Périgord by road and their increased popularity under the Second Empire, when perhaps they reached their apogee, was in part due to the fact that they arrived in the capital more quickly because of the railways.

In 1912, Périgord and Quercy produced 280 tons and the pre-war tables of Parisian hostesses were incomplete without some *feuilleté aux truffes* or a *poulet à demi-deuil*. But by 1964 production had fallen to 3-4 tons. It is thought that this rapid decrease was due to a combination of over-planting truffle oaks, the diminution in the number of men working the *truffières*, and a plague of caterpillars which virtually defoliated the oaks over a period of three consecutive years. After the Second World War, by which time many of the truffle-growing areas had become even more depopulated, it was cheaper and quicker to plant fast-growing softwood trees.

However, sustained efforts are now being made to 'cultivate' truffles and more than 100 hectares of oak and hazelnut trees, treated with mycorizes, have been planted in recent years. Mycorizes are the point of junction between the truffle and the oak. These rootlets of the 'contaminated' oak appear clothed in dense little tufts and can now be reproduced by artificial symbiosis.

The truffle is peculiar in that it is a tuber with no roots of its own, no stalks or stems, no leaves, no flowers and no true fruit. It is found growing, in a true symbiotic sense, in conjunction mainly with the 'truffle' oak – which may be *Quercus ilex*, *Quercus coccifera*, *Quercus sessiflora*, *Quercus lanuginosa* or *Quercus pendunculata* – or occasionally with hornbeam (*Carpinus betulus*), the lime tree (*Tilia*) and hazel (*Corylus avellana*). Truffles, like other mushrooms, need the right combination of sun and rain, and above all the right kind of calcareous soil. The presence of juniper, cherry and wild cherry indicate that the terrain may be favourable to their growth;

they do not flourish in the presence of chestnut, heather, gorse or foxglove. It is amusing to read that amongst the research undertaken by the botanists engaged in this work is a scientific study of the influence of the moon on the growth of truffles – which not surprisingly confirms the peasants' age-old observations.

Detecting the truffle, even in a favourable habitat, is difficult and a variety of methods have been used, including a water divining rod. They grow about eight inches below the soil and their scent, so powerful once in the air, is not perceptible to the human nose. The hovering tiny bronze-coloured truffle fly *Helomyza tuberivova* or *Tuberi perda* fairly certainly indicates their presence. Pigs and dogs can both be trained to sniff them out and it is said that in Sardinia goats are used. In the past the truffle hunter – the *caveur* – trained a sow (*truie*) who, if good, would earn her keep for fifteen years. A five-month-old piglet was chosen from the litter and fed on small morsels of truffle until she acquired a taste for them. Pieces would then be hidden and she would be encouraged to hunt for them, with acorns, chestnuts, maize, beans or potatoes as a reward. Today dogs are more generally employed and although they are easier to teach than pigs they do more damage with their paws. They are also easier to transport by car! Sheep dogs, fox terriers and, more surprisingly, poodles are the best truffle hunters. National truffle-dog trials, like sheep-dog trials in Britain, are held annually; and the champion of the 1998 competition, a German sheep dog from Cahors by the name of G. Chico, won by finding six truffles in an amazing forty-four seconds. It is interesting to record that in 1996, although the truffles were 'planted' for the contestants to find in temperatures of -15°, at St Pardoux de Mareuil, and they were frozen solid, their smell seems not to have been affected.

When the President of the Republic, Raymond Poincaré, visited Périgord in 1913, it was, alas, not the season for truffle hunting but the proud farmers wished to show him their skills. They arranged for a demonstration by one of their best dogs and the previous evening buried a few truffles in a field. All members of the party were duly impressed next day when the dogs found the truffles but imagine their astonishment when the truffles were discovered to be wrapped in tricolour ribbon! An energetic aide-de-camp had gone back in the night to prepare the surprise.

Rudyard Kipling, who wanted to write a short story about a truffle dog, took expert advice and entered into correspondence with M. Pierre Menanteau about them. Kipling kept up quite a correspondence in the spring of 1935 with Menanteau. He wrote from the California Palace, Cannes:

> Yes. I should be very grateful for any details as to the *dressage* of the truffle-hunting dogs. At what stage of their life does the training begin? Is there any sign by which a man can judge of the ability of the dog, while yet a puppy, to undertake that *métier*? Or, is the young animal introduced to ground that is full of truffles and left to follow

The truffle oak and the search for truffles (1885)

his own instincts? Also is a *small* dog – not of the sheep-dog type – as effective as a larger one? I have been told that some of the truffle-dogs are very small: and, for my purposes, I would much prefer that the dog be small.

I am specially glad to learn that the Pig is *not* an artist in the search for truffles but only an appetite at the end of a rope. That is what I always thought was the fact. I observe from your notes that the Dog is supposed to find 'amusement' in his work. Myself, I prefer to believe that he is an Artist, properly concerned for the honour of his Art! The point that interests me most is the very early age at which his training begins. I have never imagined that a puppy of three months old could be taught anything except the more elementary forms of decency.

All the 'documents' have arrived safely – the two varieties of oak – the *petit tête rouge* of the truffle – and the truffles themselves – and, most important, the acorns which I hope to plant in my own fields when I return to England this Spring.

Teem – a Treasure-Hunter was the result and was duly published, but Kipling died in January 1936 and the fate of the truffle acorns at Batemans is not known.

Truffles make their first appearance in November but they are small and efforts are being made to prevent poachers from collecting them then in an attempt to corner the early market. By early December they are officially on sale in the markets of St Silvain at Périgueux, Thiviers, Thenon, Terrasson, Sarlat and Montignac and reach their peak in late December and January in time for the festivities at Christmas and the New Year. Fair-sized truffles will weigh 200 grams; the largest one that has been found weighed 1 kilo. The high prices they fetch lead to a number of deceptions; soil, small stones, other mushrooms and even dyed carrot are buried in their crevices to increase their weight; *qu'ei un truffaire*, in the local patois, meant that a man was a cheat. But legislation to discourage fraud and the serious attempts to increase their production should change this. A number of local organizations are encouraging farmers to experiment with planting specially grown truffle oaks and financial aid is forthcoming for the purpose. The first results show that a harvest of 2 kilos per square metre can be expected in about ten years and 42 kilos in fifteen. But the *trufficulteurs* are achieving little success. Although progress is slow they continue with their efforts because the rewards are high and worth pursuing; truffles fetched 500 francs a kilo in Périgueux in November 1976, 1200-1600 francs in 1979 and 3-3,500 francs in 1998. About 130 truffle sellers turned up at Lalbenque on 20 January 1998 with approximately 300 kg of truffles. All were sold for cash within thirteen minutes, raising some 500,000 francs. In December 1998 only 12 kg of Périgordin truffles were on sale at the annual Ste Alvère market and the price per kilo soared to £400. The poor harvest was blamed on an abnormally cool summer.

The only two truffles with real gastronomic merit are the white ones of Piedmont and the black ones of Périgord although some thirty other varieties grow and are used throughout France. Despite an official ban on their use in products labelled 'truffle', some 15 tons of the thirty other varieties are harvested annually in France.

The passion for truffles has perhaps reached absurd heights if the rise in thefts of truffle hounds is anything to go by, and even the poisoning of one champion. A third of all French truffles are exported at huge prices, while the imported Chinese 'truffle' *tuber himalayensis* sells for one-fifth of the Périgordin variety. It is illegal to sell this under the label *'truffe'*.

Truffles appear in many local dishes and conserves and their cost is therefore correspondingly high. A good quality fresh whole truffle served in pastry or brioche or a cream sauce is a superlative delicacy which merits the eulogies of the publicists, and an egg which has lain with a truffle acquires its pervasive odour. Although it is heresy to say so, the small slivers of black leather from cans or bottles add little or nothing to the taste or texture of pâté or poultry and would be better omitted. It is comforting that so eminent a gastronome as Robert-Robert preferred the aroma of the truffle to the tuber itself. But there seems little point in being in pre-eminent truffle country and not at least having one good taste of them. For those who would like to try for themselves, familiarity with the descriptive labelling is a help when buying preserved trufffles:

truffes brossées: whole and cleaned
truffes pelées: whole and peeled
truffes en morceaux or *morceaux de truffes*: pieces must be not less than 5 millimetres thick; 25 per cent less expensive than whole truffles
truffes en pelures or *pelures de truffes*: peelings; just little bits
truffes preparées : with eau de vie or wine added
truffes au naturel: only water and salt added
truffes 1ère ebullition: truffles have had only one cooking, instead of two, three or four
surchoix: whole, round, black
extra: irregular and more or less black
première choix: irregular, peeled and more or less firm

If no description is given, the truffles are black but of mediocre quality. This classification to some extent constitutes an *appellation controlée*.

But of course *appellation controlée* is a term strictly applied to wine which, as one might expect, is produced in quantity in Dordogne. Because standards declined badly during and after the Second World War, especially in Monbazillac, the history of the vineyards in the department makes in some ways rather sad reading.

Morton Shand, Sichel and other authorities were reticent or condescending about most Dordogne wine. Here the vignoble was particularly hard hit by the phylloxera and, as always, quality tends to vary inversely with quantity and the ease of production. Climbing the hill up into Domme one can still make out the terracing here and there, now being smothered or broken up by scrubby vegetation, but which must have been created before 1870 on these steep slopes by years of grinding labour to accommodate vines. Even as late as 1903 Edouard Féret in his *Bergerac et ses vins* mentions four major and thirty minor growers belonging to the town itself, apart from the five pages devoted to growers in other villages within the canton of Domme. And that was after the phylloxera had run its course. An exciting new development is the recent replanting of the vineyards of the 'pays de Domme'. In 1870 they covered 2800 hectares but these all disappeared. Now – at least it is a start – 10 hectares have been planted at Bouzic, Florimont-Gaumier, Daglan, St Laurent La Vallée and Nabirat. A new *chai* has been constructed at Moncalou, and it handled the third, the 1998 vintage, and the 1999, from these new vines.

The *vignoble* of Dordogne is essentially an extension of that of Bordelais. It is not an area much visited by tourists, even today, and this helps to explain the relative unfamiliarity of the wines to foreigners. The *vignoble* extends over approximately 51,000 acres (15,600 hectares) producing in 1997 749,000 hectolitres of wine of which 648,000 – 86% – was AOC. In 1997 it brought in 526 million frances – some 16% of the department's earning from agricultural produce. (Milk made 362 million francs.)

Paul Strang, in *Wines of South-West France* (1994) gives a more up to date and detailed account of Bergerac wines, and lists all the producers as well as including a good deal of fascinating history of these vineyards. The varieties of grape grown have much diminished in number in recent years, both for red and white wines. Féret devotes nine pages to listing sixteen varieties of red, and four pages to five varieties of white grape. He also adds fascinating notes about the names they carried in different localities: the Cabernet-Sauvignon for example was known as the Machoupet in Castillon, the Carbouet in La Brède and Podensac, but as the Champigny in Blois. He does not mince words about their quality, and firmly lists them in order of merit, beginning with the Cabernet-Sauvignon (*grande finesse et un parfum suave et abondant*) and ending with the Folle Noir (*cultivée chez les petits propriétaires*) .

The years since the war have also seen a steady swing away from white towards red wine. Even so most of the Bergerac wine now produced and entitled to the AC label is still white. As usual, the ones from the *côtes* of the sloping valley sides are better than those entitled to the simple AC Bergerac, and must by law be one per cent stronger. These dry white wines made from the Sauvignon grape are pleasant enough, though in days freer of commercial pressure at the expense of quality, the only white Bergerac wine that would have justified the AC label is the sweet wine of Monbazillac.

This is the best – and the best-known – wine produced in the department. The production methods resemble those of the best Sauternes, and the grape varieties used are the same. Even at its best the wine cannot quite match the flowery lusciousness of the great Sauternes, but it is very good all the same and excellent value at its relatively modest price. The wine is produced, and the imposing château de Monbazillac owned, by a co-operative. There are about a dozen co-operatives which are responsible for producing something like half of all the wine sold each year and for selling much of the wine produced by private growers.

Such enormous strides have been made recently that it is impossible to offer advice about the best buys; improved methods of vinification and a greater number of younger producers has resulted in wines of a much higher quality.

Many of the producers now display their wares on market days in July and August and are only too delighted for one to taste: it is one way to avoid the embarrassment of turning up at the growers' *chais* and not liking the sample offered. One needs to be sure of this kind of thing, and it is a common experience for the *petit vin* that so delighted one on holiday to turn to ashes in the mouth back home. One possibility is to carry a notebook whenever eating in a restaurant, especially a good one, and to write down the details from the label of a bottle that has given pleasure. One can then seek out the grower with greater confidence in what one is going to buy.

The appellations AC Bergerac and Côtes de Bergerac are found on red wines as well as white. It was of these, one supposes, that Henri IV said as he tasted them, '*Bonne cuisine et grand vin, c'est le paradis sur terre.*' Modern wine lovers who may feel that this is to exaggerate a little will put down the king's remarks to his genius for public relations rather than his discernment.

Of the red wines, the most interesting is one called Pécharmant produced in a small area just north-east of the town of Bergerac, but little exported. The best-known growth is the château de Tiregand, long the property of the St Exupéry family. The Merlot grape forms a higher proportion of the mix here than in the Médoc, but the wine is well made and will please those who like the Merlot's rather overpowering flavour. It matures quicker than wine dominated by the Cabernet, and this is an important consideration where even a wine so good as this must be sold in fierce price competition with the equivalent wines from Bordeaux.

The best, or at least the most unexpected, red wines a traveller is likely to find in the region are in fact not produced in Dordogne at all but in the neighbouring department of Lot. The better wine of Cahors has had its own appellation for many years, and deserves it much better than many – indeed most – recent recipients. There are good co-operatives which sell very carefully made wine of consistent quality, both red and white, on behalf of a large group of local growers.

Despite its problems, the region has not lost its private growers, and unlike those of the Médoc most of them will sell their wine direct from the *chai* to interested passers-by. Of individual proprietors the best known is probably Jouffreau at Prayssac, just to the west of Cahors, who produces mainly red wine from a large estate called the Clos de Gamot under which name the wine is sold. Like that of most *vignerons* the estate was inherited, and M. Jouffreau has also successfully united modern technology to traditional skill and methods. At its best the wine has a fine, clean, fruity taste, and plenty of power without heaviness. But these results are not easily achieved, and not every year. The best vintages, though less stubborn than those made by pre-war methods, require ageing either in barrel or bottle before showing at their best. The resulting immobilization of capital, and wastage from seepage and evaporation means a fairly stiff price for the mature wine.

But – to return to Dordogne itself – apart from the AC wines already mentioned, a sweetish wine called Rosette is produced in small quantities on the hill above Bergerac to the north. To the west on the edge of the Gironde is Montravel which has three appellations: Côtes de Montravel and Haut Montravel, which are sweet-ish, and plain Montravel which is dry.

Lastly the Côtes de Saussignac, to the south, has its own appellation. Both red and white are produced, including much Bergerac sec.

A Gazetteer of the Dordogne

L'auto était en route.

Abjat (E2): heavily restored 12th c. church with interesting bell tower; château de l'Etang; 16th c. manor house; château de Grospuy; château de la Malignie

Abrillac: remains of 13th c. priory

Abzac, grotte d': *see* Eyzies, Les

Ages, château des: *see* Monsec

Agnelas, grotte de las: *see* Sourzac

Agonac (E4): pleasant small town; 10th c. château, built by Bishop Frotaire to keep the Normans out, with a 12th c. keep and 15th c. living quarters. Just outside the town good domed 11th-12th c. church of St Martin with 16th c. square belfry; abbey, Ligueux, 12th c. church restored in the 19th c.; château, which was a Benedictine abbey, with a fine 18th c. porch

Agonac, Preyssac d': *see* Preyssac d'Agonac

Aigueparse, Fontenilles d': *see* Fontenilles d'Aigueparse

Aillac: *see* Carsac et Aillac

Ajat (G5): 12th c. church with interesting tombstones; 14th-16th c. château; maison des Templiers; château de Sauveboeuf, destroyed by Richelieu in 1633 and rebuilt in Louis XIII style. One of its ornamental fountains is now in America, the other is at the château de Clairvac in Lot. Mirabeau, whose family owned the château, spent some time here

Allas les Mines: ruins of 15th c. château; château du Goudoux, 15th-16th c.

Allemans (C4): St Pierre ès Liens, a fine 12th c. church with two domes and a single nave; modern bell tower; 16th c. manor house

Allès sur Dordogne (F8): a charming village with a fine 12th c. church. It was an important Gallo-Roman centre

Ambelle, château d': *see* Ste Croix de Mareuil

Angle, rocher de l': *see* Eyzies, Les

Angoisse (H3): interesting church, 12th and 16th c with 16th and 17th c. stone statues; dolmen; château du Bouchet, a former Templar commanderie; château de Rouffiac, 16th c. with pepperpot towers

Annesse et Beaulieu (D5): dolmen; 12th c. church with 17th c. woodwork, château de Siorac, 17th c. At Beaulieu, château de Laroche Beaulieu. Domaine de Taillepetit, where Léon Bloy spent some time, and wrote *Celle qui pleure*

Antoniac, château d': *see* Razac sur l'Isle

Antonne et Trigonant (F5): château des Bories, 15th-16th c.; château d'Escoire, late 18th c.; château de Lammary, 15th and 18th c.; château de Trigonant, 15th c. Rochers de Borie Belet; côteau du Roi des Chauzes

Arborie, Jardins d': garden centre near Le Bugue with rare plants

Archignac (I6): dolmen; fine 12th c. domed church of St Etienne with capitals and a sculptured corniche

Argentine: *see* Rochebeaucourt, La et Argentine

Argentonnesse, château d': *see* Castels

Armandie, château de l': *see* Limeuil

Artigeas, château d': *see* Châtres

Atur (E5-6): restored 12th c. church and a 12th c. lanterne des morts

Aubas (H6): romanesque church with 11th c. capitals; 16th c. stone retables and 17th c. woodwork. A Merovingian stone sarcophagus in courtyard of house in village; château de la Fleunie; château de la Petite Filolie

Auberoche, château d': *see* Fanlac

Auberoche, château fort, and Chapelle St Michel: *see* Change, Le

Aubespin, château de l': *see* Monsaguel

Aucors, château d': *see* Beaussac

Audi, abri d': *see* Eyzies, Les

Audrix-Le Bugue (F8): 12th and 14th c. church with fortified apse; gouffre de Proumeyssac

Augignac (E2): Gallo-Roman sites of Le Meynichar and Les Morandies; romanesque church with 12th c. dome; ruins of 15th c. manor house

Auriac du Périgord (H6): 12th c. fortified church, restored 15th c.; fine 18th c. belfry and stairway. Les Olivoux, site of important Roman villa of which little now remains; chapelle de St Rémy; built about 1465 by Antoine La Cropte;

château de la Faye, 12th c. keep and 14th c. living quarters; Museum Abeilles du Périgord, miellerie et elevage

Ayguevive, château d': *see* Cénac et St Julien

Ayguevive, château d': *see* St Vincent de Cosse

Azerat (G5): château, medieval and 18th c.; attractive houses and public buildings. Chapelle Notre Dame de Bonne Espérance, gothic pilgrimage church for children who are ill

Bachellerie, La (H5): the village, known as Cern or Sern until about 1730, underwent destruction by the English and was greatly reduced during the Wars of Religion but is now flourishing; château de Rastignac

Badefols d'Ans (H5): pretty village with good views; 12th c. domed church with 18th c. belfry; 14th-15th c. château which belonged to the Born family but changed hands frequently; burned in 1945 but partially restored

Badefols sur Dordogne (F8): ruins of 15th and 16th c. château destroyed by Lakanal in 1793

Badegoule, grotte de: *see* Lardin, Le

Badeix, priory of: *see* St Estèphe

Baisse, château de la: *see* Milhac d'Auberoche

Balutie, gisement de la: *see* Montignac sur Vézère

Baneuil, château de: *see* Lalinde

Bannes, château de: *see* Beaumont du Périgord

Bara Bahau, grotte de: *see* Bugue, Le

Bardou: 12th c. church with fine doorway; 15th-17th c. château

Bardouly, château de: *see* St Aubin de Cadelech

Barradis, château de: *see* Monbazillac

Barrière, Château: *see* Périgueux

Barrière, Château: *see* Villamblard

Barry, château du: *see* Marcillac St Quentin

Bars (G6): interesting church in the heart of the forêt Barade

Bassac: *see* Beauregard et Bassac

Bassillac (F5): 12th c. church rebuilt during renaissance, with 17th c. retable; château de Rognac, 16th c., built by Père Trincard, Henri IV's almoner, now restored; moulin de Rognac, 17th c.; château Goudeau; château Pouyet; Par de Chasse de Meycourby

Bastide, La: *see* Monestier La Bastide

Batut, château de la: *see* St Chamassy

Baudeix: *see* Piégut Pluviers

Bauzens: St Barthélemy, church with fine pure romanesque portal and unusual stone pulpit. It was a priory dependent on the abbey of Tourtoirac, but only the church and dovecote are still extant

Bayac: 16th c. château; gisement de la Gravette

Beaulieu, château de: *see* Mareuil sur Belle

Beaulieu: *see* Annesse et Beaulieu

Beaumont de Périgord (E8): château de Luzier, 17th c.; château de Bannes, 15th-16th c. with vestiges of 13th c. fort; Chapelle Notre Dame de Belpey (Bel-pech, a fine hill in patois), which was a priory belonging to Cadouin and enlarged in 15th c.; dolmen de Blanc; dolmen de Pincarelle

Beaupouyet (B7): interesting church with 12th c. choir and good capitals; modern château de Fournils

Beauregard de Terrasson (H5): château de Beauregard de Terrasson: church with 12th c. remains; château de Mellet, 17th and 18th c.

Beauregard et Bassac: English bastide founded 1281 by Edward I; heavily restored church; château now children's holiday home; dolmen. Bassac: 12th c. church with interesting doorway

Beauregard, château de: *see* Mareuil sur Belle

Beauregard, Clermont de: *see* Clermont de Beauregard

Beauronne (C6): domed romanesque church with interesting archaic capitals. The village was renowned in the past for its production of pottery, a craft whch has been revived

Beauséjour, château de: *see* St Léon sur l'Isle

Beauséjour, château de: *see* Tocane St Apre

Beaussac (D3): 12th and 13th c. church. château d'Aucors; château de Bretanges, 15th and 17th c., inhabited by Alain de Moneys who was assassinated and burned by the peasants in 1871 at Hautefaye; château de Poutignac

Beauvais, château de: *see* Lussas et Nontronneau

Belaygue, priory of: *see* Gonterie Boulouneix, La

Belcayre, château de: *see* Thonac

Belet, château de: *see* St Aquilin

Beleymas (D7): 12th c. church heavily restored; retable from the Chapel of the Visitation at Périgueux with the only known depiction of St François de Sales in France

Bellegarde, château de: *see* Lamonzie Montastruc

Bellevue, château de: *see* Monbazillac

Bellussière, château de: *see* Rudeau Ladosse

Belpey (Belpech), Chapelle Notre Dame de: *see* Beaumont du Périgord

Belvès (G8): charming small town recently much restored; troglodytic habitations beneath the place furnished to show medieval life; château with square keep, church of Notre Dame de Montcucq, 14th and 15th c., was a Benedictine priory and has good woodwork; ruined Dominican chapel with an octagonal bell tower; dolmen de Langlade; Musée Organistrum et Vielles à roue du Périgord Noir; troglodytic site; ruins of a *filature* 1 km away

Berbiguières (G8): fine large château with remarkable façade, owned by Caumont family from 1368 for two centuries. Greatly enlarged in 15th c. by the end of which it had become a substantial fortress. Much destroyed by fire in early 18th c. and bought and sold by proprietors including property speculators from 1723 to 1983 though some restoration work intermittently undertaken. It now belongs to an Englishman who is restoring it to its former glory with painstaking care

Bergerac (D8): château de Lespinassat, 18th c.; Musée d'Intérêt National du Tabac; château de Mounet Sully (shut); Institut du Tabac, garden; Maison des Vins; Cloître des Récollets; Musée d'Art Sacré; Musée Ethnographique du Vin, de la Tonnellerie et de la Battelerie

Bernadières, château des: *see* Champeaux et La Chapelle Pommier

Bernifal, grotte de: *see* Meyrals

Bernou, gisement de: *see* Bourdeilles

Bersac, château de: *see* Lardin, Le

Bertis: *see* Vergt de Biron

Besse (G9): church of St Martin; dolmen du Roc de Travers

Bessède, forêt de: despite frequent fires, this forest is still very imposing

Beynac et Cazenac (H8): château de

Beynac; good village church recently restored with a good 17th c. retable; Musée Parc Archéologique. Cazenac; 15th c. gothic church; grotte de Cro Bique

Beynac: château de, *see* St Saud Lacoussière

Beyssac, château de: *see* Sireuil

Bézenac: Gallo-Roman site

Bigaroque, La: *see* Coux et Bigaroque, La

Bil, falaises de: *see* Eyzies, Les

Biras (E4): 12th c. church; château de la Cote

Biron, château de (F9-10): near Monpazier, 13th and 18th c., more finished rooms are now open to visitors as a result of filming *Les Visiteurs 2* having been made there; Notre Dame du Bourg

Blanc, Le: dolmen, *see* Beaumont du Périgord

Blanzac, château de: *see* Change, Le

Boiras, château de: *see* Vergt

Boisse: dolmen

Boisset, château de: *see* St Aquilin

Boisseuilh (H4): 12th c. church with Limousin influence; 19th c. reconstructed château

Boissière d'Ans, La (G5): 12th c. church with 16th c. chapels; château des Brouillets, which belonged to Jeanne

d'Albret, Henri IV's mother, 15th c. ruins

Boissière, Pech de la, gisement: *see* Carsac et Aillac

Bonaguil, château de (Lot et Garonne): magnificent medieval fortress

Bonarme, dolmen de: *see* Siorac de Ribérac

Bonnetie, château de la: *see* Sarliac sur l'Isle

Bonneville et St Avit de Fumadières (A8): 15th c. church with renaissance doorway, small 16th c. manor house in which Pierre Loti lived for a time; château de Valadou

Borde, château de la: *see* Change, Le

Bordeix, Le (E2): Gallo-Roman site

Borderie, château de la: *see* Monbazillac

Boreau, château de: *see* Cornille

Borie Belet, rochers de: *see* Antonne et Trigonant

Borie Petit, château de: *see* Champcevinel

Borie Saulnier, château de la: *see* Champagnac de Belair

Borie, château de La: *see* Cubjac

Borrèze: 12th c. church restored in 15th c.; ruins of château de Caviale; dolmen

Boschaud, abbaye de: *see* Villars

Boslaurent, château de: *see* Chapelle Faucher, La

Bost: dolmen

Bosvieux, château de: *see* St Vincent sur l'Isle

Bouchet, château du: *see* Angoisse

Bouillac (F8): 12th c. church with 14th c. portal; dolmen

Boulazac (E5): an expanding industrial suburb of Périgueux; château du Lieu Dieu, 14th-15th c., restored 19th c.

Boulouneix: *see* Gonterie Boulouneix, La

Bouniagues: presbytery with renaissance doorway

Bouquerie, La: 12th c. church with gothic additions and 14th c. portal

Bouquet, château de: *see* Sorges

Bourbet, château du: *see* Cherval

Bourdeilles (D4): town of; 12th and 16th c. châteaux de, scrupulously restored; medieval bridge; maison des Sénéschaux; gisements de La Chèvre, Bernou and Fourneau du Diable

Bourdeix, Le: romanesque church with 15th c. gothic nave. 12th c. domed keep on the square

Bourg, church of Notre Dame du: *see* Biron

Bourg des Maisons (C4): Ste Marie, a fine single naved romanesque church which in 1134 belonged to the abbey of Sarlat. It has two domes; the west front is 19th c.; 17th c. frescoes. Manoir du Reclaud; château de Tinteillac

Bourg du Bost (B4): Notre Dame, romanesque church, oval dome, painted ceiling and frescoes in the choir with good 17th c. retable, and 17th c. French school painting 'L'Enfant Jésus adoré par une princesse'

Bourgonnie, château de la: *see* Paleyrac

Bourlie, château de la: *see* Urval

Bournat: village of, at Le Bugue

Bourniquel: heavily restored romanesque church; château de Cardou, 15th and 16th c.; gisement de Champs Blancs or Jean Blancs; gisement de Malpas

Bouteilles St Sébastien (C4): romanesque church with fine saintongeais apse with 15th c. defensive chamber above; château de la Richardie, 17th c.

Bouyssieral, Breuil de: *see* St André d'Allas

Bouzic (H9): romanesque church with interesting capitals; 18th c. Virgin; grotte du Trou de Vent

Brantôme (E4): abbey; fine bridge; monks' garden, Medici fountain; Musée Fernand Desmoulins; Musée Rêve et Miniatures; caves; church of St Pardoux de Feix; château de la Hierce, in centre of town, 16th c., typical renaissance style, with botanical gardens; dolmen de Pierre Levée; abbey and troglodytic site; château de Richemont

Braulem, château de: *see* Calviac

Bretanges, château de: *see* Beaussac

Breuil de Bouyssieral: *see* St André d'Allas

Breuil, château du: *see* Verteillac

Bridoire, château de: *see* Ribagnac

Brognac, château de: *see* Teyjat

Brouillets, château des: *see* Boissière d'Ans

Bruc: tiny village with interesting 14th-15th c. church

Brunies, château des: *see* Chapelle Gonaguet, La

Bruzac, château de: *see* St Pierre de Côle

Bugue, Le (F7): rows of houses with wrought iron balconies give this agreeable small town on the Vézère a slightly Spanish look. It was the birthplace of the little known Jean Rey (1583-1645) who invented the clinical thermometer and discovered, earlier than Lavoisier, the principle of conserving matter. Grotte de Bara Bahau, cave, engravings; Gouffre de Proumeyssac; Aquarium du Périgord Noir; Le Village de Bournat; Les Jardins d'Arborie; Maison de la Vie Sauvage; Musée de la Paléontologie

Buisson, Le (F8): a small town. 14th c. church of St Pierre ès Liens nearby at Cabans

Bussac: fortified 12th c. church

Busserolles (E1): picturesque small town with a finely proportioned romanesque church

Bussière Badil (D1): interesting church with good capitals

Cabans: *see* Buisson, Le

Cabrerets (Lot): grotte de Pech Merle

Cadelech: *see* St Aubin de Cadelech

Cadouin (F8): cloister; Musée du Suaire; Musée de la Vélocipède

Calès (F8): village perched high above the Dordogne with a good view; fine 12th c. church houses a statue of Notre Dame du Lac – a Virgin which was an object of veneration to the gabarriers

Calviac: 13th-14th c. church. Site of abbey where St Sacerdos, later bishop of Limoges, was abbot. He was beatified for curing lepers. His relics were taken to Sarlat cathedral in the 16th c. Château de Braulem; château de Monteil; château de Fonnoyer

Campagnac, château de: *see* St Pardoux et Viélvic

Campagne (G7): 12th c. church re-worked 15th c. Original château razed by Charles VII; rebuilt 15th c. and now excessively restored and used as a store by the museum at Les Eyzies. Very pretty village with a communal washing tub with an elegant balustrade; Le Solleilal, champignonnière in the old stone quarries

Caneau, château de: *see* St Front la Rivière

Caneda, Le: on the outskirts of Sarlat; 12th c. Templar church

Canet, villa du: *see* Port Ste Foy

Cantillac: 12th c. church

Cap Blanc, abri du: *see* Marquay

Cap del Roc, château de: *see* Manaurie

Capdropt (Capdrot) (F9): the village lies on a plateau overlooking the Dropt - hence its name. 12th c. church transformed into a collegiate church by Pope John XXII; 17th c. wooden Virgin

Cardou, château de: *see* Bourniquel

Carennac (Lot): priory and cloister; Maison de la Dordogne Quercynoise; Musée des Alambics et Aromathèque

Carlucet: *see* St Crépin et Carlucet

Carlux (I7-8): impressive ruins of 12th c. château which belonged to the viscounts of Turenne; château de Rouffilhac; garden at Cadiot

Carnedie, La, Gallo-Roman site of: *see* Piégut Pluviers

Carpe Diem, grotte de: *see* Manaurie

Carrieux, château de: *see* Liorac

Carsac de Gurson (A7): 12th c. church with arcaded tower and fine façade. The château de Gurson is now in ruins. Henry III gave it to Jean de Grailly in 1277 and it was almost entirely rebuilt in the 18th c. Montaigne spent many hours there

Carsac et Aillac: château de la Gazaille, part 15th c.; gisement du Pech de la Boissière; gisement de Pech de l'Aze. Aillac: 14th c. church with 12th c. font. Ruins of château taken by the English in 1355

Carvès: 12th c. church; 18th c. retable

Cassagne, La (I6): pretty village with fine 12th c. church and 16th c. presbytery, the remains of a priory; 16th c. cross in cemetery. The village also has a barn, the lower room of which is covered in 12th c. ogival vaulting, which is known as the Temple, doubtless because of some association with the Knights. Gallo-Roman site nearby known as the Source de Ladoux; La Grange Dimière – Musée SEM

Castanet, abri de: *see* Sergeac

Castelet, manoir du: *see* Domme

Castelmerle, gisement de: *see* Sergeac

Castelnaud La Chapelle (H8) (so-called since the amalgamation of Castelnaud Fayrac and La Chapelle Pechaud in 1975): château de Fayrac; château des Milandes; château de Lacoste, 18th c., park and garden; château de Castelnaud; Musée de la Guerre du Moyen-Age; Ecomusée de la Noix du Périgord

Castels (G8): ruined 12th c. church of St Martin du Vieux Castels; château d'Argentonnesse, 18th c. Nearby is the chapelle de Redonespic, a fine church, though difficult to reach

Castelviel, château de: *see* St Pompont

Castillonès (Lot-et-Garonne): a French bastide, with an interesting church

Caudon, château and chapelle de: *see* Domme

Cause de Clérans: church and the ruins of 13th c. château with a keep; mentioned in one of Bertrand de Born's *sirventes*

Caussade, château de: *see* Trélissac

Cayreleva(t), dolmen de: *see* Siorac de Ribérac

Cazenac et Beynac: *see* Beynac

Cazoulès: the river Dordogne enters the department here. Heavily restored church. Château de Font Haute, 16th c.; manoir du Raysse, 17th c.

Celles (C4): exceptional fortified 12th c. church containing a 17th c. painting of Stes Radegonde and Catherine. Château de Montardy, where the Marquis de Lau d'Allemans entertained Malebranche in 1688

Cellier, abri: *see* Tursac

Cénac et St Julien: Cénac fine priory church. St Julien is the port of Cénac and is a tiny pretty hamlet with a roman-esque church on the river facing La Roque Gageac. Château de Monbette; château de Sibeaumont; château de Costecalve; château d'Ayguevive; château de Fondaumier, where Albéric Cahuet lived and where the action of *Pontcarral* took place. Grotte du Comte

Cendrieux (F7): 12th c. domed church

with doorway reworked 18th and 19th c.; 17th c. manoir

Cercles (D4): good romanesque church, former priory of St Cybard with gothic additions; fine doorway and capitals

Chabans, château de: *see* St Léon sur Vézère

Chalagnac: 12th c. church reworked 16th c. with good 14th c. doorway. Château de Rossignol; dolmen

Chaleix (or Chalais) (F3): badly restored romanesque church; 17th c. stone statue of St John the Baptist in churchyard. Château de Malaveix, 16th c. Foundry of Malaveix of Gallo-Roman origin, transformed by its ironmaster owner into an elegant country house

Champagnac de Belair (E4): small town on the Dronne. 16th c. church of St Christophe with a fine porch and a 17th c. retable; château de la Borie Saulnier, Gallo-Roman site

Champagne et Fontaine (C3): 12th c. church of St Martin de Champagne fortified in 16th c.; 17th c. retable. Fontaine; 12th c. church of St John the Baptist which was a priory belonging to Fontevrault and restored in the 17th c. château de Clauzuroux, renaissance building with an 18th c. gateway

Champcevinel: château de Borie Petit, belonged to the canons of St Front, well restored

Champeaux et La Chapelle Pommier (D3): Champeaux: 12th c. church with 16th c. additions; La Chapelle Pommier:

12th c. church; château des Bernard-
ières, 12th and 18th c. Brantôme was a
frequent visitor here. Château de
Puycheny, 15th c.

Champniers et Reilhac (E1): Champniers: 12th c. church with limousin bell
tower, 12th c. font and 18th c. retable.
15th and 17th c. château where the
Marquis de Lau d'Allemans entertained
Fénelon and Malebranche. Reilhac:
domed 12th c. church of St Paul built of
granite; ruined 18th c. château, which
once belonged to the Templars. It was
listed in 1742 as being the property of
the Knights of Malta. Gallo-Roman site
of La Fraysse

Champs Blancs, gisement de: *see*
Bourniquel

Chancelade (E5): abbey; vestiges of
Gallo-Roman occupation; abri de
Raymonden; chapel of St Jean

Change, Le (F5): well sited village on
the Auvézère with mill and bridge; the
dome of the 12th c. church is heavily
restored. Château-fort and chapelle St
Michel d'Auberoche; château de la
Sandre, 15th c. with a 13th c. tower still
extant; château de la Faurie, 15th c. with
a 16th c. tower; château de Ribeyrolles;
château de Blanzac: château de la Borde;
château du Roc

Chantérac (C5): fortified romanesque
church enlarged 16th c. 16th-17th c.
château which belonged to La Cropte

Chapdeuil (D4): a small town with old
houses; fine 12th c. keep with 15th c.
battlements surrounded by a moat

Chapelet du Diable: *see* St Estèphe

Chapelle Faucher, La (E4): small village on the Côle with a domed
romanesque church restored 16th c.;
13th-16th c. château taken by Coligny
in 1569 and Sauveboeuf during the
Fronde, destroyed by fire this century;
12th c. Templar chapel of Jumilhac le
Petit; château de Boslaurent, 15th-17th
c.; Notre Dame de Puymartin, ruins of
a priory; gisement de Rochecaille;
château de La Chapelle Faucher

Chapelle Gonaguet, La (D5): château
des Brunies. Merlande: Priory chapel

Chapelle Montabourlet, La: fortified
15th c. church with 17th c. altar and
18th c. Virgin

Chapelle Péchaud, La: pretty 12th c.
church with fine apse, decorated corbels
and a good 18th c. doorway

Chapelle Pommier, La: *see* Champeaux
and La Chapelle Pommier

Chapelle St Robert, La (D2): small
pretty church

Chapoulie, château de la: *see* Peyrignac

Charreaux, La Tour des: *see* St Médard
d'Excideuil

Chassaignes: early 12th c. church of St
Jean Baptiste, heavily restored; château
du Pauly; château de la Ro(u)velle

Château L'Evêque (E5): bishop's
palace started in 14th c. by Adhémar de
Neuville, Bishop of Périgueux, rebuilt
16th c.; modern neo-gothic church
which preserves some remains of earlier
constructions. St Vincent de Paul (1581-
1660), renowned for his charitable

foundations, the Filles de la Charité and the Prêtres de la Mission, was ordained here in 1600. Gentilhommière de Cluzel

Château Missier: church of St Quitterie

Chatelard, château de: *see* Teyjat

Châtres (H5): modern church with 12th c. doorway. There was an Augustinian abbey at Châtres Bas, but no traces remain. St Waast, who converted Clovis to Christianity, was born at Branquelion nearby and is commemorated by a modern fountain; château d'Artigeas, ruins

Chavagnac: dolmen; 12th c. church; 14th c. watch-tower. Gentilhommières de la Fauconnie Haute et de la Fauconnie Basse

Chavaroche, château de: *see* Vieux Mareuil

Chenaud (A5): Church of St Pierre and St Paul consecrated in 1100, rebuilt in the 19th c.

Cherval (C3): fortified domed church of St Martin; château du Bourbet; garden at Limodore

Cherveix Cubas (H4): busy small junction with 12th c. church and a lanterne des morts in the cemetery. Cubas: church with statue of St Roch; St Martial Laborie, domed 12th c. church with statue of Ste Valerie

Chèvre, gisement de la: *see* Bourdeilles

Cheylard, chapelle du: *see* St Geniès

Chourgnac d'Ans (G5): Musée des Rois d'Araucanie

Claud, château du: *see* Salignac-Eyvigues

Clauzuroux, château de: *see* Champagne et Fontaine

Clermont de Beauregard (E7): heavily restored romanesque church by the side of ruins of 14th c. castle; château de la Gaubertie, 16th and 17th c. building, completely restored in the early years of the 20th c. There is a small 17th c. chapel by its side

Clottes: *see* Nojals et Clottes

Cluzeau, grotte du: *see* Villars

Cluzeau, manoir du: *see* Proissans

Cluzel, gentilhommière de: *see* Château l'Evêque

Colombier (D8): 12th c. church, reconstructed in the 16th c., with a good renaissance doorway; château de la Jaubertie, given by Henri IV to his mistress Gabrielle d'Estrées about 1592. It was restored in the 19th c. and furnished with paintings and sculptures from the château of St Cloud, but is now very dilapidated

Coly: small 12th c. church restored in the l6th c.

Combarelles, grotte des: *see* Eyzies, Les

Combe Capelle, gisement de Roc de la: *see* St Avit Sénieur

Combe, gisement de la: *see* Valajoulx

Combe, Grenal, abri de: *see* Domme

Combéranche et Epeluche: Combéranche: 12th c church; Templar commanderie. Epeluche: 12th c. church with gothic additions

Commarque, château de: *see* Marquay

Comte, grotte du: *see* Cénac et St Julien

Condat sur Trincou (E4): village perched on cliff above confluence of Côle and Trincou; 12th c. church built on remains of Gallo-Roman necropolis where some hundreds of sarcophagi were found. A three-headed statue of Hercules (now in the museum at Bordeaux) was discovered there in 1800. Dolmen de Pierrelevade; château de Montplaisir, 16th and 17th c.

Condat sur Vézère (H6): village at the confluence of the Vézère and Coly (*condat* means confluence in Celtic). The tiny and beautifully kept hamlet has a restored 12th c. church, and fortified living quarters, some small towers on some of the houses which were once part of a Templar and later Hospitaller commanderie

Conne de Labarde: 16th c. church with curious lop-sided bell tower

Connezac (D3): 12th c. church reconstructed in the 16th c. with a good doorway; château, 17th c.

Conty, château de: *see* Coulaurès

Coquille, La (G2): château la Meynardie

Corgnac sur l'Isle (F4): a small village with a fine medieval bridge and a heavily restored 12th c. church; château de Laxion, magnificent 16th c. building put up by Antoine Chapt de Rastignac during the Wars of Religion and untouched since

Cornille: romanesque church; château de la Luminade; château de la Forêt; château de la Fayardie; château de Boreau

Costecalve, château de: *see* Cénac et St Julien

Cote, château de la: *see* Biras

Coubjours: romanesque church with 16th c. pietà; 18th c. manoir

Coudonie, château de la: *see* Fanlac

Cougnac, grotte de: *see* Gourdon

Coulaurès (G4): small town at confluence of the Isle and the Loue; church of St Martin, 12th c. with 14th c. fresco and gothic additions, restored; dolmen; chapelle de Notre Dame du Pont, 17th c.; château de Conty, 16th c. and later; château de la Cousse, 17th-18th c.

Coulonges, château de: *see* Montignac sur Vézère

Coulouneix (E5): château de la Rolphie, 16th c., with ruins of fine renaissance staircase and ceiling; La Maladrerie, 12th c. house known as the 'Maison des Anglais'; Gallo-Roman remains

Coursac: domed 12th c. church; château de la Jarthe, 14th-16th c., the home of the Du Puy family who furnished Périgueux with more than 30 mayors and consuls

Cousse, château de la: *see* Coulaurès

Coutoux, dolmen de: *see* Valeuil

Coutures: 12th c. domed church of St Saturnin, reworked 18th c., with a 17th c. retable; small pavilion on arcaded base

Coux et Bigaroque, Le (G8): Coux: 12th c. church with fine doorway. Bigaroque: pretty village with 12th c. church and ruins of château which belonged to the archbishops of Bordeaux

Couze St Front (E8): on the river Dordogne near its confluence with the Couze; troglodytic dwellings; romanesque church. Now a centre for making tannin and paper and growing mushrooms. St Front, 12th c. church with interesting capitals; Moulin La Rouzique; Ecomusée du Papier

Crète, La: *see* Etouars

Creyssac: heavily restored 12th c. church

Creysse (D8): Bella Riva, centre for river trips in gabarres; château de Tiregand, park; Préhistoire, vin de Pécharmant; Musée Aquarium de la Rivière Dordogne

Cro Bique, grotte de: *see* Beynac

Cro de Granville, grotte de: *see* Rouffignac

Cro Magnon, grotte de: *see* Eyzies, Les

Crognac, château de: *see* St Astier

Croze, château de la: *see* Sireuil

Croze, grotte de la: *see* Eyzies, Les

Cubas: *see* Cherveix Cubas

Cubjac: a small town on the Auvézère which has a goat cheese named after it; château de la Sudrie, 17th c.; château de La Borie

Cumond: domed church of St Antoine Cumond, 12th c. sculpted doorway and traces of frescoes

Cunège: 12th c. church with a good doorway

Daglan (H9): a pretty village with 12th c. church of little interest and 18th c. houses; château de Pauliac; château de Peyruzel, fortified, 17th c., unusual in that it is in the shape of a Greek cross. 150 stone huts build by vignerons have been listed and the Musée de la Pierre Sèche is in one of them

Dalon, abbaye du: *see* Ste Trie

Dévars du Mayne, château de: *see* Nanthiat

Doissat (G9): fine extensive grove of walnut trees

Domme (H8): château de Giversac, owned by the Banque de France and used as a holiday home; château de Caudon; chapelle de Caudon, a disused chapel cut in the cliff on the river road to Domme, built for Catholic worship when Domme was in the hands of the Protestants; manoir du Castelet; abri de Combe Grenal; dolmen de Giversac; grotte de la Halle; Musée des Arts et Traditions Populaires; Porte des Tours Prison des Templiers

Douchapt: village well situated on the Dronne with a 12th c. church of St Pierre ès Liens with interesting porch and decorated capitals; dolmen

Douville: 16th c. church; château de St Mamet, 12th c.; château de Lestaubière; château de Roussille; ruins of the fortress of Waiffre, Duke of Aquitaine, 7th-8th c.

Douze, La (F6): charming small romanesque church on outskirts of town

Douzillac (C6): sited above the Isle with a 12th c. church, revaulted in the 16th c; château de Mauriac, 16th c.

Dulgarie, château de la: *see* Sarliac sur l'Isle

Durantie, château de la: *see* Lanouaille

Dussac (G3): domed romanesque church; château, built in 1778; now a school

Duvigneau, château de: *see* St Seurin de Prats

Echourgnac (B6): small village in the heart of the Double with a community of nuns at Notre Dame de Bonne Espérance where cheese is made; Ferme du Parcot Habitat de la Double

Eglise Neuve de Vergt (E6): church uninteresting save for modern glass windows of Breton inspiration

Enfer, grotte du gorge d': *see* Eyzies, Les

Epeluche: *see* Combéranche et Epeluche

Escoire, château d': *see* Antonne et Trigonant

Etang, château de l': *see* Abjat

Etouars: restored 12th c. church with a 17th c. retable. Gallo-Roman site at La Crète

Evêques, château des: *see* Issigeac

Excideuil (G4): busy small town on the Loue at the confines of the Limousin and Périgord; heavily restored 12th-15th c. church with gothic doorway. It was a Benedictine priory and contains a pietà and a good 17th c. retable. Remains of 11th-12th c. château which belonged to the viscounts of Limoges and subsequently to Jeanne d'Albret, Henri IV's mother. It passed to the Talleyrand family but fell into disuse at the Revolution, There are two keeps and two renaissance buildings

Eybènes: *see* Eyvigues et Eybènes

Eyliac: 12th c. domed church enlarged in 16th c. when the sacristy was frescoed. 15th-17th c. manoir

Eymet (C9): bastide; Musée Archéologique et Historique

Eyrenville: a small village on the very edge of the department with a 12th c. domed church reworked in the 16th c.

Eyrignac, manoir d': *see* Salignac-Eyvigues

Eyssendiéras, château d': *see* St Médard d'Excideuil

Eyvigues et Eybènes: good 12th-16th c. church with 12th c. font. Dolmen

Eyzies de Tayac, Les (G7): grotte d'Abzac; rocher de l'Angle; abri d'Audi; falaises de Bil: grotte des Combarelles: grotte de Cro Magnon; grotte de la Croze; grotte de Font de Gaume; grotte du Grand Roc; grotte du Gorge d'Enfer; abri Lartet; gisements de Laugerie Haute et Laugerie Basse; gisement de la Mouthe; gisement de Pataud; grotte du Poisson; La Micoque gisement; jardin botanique; Musée de la Spéléologie; Musée National de Préhistoire; Roc de Cazelle prehistoric park, troglodytic fort

Fage, château de: *see* Pomport

Fages, château de: *see* St Cyprien

Fanlac (G6): 12th c. church extended in the 17th c. The bas relief on the north wall depicts Jean de la Jalage who served Maréchal de Boucicaut (who commanded the French army at the battle of Agincourt) and settled at Fanlac after the destruction of the fortress at Montignac in 1398. There is a fine 17th c. stone cross in front of the church. Eugène Le Roy made *Jacquou le Croquant*'s curé Bonal live in the presbytery here. Château d'Auberoche, 14th and 17th c. château du Sablou; château de la Coudonie

Fauconnie, gentilhommières de la Haute et Basse: *see* Chavagnac

Faurélie, château de la: *see* Mauzens et Miremont

Faurélie, gisement de la: *see* Manaurie

Faurie, château de la: *see* Change, Le

Faurie, croix de la: *see* Paulin

Faux: dolmen

Fayardie, château de la: *see* Cornille

Faye, château de la: *see* Auriac du Périgord

Faye, cross and château de la: *see* St Sulpice de Mareuil

Faye, église de: *see* Ribérac

Fayolle, château de: *see* Tocane St Apre

Fayolles, château de: *see* Saussignac

Fayrac, château de: *see* Castelnaud

Fénelon, château de: *see* Ste Mondane

Ferrassie, gisement de la: *see* Savignac de Miremont

Festalemps: domed romanesque church of St Martin with traces of frescoes and an early 16th c. belfry. The nave was re-roofed in the 19th c. and the church contains a 17th c. polychrome retable

Feuillade, La: much restored 12th c. church; 17th c. château

Filolie, château de la: *see* Thiviers

Filolie, château de la Grande: *see* St Amand de Coly

Filolie, château de la Petite: *see* Aubas

Fixade, dolmen de: *see* Piégut Pluviers

Flaugeac: 15th c. church

Fleix, Le (B8): small town on a bend (flexus) of the Dordogne. The château is now a Protestant church

Fleunie, château de la: *see* Aubas

Fleurac (G7): 12th c. church with 15th c. additions; 19th c. neo-gothic château inhabited by St Exupéry family from 12th-17th c., fine park; château de Peuch; château de Souffron; château de Fleurac

Florimont Gaumier: Florimont: restored 12th c. church and font; 18th c. retable; château de Pechembert; Gallo-Roman site. Gaumier: old mill

Fondaumier, château de: *see* Cénac et St Julien

Fongalop: 12th c. church restored in the 16th c.

Fonnoyer, château de: *see* Calviac

Fonroque (C9): an English bastide; church with 14th c. defensive bell tower

Fonrousse, château de: *see* Monbazillac

Font de Gaume, grotte de: *see* Eyzies, Les

Font Haute, château de: *see* Cazoulès

Fontaine: *see* Champagne et Fontaine

Fontenilles d'Aigueparse (G9): 12th c. church, fortified in the 13th c.

Fontjuliane, château de: *see* St Julien d'Eymet

Fonvieille, manoir de: *see* Monbazillac

Force, La: *see* Laforce

Forêt, château de la: *see* Cornille

Forêt, gisement de la: *see* Tursac

Forge, château de la: *see* Savignac Lédrier

Forge d'Ans, château de la: *see* St Pantaly d'Ans

Fossemagne: 12th-14th c. church on the edge of the forêt Barade

Fougueyrolles: 15th c. church heavily restored with a huge 16th c. stone retable

Fouleix: 12th c. domed church restored in the 19th c.

Fourneau du Diable, gisement: *see* Bourdeilles

Fournils, château de: *see* Beaupouyet

Fratteau, château de: *see* Neuvic sur l'Isle

Fraysse, La: Gallo-Roman site of: *see* Champniers et Reilhac

Frugie, château de: *see* St Pierre de Frugie

Gabillou (G5): 12th c. church with 17th c. additions; château de Vaudre, 14th-17th c.

Gabillou, grotte de: (also known as grotte de las Agnelas): *see* Sourzac

Gageac et Rouillac (C8): Gageac: on a plateau above the river Dordogne, with an 18th c. church. Rouillac: a 14th c. château which belonged to Geoffroy de Vivans' family

Gageac, La Roque: *see* Roque Gageac, La

Gamenson, château de: *see* St Laurent des Hommes

Gane, gisement de la: *see* Grolejac

Gardonne: a small town on the Dordogne. All traces of the 13th c. château have disappeared

Garraube, château de la: *see* Liorac

Gaubertie, château de la: *see* Clermont de Beauregard

Gaugeac: 14th-16th c. church heavily restored; château de St Germain

Gaume, Font de grotte de: *see* Eyzies, Les

Gaumier: *see* Florimont Gaumier

Gauterie, domaine de la: *see* St Paul Lizonne

Gazaille, château de la: *see* Carsac et Aillac

Genis (H4): 12th c. domed church restored with Limousin influences; ugly modern health resort at nearby Clairvivre

Gentiac, château de: *see* Liorac

Gérauds, château des: *see* St Martin de Ribérac

Gevaudon, château de: *see* Monpazier

Giversac, château de, and dolmen de: *see* Domme

Gonterie Boulouneix, La (D4): domed church with saintongeais façade. All that remains of the priory of Belaygue, a dependency of the Benedictine abbey of Ligueux, is a ruined 12th c. church with a fine doorway. Gisements de la Tabaterie et de Roc Plat

Gorge d'Enfer, grotte de: *see* Eyzies, Les

Goudeau, château: *see* Bassillac

Goudoux, château du: *see* Allas les Mines

Gourdon (Lot): a charming small market town perched on a hill; grotte de Cougnac

Gouts Rossignol: strange church; château de Jaurias, early 18th c. house with central courtyard; château de la Vassaldie, 18th c.

Gramat (Lot): gouffre de Padirac

Grand Brassac (D4): church of St Pierre and St Paul with three domes and a sculpted porch; château de Maroitte; gisement de Rochereuil

Grand Castang: romanesque church, heavily restored

Grand Roc, grotte du: *see* Eyzies, Les

Grande Filolie, château de la: *see* St Amand de Coly

Granges d'Ans: 12th c. church, heavily restored; château de Redon, rebuilt this century

Grateloup, château de: *see* St Sauveur

Graulet, château de: *see* Ste Eulalie d'Eymet

Graulges, Les: domed romanesque church with saintongeais façade and a decorated cross in churchyard

Gravette, gisement de la: *see* Bayac

Grénerie, château de la: *see* Verteillac

Grèze, grotte de la: *see* Marquay

Grèzes: 12th c. church, restored; 14th c. château

Grézignac, manoir de: *see* Sarliac sur l'Isle

Griffoul, château de: *see* Vitrac

Grignols: 14th-15th c. gothic church with good sculpted vault bosses. Fortress built from 12th-17th c. with its moat still there. It belonged to the Talleyrand and later the Du Puy families whose device is used as a decoration on the chimneys and windows

Grives: restored 12th c. church with a 17th c. altar screen

Grolejac (I8): village on the river Dordogne with an attractive manoir and houses. 12th c. church with 17th c. woodwork; gisement de la Gane

Grospuy, château de: *see* Abjat

Gurson, Carsac de: *see* Carsac de Gurson

Hautefort (H5): château; ancien hospice founded 1669 by the Marquis of Hautefort for the relief and spiritual succour of the poor; château de Hautefort, park and gardens; châteaux des Charreaux, jardin anglais; Musée de la Medicine (ancien hospice)

Herm, château de l': *see* Rouffignac

Hierce, château de la: *see* Brantôme

Hospitalet, L' (Lot): grotte des Merveilles

Hurtevent, château de: *see* Paunat

Igonie, manoir d': *see* St Sulpice d'Excideuil

Isle, manoir de l': *see* Paulin

Issac (C6-7): 12th c. domed church; château de Montreal, with 11th c. ramparts, a vaulted staircase and towers, and renaissance living quarters. The 16th c. chapelle de la Ste Epine contains the tomb of its founder François de Pontbriand and his wife, and the Holy Thorn carried by Sir John Talbot at the battle of Castillon

Issigeac (D9): château des Evêques; fine bishop's palace

Jaillac, château de: *see* Sorges

Jarthe, château de la: *see* Coursac

Jaubertie, château de la: *see* Colombier

Jaure: restored romanesque church; 15th-17th c. château

Jaurias, château de: *see* Gouts Rossignol

Javerlhac (D2): Fernand Desmoulins (1853-1914 born here; Forge Neuve, the former Manufacture Royal which belonged to the Comte d'Artois and made artillery for the navy; slipper factories; 13th c. church of St Etienne burned down by the Duke of Cambridge, the Black Prince's brother, in 1369 and reconstructed 15th c., decorated capitals and tombs of the d'Aguesseau family; château, 13th and 15th c.; dolmen

Jayac (I6): 12th c. church restored this century with a 16th c. pietà; 15th c. château with a 12th c. keep

Jean Blancs, gisement de: *see* Bourniquel

Jemaye, La (B5): a village in the Double forest. It has a 12th c. church with a fine doorway, and is surrounded by lakes

Jor, côte de: *see* Thonac

Jovelle, château de: *see* Tour Blanche, La

Jumilhac le Grand (G3): Eugène Le Roy worked there for several years; 15th-17th c. château which now belongs to the Comte du Pin; château de Jumilhac le Grand; Musée de l'Or. It was a centre for iron forges at the end of the Hundred Years War which enriched the locals until the 19th century when a commercial treaty with the English ruined them

Jumilhac le Petit, Templar chapel: *see* Chapelle Faucher, La

Justices, Les, polissoir: *see* Mauzens et Miremont

Labrousse, château de: *see* St Sulpice d'Excideuil

Lachaud, grotte de: *see* Terrasson

Lacoste, château de: *see* Castelnaud

Ladornac: romanesque church, was an Hospitaller preceptory, renovated 16th c.; curious 18th c. font

Ladosse: *see* Rudeau Ladosse

Ladoux, source de: *see* Cassagne, La

Ladouze: *see* Douze, La

Ladres, chapelle des: *see* St Pierre de Côle

Lafaye, château de: *see* Ste Orse

Laffinoux, château de: *see* Lalinde

Laforce (C8): a small town with one dramatic ruin of the château which belonged to the Caumont Laforce family. The building was virtually completely destroyed by Lakanal during the Revolution. 14th c. Protestant chapel, and old people's home founded by John Bost; manoir de Riandolle

Lalinde (E8): château de Laffinoux, with 15th c. and 17th c. pavilions; château des Landes, 17th-18th c. Maine de Biran visited his niece who lived here; château de la Rue, ruins of the 15th c. building based on the 13th c. foundations; château de Baneuil, 14th c.; romanesque church with 11th c. choir and bell tower

Lambertie, château de: *see* Miallet

Lammary, château de: *see* Antonne et Trigonant

Lamonzie Montastruc (D7): romanesque church; château de Bellegarde, modern; château de Montastruc, beautiful 17th c. château built on a raised platform

Lamonzie St Martin (C8): church heavily restored; 16th c. château

Lamothe Montravel: remains of a château which belonged to the archbishops of Bordeaux. Monument commemorating the battle of Castillon

Landes, château des: *see* Lalinde

Langlade, dolmen de: *see* Belvès

Langlade, manoir de: *see* Proissans

Lanouaille (H4): a busy small town with market; château de la Durantie, a fine set of yellow stone farm buildings and house which belonged to Bugeaud

Lanquais, château de (E8): harmonious, rather grand château, 14th to 16th c.

Lanvège, tours de: *see* Saussignac

Lapouyade, château de: *see* Sceau St Angel

Laprade, château de: *see* Saussignac

Laprouges, dolmen de: *see* Valeuil

Lardimalie, château de: *see* St Pierre de Chignac

Lardin, Le-St Lazare (H6): important centre for the manufacture of glass until the end of the First World War. A factory which extracted material from chestnuts for dye work and tanneries was founded in 1906 and went on in 1923 to produce cellulose but it became a paper-works in 1933. The factory is now modernised and has become an important producer of paper and the town is busy and prosperous. Château de Bersac, 18th c. retable; grotte de la Machonie; grotte de Badegoule; château de Peyraux, medieval with a 15th c. tower, reworked in thc 18th c. It belonged to the Royère family, one of whose members returned from the Crusades with Arab horses

Laroche Beaulieu, château de: *see* Annesse et Beaulieu

Lartet, abri: *see* Eyzies, Les

Larzac: romanesque church with 15th c. doorway

Lascaux, grotte de: *see* Montignac

Lasserre, château de: *see* Marcillac St Quentin

Laugerie Haute and Laugerie Basse, gisements de: *see* Eyzies, Les

Laussel, château de, and gisement de: *see* Marquay

Lauvie, château de La: *see* Simeyrols

Lauterie, château de: *see* Trélissac

Lauzun (Lot et Garonne): fine 16th c. château; home of Duc de Lauzun

Lavalade, château de: *see* St Paul Laroche

Laxion, château de: *see* Corgnac sur l'Isle

Lèches, Les: ruined priory at Tresseyroux. It was a Benedictine priory attached to Ligueux abbey and has a fine doorway

Léguillac de Cercles (D4): a good fortified romanesque church with two domes and an interesting bell tower; façade rebuilt; dolmen

Lempzours (F4): 12th c. church which was a priory, with an 18th c. retable

Léparon: *see* St Michel de l'Ecluse et Léparon

Lespinassat, château de: *see* Bergerac

Lestaubière, château de: *see* Douville

Lestignac: gothic church with 17th c. retable

Leyzarnie, château de: *see* Manzac sur Vern

Libourne (Gironde): a thriving wine town of some considerable interest. Now also a centre for all misdirected post in France, handling 25-30,000 letters and packets daily, and employing 60 postmen

Lieu Dieu, château du: *see* Boulazac

Ligueux: *see* Agonac

Limeuil (F7): bridges over the Dordogne and Vézère built in 1891; church of Ste Catherine with a black Vierge des Bateliers; 15th c. gateway; château de la Pechère; château de la Vitrolle; château de l'Armandie; Chapelle de St Martin; La Maisonette, Jardin Musée

Limeyrat (G5): 12th c. church by the side of 14th-17th c. château

Liorac: restored 12th c. fortified church; château de la Garraube, 17th c.; château de Carrieux; château de Gentiac, 17th c.; château de la Ricardie; dolmen

Lisle (D4): charming small town, with a romanesque and gothic church restored in the 16th c.; 16th c. château with a fine staircase

Liveyre, gisement de: *see* Tursac

Lolme: restored romanesque church

Longas, château de: *see* Ste Foy de Longas

Lortal, château de: *see* Manaurie

Losse, château de: *see* Thonac

Lostanges, château de: *see* Ste Alvère

Loubéjac (G10): the southernmost village in Dordogne with a romanesque church with an octagonal bell tower. Fountain of the three bishops (Périgueux, Agen and Cahors); château de Sermet, a 13th and 17th c. building with Templar associations. Dolmen

Luminade, château de la: *see* Cornille

Lusignac (C4): 12th c. church with 16th c.

pietà and 17th c. retable. 14th-18th c. château

Lussas et Nontronneau (D3): Lussas: romanesque church with 13th c. porch. Nontronneau: romanesque church heavily restored 16th c. with a 17th c. retable; château de Beauvais, 15th-16th c.; Gallo-Roman site

Luzier, château de: *see* Beaumont du Périgord

Machonie, grotte de la: *see* Le Lardin-St Lazare

Madeleine, gisement de la: *see* Tursac

Maine, château du: *see* Siorac de Ribérac

Mairie, grotte de la: *see* Teyjat

Maladrerie, La: *see* Coulouneix

Malartrie, château de: *see* Roque Gageac, La

Malaveix, château de and foundry: *see* Chaleix

Malfourat, moulin de: *see* Monbazillac

Malignie, château de la: *see* Abjat

Malpas, gisement de: *see* Bourniquel

Manaurie (G7): its romanesque church is restored; grotte de Carpe Diem; gisement de la Micoque; château de Lortal; château de Recaudou; château de Cap del Roc; gisement de la Faurélie

Manzac sur Vern: a badly disfigured romanesque church which was the oratory of a priory of the abbey of Brantôme; château de Leyzarnie, now an institution

Marafy, château de: *see* Vieux Mareuil

Marais, château du: *see* St Chamassy

Marcillac St Quentin: romanesque church; St Quentin: an 11th-12th c. church with 17th c. woodwork; château de Lasserre; château du Barry

Mareuil sur Belle (C3): château de Mareuil; Musée de la Pierre Taillée; St Pardoux de Mareuil, a particularly fine tiny romanesque church with a charentais façade, and a pretty bell tower; St Priest de Mareuil, 12th c. church; château de Beauregard; château de Monbreton; château du Repaire: château de Beaulieu

Marnac: 12th c. church restored in the 16th c. Château de Retou 15-17th c.

Maroitte, château de: *see* Grand Brassac

Marquay (H7): a rather dull domed romanesque church; château de Laussel, 15th-16th c.; château de Puymartin, although now largely a 19th c. restoration, the château was built in the 15th and 16th c. on 14th c. foundations. The restoration was by Léon Prouin, a Bordelais pupil of Viollet Leduc, but it is interesting nonetheless. It has some good paintings and statues and the furniture is particularly attractive and remarkable in that it has always been in the house. The house is said to be haunted by a 'white lady'. Château de Commarque; gisement de Laussel; grotte de la Grèze; Cap Blanc rock shelter, engravings

Marqueyssac, château de: *see* St Pantaly d'Ans

Marqueyssac, château de: *see* Vézac

Marsac: romanesque church; dolmen

Marsalès: a restored romanesque church and a 16th c. and 18th c. château

Marsalet, château de: *see* Monbazillac

Martel (Lot): house where Henry Courtmantel died

Marthonie, château de la: *see* St Jean de Côle

Martinie, château de la: *see* Segonzac

Marzac, château de: *see* Tursac

Marzac, château de Petit: *see* Tursac

Mas Robert, château de: *see* Vitrac

Masnegre, château de: *see* Valojoulx

Matecoulon, château de: *see* Montpeyroux

Mauriac, château de: *see* Douzillac

Mauzac: dolmen

Mauzens et Miremont (F7): a pretty romanesque fortified church restored in the 16th c.; château de Miremont; grottes de Miremont and polissoir at Les Justices; château de la Faurélie

Mayac (F-G4): domed romanesque church with fine doorway. 17th-18th c. château

Mège, abri: *see* Terrasson

Mellet, château de: *see* Beauregard de Terrasson

Mensignac: restored romanesque church

Merlande: *see* Chapelle Gonaguet, La

Merlins, château des: *see* St Martin de Freyssingeas

Mescoules: 14th c. church; château de la Pleyssade

Mespoulet, château de: *see* St Pompont

Meycourby, Par de Chasse de: *see* Bassillac

Meyfrénie, château de la: *see* Verteillac

Meynardie, château la: *see* Coquille, La

Meynichar, Le, Gallo-Roman site: *see* Augignac

Meynichoux, château de: *see* St Aquilin

Meyrals (G7): a romanesque church with an 18th c. retable given by Christophe de Beaumont, Archbishop of Paris; château de la Roque, 15th-16th c., on triangular plan; grotte de Bernifal cave, paintings, engravings

Miallet (F2): restored romanesque church; château de Lambertie, 15th-16th c., restored in the 19th c.

Micoque, gisement de la: *see* Manaurie

Milandes, Les (G8): château des Milandes; Musée de la Fauconnerie, spéctacle des rapacés; Musée Josephine Baker

Milhac: *see* Peyrillac et Milhac le Sec

Milhac d'Auberoche: romanesque church; château de la Baisse, 15th-16th c.

Miremont, château and grottes: *see* Mauzens et Miremont

Missier, Château: *see* Château Missier

Molières (F8): château; manoir de Sautet; Maison de la Noix en Pays des Bastides

Monbazillac (D8): château de Monbazillac, and museum; château de Barradis; château de Bellevue; château de la Borderie; château de Fonrousse; château de Marsalet; château de Rauly; château de la Ro(u)quette; château de Theulet; château de Touron; manoir de Fonvieille; moulin de Malfourat

Monbette, château de: *see* Cénac et St Julien

Monbos (C9): a good romanesque church with interesting capitals

Monbreton, château de: *see* Mareuil sur Belle

Monclar, château de: *see* Villamblard

Monestier La Bastide: remains of an incomplete English bastide; gothic church

Monmadalès: dilapidated romanesque church

Monpazier (F9): fine bastide town; château de Monpazier; château de Gevaudon

Monrecour, château de: *see* St Vincent de Cosse

Monsaguel: restored romanesque church with good doorway; château de l'Aubespin, 14th-15th c.

Monsec (D3): fortified 16th c. church with renaissance doorway; château des Ages, 14th-16th c.

Montagnac, château de: *see* St Saud Lacoussière

Montagnac d'Auberoche: restored romanesque church

Montagrier (D4): a small town on a plateau above the Dronne, with a fine domed 12th c. church, a former priory of Brantôme. It has, alas, badly restored apsidal chapels in an unusual trefoil shape

Montaigne, château de: *see* St Michel de Montaigne

Montanceix, château de: *see* Montrem

Montardy, château de: *see* Celles

Montastruc, château de: *see* Lamonzie Montastruc

Montazeau: château de la Ségur Montazeau in which Montaigne's granddaughter lived

Montbrun, château de: *see* Verdon

Montcaret (A8): a small village with a

Gallo-Roman villa. One of the best mosaic floors in the department has been found there. It is thought to have been the site of a battlefield. The objects found on the site are now housed in the Musée Tauziac. There is also an 11th-12th c. church, with interesting capitals, which was a priory of St Florent de Saumur

Montcheuil, château de: *see* St Martial de Valette

Montcucq, Notre Dame de: *see* Belvés

Montferrand du Périgord: small town with a romanesque church and pretty 16th c. houses and market; château, 12th-15th c.; château de Regagnac, 15th-16th c.

Montfort, château de: *see* Vitrac

Montignac sur Vézère (H6): (tickets) Lascaux II: cave, paintings (facsimile); gisement du Regourdou; château de Coulonges; château de Planchat; gisement de la Balutie; Musée Ours Vivants; Musée Eugène Le Roy

Montpeyroux (A7): fine romanesque church with elegant saintongeais apse; château de Matecoulon 17th-18th c., in U-shape

Montplaisir, château de: *see* Condat sur Trincou

Montpon Ménestérol (B7): small town on the river Isle with a romanesque church restored in the 16th c. with 18th c. woodwork. Renowned for its organs of which it has six. Chartreuse de Vauclaire, part of which is now a psychiatric hospital, has gothic frescoes

Montréal, château de: *see* Issac

Montrem: romanesque church; château de Montanceix, 14th-17th c.

Montsigoux, château de: *see* St Pierre de Frugie

Morandies, Les, Gallo-Roman site: *see* Augignac

Mothe, château de la: *see* St Privat des Près

Moustier, Le: *see* Peyzac le Moustier

Mouthe, gisement de la: *see* Eyzies, Les

Mouzens: restored romanesque church

Mussidan (C6): an industrial town at the confluence of the Isle and the Crempse built on a site which has been known since the 10th century. The town is twinned with Woodbridge, Suffolk. The church is modern. Dolmen. Musée des Arts et Traditions Populaires du Périgord (Musée André Voulgré)

Nabirat: 17th c. church with 18th c. furniture

Nadaillac: interesting small village 12th c. church of St Denis which was a priory dependent on St Amand de Coly. Dolmen

Nailhac: 12th c. church restored 16th c.

Nanchapt, manoir de: *see* Tour Blanche, La

Nantheuil de Bourzac: romanesque church with a 16th c. porch; calvary; château

Nantheuil de Thiviers: picturesque village with a 12th c. domed church of St Etienne having a 17th c. retable

Nanthiat: romanesque church. 16th c. calvary; altar by François de Journiac in market square; château Devars du Mayne, 18th c. with renaissance pavilion

Narbonne, château de: *see* St Just

Nastringues: fine romanesque church with gothic portal

Negrondes: dolmen

Neuvic sur l'Isle (D6): château de Fratteau; château de Mellet, botanical garden

Nojals et Clottes (E9): Rucher école; allée couverte de Blanc; dolmen de Peyrelevade

Nontron (E2): Gallo-Roman remains; dolmen de Poperdu; 18th c. château de Nontron; Musée des Poupées et Jouets d'Antan

Nontronneau: *see* Lussas et Nontronneau

Notre Dame du Bourg: *see* Biron

Notre Dame d'Espérance: *see* Echourgnac

Notre Dame de Bonne Espérance, chapelle de: *see* Azerat

Notre Dame de Montcucq: *see* Belvès

Notre Dame de Pitié, chapelle de: *see* Plazac

Notre Dame de Puymartin: *see* Chapelle Faucher, La

Notre Dame du Pont, chapelle de: *see* Coulaurès

Objat: busy small market town

Oche, château d': *see* St Priest les Fougerès

Olivoux, Les: *see* Auriac du Périgord

Orliac (G9): T-shaped church roofed with lauzes

Orliaguet: romanesque church with a 12th c. font and an 18th c. Virgin and retable

Pagnac, château de: *see* Villac

Paleyrac: château de la Bourgonnie, 15th-17th c.

Paluel, château de: *see* St Vincent le Paluel

Panassou, château de: *see* St Vincent de Cosse

Panisseau, château de: *see* Thénac

Papessus: *see* St Michel de Montaigne

Parcoul (A5): a small town above the Dronne, with a romanesque church with a good saintongeais apse

Pas du Miroir: *see* Peyzac le Moustier

Pataud, gisement de: *see* Eyzies, Les

Pauliac, château de: *see* Daglan

Paulin: romanesque church, ruined château; croix de la Faurie; manoir de l'Isle

Pauly, château du: *see* Chassaignes

Paunat (F7): abbey church of Notre Dame; château de Hurtevent, 18th c. façade

Paussac St Vivien (D4): curious fortified 13th c. domed romanesque church of St Timothé at Paussac. St Vivien: restored romanesque church with good doorway. Château de Peignefort; dolmen de Peyrelevade; dolmen de Peyre d'Ermale

Pavillon, château du: *see* Sorges

Pécany, château de: *see* Pomport

Pech de l'Aze, gisement de: *see* Carsac et Aillac

Pech de la Boissière, gisement de: *see* Carsac et Aillac

Pech Merle, grotte de: *see* Cabrerets

Pech St Sourd, fort du: *see* St Cirq du Bugue

Pechembert, château de: *see* Florimont et Gaumier

Pechère, château de la: *see* Limeuil

Pechmejot, château de: *see* Ste Foy de Belvès

Peignefort, château de: *see* Paussac et St Vivien

Pelvézy, château de: *see* St Geniès

Perdigal, manoir du: *see* St Chamassy

Périgueux (E5): a fine city with much to see. Roman Arènes and Tour de Vésone; the cathedral of St Front and St Etienne de la Cité; many renaissance buildings in mostly pedestrianized streets; château Barrière; Musée du Périgord; Musée Militaire

Petit Bersac (B4): Musée Gallo-Romain

Petit Marzac, château de: *see* Tursac

Petite Filolie, château de la: *see* Aubas

Petits Bois, Les: Gallo-Roman site

Peuch, château du: *see* Fleurac

Peyraux, château de: *see* Lardin, Le

Peyre d'Ermale, dolmen de: *see* Paussac et St Vivien

Peyrebrune, dolmen de: *see* St Aquilin

Peyrelevade, dolmen de: *see* Nojals et Clottes

Peyrelevade, dolmen de: *see* Paussac et St Vivien

Peyrelevade, dolmen de: *see* Rampieux

Peyrelongue, dolmen de: *see* St Laurent la Vallée

Peyrignac: château de la Chapoulie, 15th c. with an octagonal dovecote

Peyrillac et Milhac le Sec (I7): Peyrillac: a village on the Dordogne; church has 15th c. portal. Milhac le Sec: restored romanesque church with a fine view; château du Saulou 15th c.

Peyruzel, château de: *see* Daglan

Peyzac le Moustier (G7): a charming small village by the Vézère with a good 15th c. church; grotte du Moustier; romanesque church at Le Moustier; La Roque St Christophe, impressive evidence of prehistoric dwellings inhabited throughout the middle ages; Le Ruth, gisement, Collection Pagès; Pas du Miroir, path cut out of the rock face, so-named because of the reflection of the river; Expo Musée 'Fossiles, Préhistoire'

Piégut Pluviers (E2): a small town where the 13th c. tower is the only remaining part of the château. Pluviers: 12th c. church. Baudeix: ruins of a 12th c. Grandmontain priory. Dolmen de Fixade; megalithic chamber of La Couraine at St Barthelémy; Gallo-Roman site at La Carnedie

Pierre Levée, dolmen de: *see* Brantôme

Pierrelevade, dolmen de: *see* Condat sur Trincou

Pincarelle, dolmen de: *see* Beaumont du Périgord

Pitray, château de: *see* St Seurin de Prats

Plaisance: romanesque church

Planchat, château de: *see* Montignac sur Vézère

Plazac (G6): small town with a pretty romanesque church with a good bell tower, picturesque cemetery and 14th c.

presbytery; chapelle Notre Dame de Pitié, 16th c. frescoes and wooden pietà

Pleyssade, château de la: *see* Mescoules

Pluviers: *see* Piégut Pluviers

Poisson, grotte du: *see* Eyzies, Les

Pommier, château de: *see* St Front la Rivière

Pomport (C8): château de Fage; château de Pécany; château de Sanxet and Musée de Voitures Anciennes; ruined romanesque church at St Mayme

Poncie, château de la: *see* St Jean d'Estissac

Pont, château du: *see* Villac

Ponteyraud: church with romanesque choir

Poperdu, dolmen de: *see* Nontron

Port Ste Foy (B8): La maison de Fleuve, Musée de la Batellerie; villa du Canet with Gallo-Roman mosaics

Poujade, château de la: *see* Urval

Poutignac, château de: *see* Beaussac

Pouyet, château: *see* Bassillac

Pradelle, manoir de: *see* Ste Alvère

Prats, château de: *see* St Seurin de Prats

Prats de Carlux: restored romanesque church with wooden altar retable; château du Sirey, 15th c.

Prats du Périgord: romanesque church fortified in 15th c. château, 16th c.

Prémillac, château du: *see* St Sulpice d'Excideuil

Pressignac Vicq: romanesque church

Preyssac d'Agonac (G4): romanesque church with 16th c. additions; gentil-hommière de Cluzel

Preyssac d'Excideuil: 12th c. church with 13th c. bell tower

Proissans (H7): the church has a romanesque choir; château de la Roussie, 15th-17th c.; manoir du Cluzeau, 14th c.; manoir de Langlade

Proumeyssac, gouffre de: *see* Bugue, Le

Puid, château du: *see* St Sulpice de Roumagnac

Puy St Astier, château de: *see* St Astier

Puycharneau, château de: *see* St Estèphe

Puycheny, château de: *see* Champeaux et la Chapelle Pommier

Puyfaiteau, château de: *see* St Martial de Valette

Puyferrat, château de: *see* St Astier

Puyguilhem, château de: *see* Villars

Puyguilhem, commune de Thénac (C9): not to be confused with the château of Puyguilhem near Villars. The town derived its importance from its site at the confines of Périgord and Agenais. It was here that the first cannon shots of the Hundred Years War were fired. Only defensive works of the castle now remain

Puymartin, château de: *see* Marquay

Puymartin, Notre Dame de: *see* Chapelle Faucher, La

Queyssac (D7): 12th c. church with good capitals

Quinsac: small town on the Dronne, with an old bridge; château de Vaugoubert, 18th c.

Ramefort, château de: *see* Valeuil

Rampieux: dolmen de Peyrelevade

Rastignac, château de, near La Bachellerie

Rauly, château de: *see* Monbazillac

Raye, château de la: *see* Vélines

Raymonden, abri de: *see* Chancelade

Raysse, manoir du: *see* Cazoulès

Razac sur l'Isle: romanesque church reworked 16th c.; château d'Antoniac, belonged to Lagrange-Chancel

Recaudou, château de: *see* Manaurie

Reclaud, manoir du: *see* Bourg des Maisons

Redon, château de: *see* Granges d'Ans

Redonespic, chapelle de: *see* Castels

Regagnac, château de: *see* Montferrand du Périgord

Regourdou, gisement du: *see* Montignac sur Vézère

Reignac, fortress of: *see* Tursac

Reilhac: *see* Champniers et Reilhac

Repaire, château du: *see* Mareuil sur Belle

Repaire, château du: *see* St Aubin de Nabirat

Retou, château de: *see* Marnac

Riandolle, manoir de: *see* Laforce

Ribagnac (D8): restored romanesque church; château de Bridoire, known to have existed before the 12th c., it belonged to Marguerite de Turenne, Dame de Bergerac in 1274. The fine 15th c. building was restored in the 19th and 20th c.

Ribérac (C5): busy town with a good market; église de Faye

Ribeyrolles, château de: *see* Change, Le

Ricardie, château de la: *see* Liorac

Richardie, château de la: *see* Bouteilles St Sébastien

Richemont, château de: *see* Brantôme

Richemont, château de: *see* St Crépin de Richemont

Rigale, château de la and tower: *see* Villetoureix

Rivière, château de la: *see* St Sulpice de Mareuil

Ro(u)quette, château de la: *see* Monbazillac

Ro(u)velle, château de la: *see* Chassaignes

Roc de la Combe Capelle, gisement de la: *see* St Avit Sénieur

Roc de Travers, dolmen du: *see* Besse

Roc Plat, gisement de: *see* Gonterie Bouloneix, La

Roc, château du: *see* Change, Le

Roc, château du: *see* St André d'Allas

Roc, grotte du Grand: *see* Eyzies, Les

Rocanadel, château de: *see* Veyrignac

Roche Chalais, La (A5): a town on the Dronne with a fine view; centre for manufacturing shoes and some metallurgical works; on the route to St James of Compostela; ruins of feudal château; La Valouze, gardens

Roche, château de la: *see* St Pantaly d'Excideuil

Roche, gisement de: *see* St André d'Allas

Rochebeaucourt, La, et Argentine (C3): a small town on the Nizonne with a 13th c. church built by the Cluniacs. The château was destroyed in 1944 but there are still impressive remains. Dolmen. Argentine: a romanesque church which can be reached by foot only

Rochebois, château de: *see* Vitrac

Rochecaille, gisement de: *see* Chapelle Faucher, La

Rochecourbe, château de: *see* Vézac

Rochereuil, gisement de: *see* Grand Brassac

Rochette, gisement de: *see* St Léon sur Vézère

Rognac, château de and moulin de: *see* Bassillac

Roi des Chauzes, côteau du: *see* Antonne et Trigonant

Rolphie, château de la: *see* Coulouneix

Roque Barbel, gisement de: *see* Tursac

Roque Gageac, La (H8): village and troglodytic site; manoir de Tarde; 16th c. château de la Malartrie; 19th c. dolmen

Roque St Christophe: *see* Peyzac Le Moustier

Roque, château de la: *see* Meyrals

Rossignol, château de: *see* Chalagnac

Rouffiac, château de: *see* Angoisse

Rouffignac (G6): château de l'Herm, chimney and renaissance doorway; grotte de Cro de Granville; grotte aux Cent Mammouths, with engravings and drawings

Rouffignac de Sigoulès: domed 12th c. church

Rouffilhac, château de: *see* Carlux

Rouillac: *see* Gageac et Rouillac

Roumagnac, château de: *see* St Sulpice de Roumagnac

Roumeilhac (Roumaillac), château de: *see* Tour Blanche, La

Roussie, château de la: *see* Proissans

Roussille, château de: *see* Douville

Rudeau Ladosse: château de Bellussière, romanesque tower

Rue, château de la: *see* Lalinde

Ruth, gisement de: *see* Tursac

Sablou, château du: *see* Fanlac

Sadillac: domed romanesque church with good capitals. It was a priory of Moissac. 16th c. château

Sagelat: small town on the Nauze. Church very restored but a harmonious ensemble

Salignac-Eyvigues (I7): château de Salignac, fine 15th-17th c. building with some relics of Fénelon; 16th c. manoir du Toulgou, where La Calprenède was born; château du Claud, fine 15th-16th c. buildings; Musée Vivant de Plein Air Arts et Traditions Populaires. Gardens at manoir d'Eyrignac

Salles de Belvès: domed roman-esque church, modern roof over nave

Salon (E6): restored romanesque church

Sandre, château de la: *see* Change, Le

Sanxet, château de: *see* Pomport

Sardy, château de: *see* Vélines

Sarlande: a small town on the Loue with romanesque and gothic church with a 14th c. doorway

Sarlat (H7): wonderfully preserved and restored small town with many enchanting buildings; cathedral; Musée Automobile; Temniac, ruins of bishops' palace

Sarliac sur l'Isle (F5): romanesque church; restored 16th c. château de Sarliac; château de la Bonnetie; château de la Dulgarie; manoir de Grézignac, 16th c.

Sarrazac: small town with a gothic church

Saulnier, château de: *see* St Front la Rivière

Saulou, château du: *see* Peyrillac et Milhac le Sec

Saussignac (C8): 17th c. château built by the notorious Duc de Lauzun's father, and visited by Brantôme, Montaigne and, probably, Rabelais. Ruins of tours de Lanvège, 14th c.; château de Fayolles, 16th c.; château de Laprade.

Sautet, manoir de: *see* Molières

Sauveboeuf, château de: *see* Ajat

Savignac de Miremont (F7): La Ferrassie, gisement abri

Savignac Lédrier (H4): badly restored romanesque church with an 18th c. retable; fine château de la Forge, 16th-17th c. with a foundry

Sceau St Angel (E3): romanesque church with fine apse; château de Lapouyade

Segonzac (C5): domed romanesque church Notre Dame de la Visitation, enlarged in the 16th c.; château, 15th c., restored 18th c.; château de la Martinie fine 15th c. and renaissance building; dolmen

Ségur Montazeau, château de la: *see* Montazeau

Septfonds, château de: *see* Trélissac

Sergeac (G7): good romanesque church with a fine doorway; remains of a Templar commanderie established 1275; 16th c. crucifix; gisement de Castelmerle; abri de Castanet

Sermet, château de: *see* Loubéjac

Serre, manoir de la: *see* Sireuil

Sibeaumont, château de: *see* Cénac et St Julien

Sigoulès (C8): small town, renowned for its wine

Silvie, gisement de la: *see* St Vincent de Paluel

Simeyrols: romanesque church with 17th c. statues of St Cosme and St Damien; château de la Lauvie, 18th c.

Siorac de Ribérac (C5): fine fortified

romanesque church; château du Maine; dolmens de Bonarme and Cayreleva(t)

Siorac en Périgord (G8): small town on the Dordogne with remains of 17th c. château; Musée du Château, objets de cuisine, poteries du terre et du feu

Siorac, château de: *see* Annesse et Beaulieu

Sireuil (G7): small town with a domed romanesque church; 17th c. foundry; château de Beyssac, 16th c.; château de la Croze; manoir de la Serre

Sirey, château du: *see* Prats de Carlux

Solvignac, château de: *see* Vézac

Sorcier, gisement and grotte du: *see* St Cirq du Bugue

Sorges (F4): a small town renowned as a truffle centre. It has a romanesque church with renaissance doorway; château du Pavillon; château de Jaillac, 15th c.; château de Bouquet; Ecomusée Musée de la Truffe et les sentiers de découverte des truffières

Souffron, château de: *see* Fleurac

Souillac (Lot): attractive small town on N20 with a most beautiful romanesque abbey; Musée de l'Automate; Musée d'Attelages de la Belle Epoque

Sourzac (C6): small town on the Isle with a romanesque and gothic church which was part of a priory; pretty petrifying fountain; grotte de las Agnelas or Gabillou

Sudrie, château de la: *see* Cubjac

St Aigne: modern church with a romanesque porch restored during the renaissance

St Amand de Coly (H6): abbey church; château de la Grande Filolie

St Amand de Vergt: domed romanesque church

St André d'Allas (H7): St André; romanesque church. Allas l'Evêque, 12th-15th c. church; château du Roc 17th c.; gisement de Roche. Group of cabanes at Breuil de Bouyssieral

St Antoine d'Auberoche: fortified 12th c. church with an 18th c. retable

St Antoine de Breuilh: 12th c. church

St Antoine Cumond (B5): restored romanesque church with a fine 12th c. doorway; château 17th c.

St Aquilin: renaissance church with an 18th c. retable; château de Meynichoux; château de Belet, 15th c.; château de Boisset; dolmen de Peyrebrune

St Astier (D5): lively small town on the Isle with cement and shoe-making industries. Elie Salomon, a priest living *c.*1200, wrote his treatise *Scientia artis musicae* here. 12th c. church with a good crypt, restored in the 15th c. when the fine square bell tower was built. Interesting renaissance houses in the town. Château de Crognac, 18th c; some 14th c. remains and cluseaux; château d'Excideuil; château de Puyferrat, 15th c.; château de Puy St Astier, 15th c. chapelle des Bois, a modern building on the site of St Astier's hermitage. St Astier was born in 560

St Aubin de Cadelech: romanesque church at Cadelech; château. Château de Bardouly

St Aubin de Nabirat: ruined romanesque church; 18th c. retable in new church; château de Repaire, 15th and 17th c. ruins

St Aulaye (B5): small town on the Dronne; bastide built 1288 by Pierre de Brémont. The romanesque church Ste Eulalie was restored in the 16th and 19th c. but has a saintongeais façade and decorated capitals in choir; Musée du Cognac, du Vin et du Pineau

St Avit de Fumadières: *see* Bonneville et St Avit de Fumadières

St Avit Rivière (F9): tiny village with a church with fine belfry

St Avit Sénieur (F8): abbey church; Musée Géologique, salle archaéologique; gisement de la Roc de la Combe Capelle

St Barthelémy: *see* Piégut Pluviers

St Barthelémy du Bussière: picturesque village with a 12th c. church reworked in the 16th c.

St Cernin: *see* Vergt de Biron

St Chamassy (F8): restored 12th c. church; château de la Batut 16th-18th c.; château du Marais; château de Verliac; manoir du Perdigal, 16th c. dolmen

St Cirq du Bugue (G7): grotte and gisement du Sorcier with engravings; fort du Pech St Sourd

St Clément: *see* St Romain et St Clément

St Crépin d'Auberoche: romanesque church restored in the 16th c.

St Crépin de Richemont (D3): romanesque church rebuilt in the 16th c.; château de St Crépin, modern; château de Richemont built in the 16th c. by Brantôme who died there in 1614; the funerary chapel houses his self-composed epitaph

St Crépin et Carlucet (H-I7): manoir de Cipières; Carlucet: fine lauze-roofed 12th c. church; adjoining cemetery has arcaded tomb emplacements

St Cybranet: unremarkable small town with good shops

St Cyprien (G8): busy small town with fine houses, especially the Maison Beaumont. Massive 14th c. church, heavily restored, with 17th c. retable and woodwork, it was part of an Augustinian abbey whose buildings have been used as a tobacco warehouse. It contains the heart of Christophe de Beaumont, Archbishop of Paris. Château de Fages, 16th-17th c., restored. It has a small chapel with an ornate renaissance porch

St Cyr les Champagnes: interesting village and romanesque church

St Estèphe (E2): picturesque town with a fine lake; 12th c. church with 16th c. additions; rocks known as la Casse Noisette and Chapelet du Diable. Château du Puycharneau; priory of Badeix, ruins

St Front la Rivière: domed 12th c.

church; château de Caneau; château de Pommier; château de St Front, 15th c.; château de Saulnier, 16th c.

St Front sur Nizonne: domed 12th c. church

St Front: *see* Couze and St Front

St Geniès: a most beautiful village with a fine romanesque church, 16th c. bell tower, the remains of an early keep, and pretty château; chapelle du Cheylard, 14th c. frescoes; château de Pelvézy, 15th-16th c., in which St Louis is reputed to have stayed on his way to visit the Holy Shroud at Cadouin

St Germain, château de: *see* Gaugeac

St Germain des Près: picturesque small town which was a centre of iron founding and renamed during the Revolution as Germain le Ferrigineux; restored romanesque church; at La Moranchie a monument to British airmen killed during the Second World War; château de St Germain; château de St Pierre

St Germain du Salembre: industrious small town with a 12th c. fortified church with gothic additions

St Geyrac: romanesque church with gothic additions; château de la Taleyrandie

St Hilaire d'Estissac: interesting romanesque church and manoir

St Innocence: small rustic church with a 15th c. doorway

St Jean, chapel of: *see* Chancelade

St Jean de Côle (F3): 12th c. trefoil shaped church with decorated capitals; 11th c. priory destroyed but part of 16th c. cloister remains; colonnaded house next door was the miller's house with 15th c. towers and a 17th c. wing; château de la Marthonie

St Jean d'Estissac: 12th c. church restored in the 16th c.; château de la Poncie, 15th c.

St Jean d'Eyraudi: restored romanesque church

St Jory de Chalais (F3): badly deformed romanesque church; château de la Grange; dolmen

St Jory Lasbloux (G4): pretty village with a romanesque church and 16th-18th c. manoir. The large number of mills in the vicinity were a source of inspiration to Eugène Le Roy when he was writing *Le Moulin du Frau*

St Julien: *see* Cénac et St Julien

St Julien de Bourdeilles: restored romanesque church

St Julien de Crempse: restored romanesque church

St Julien d'Eymet: romanesque church; château de Fontjuliane

St Julien de Lampon: a lively small village on the Dordogne with an unremarkable church with 16th c. mural paintings; château de la Tourette, dilapidated 16th c. building which was once part of a line of fortifications with Fénelon and Rocanadel

St Just (D4): Musée du Ver de Soie Magnanerie de Gourmandie; restored and dilapidated romanesque church; château de Narbonne, 15th-16th c.; dolmen

St Laurent des Batons (E7): restored romanesque church; Château de St Maurice, 15th-16th c.

St Laurent des Hommes (B6): gothic church with a 17th c. retable; château de Gamenson 17th c.; château de la Vigerie

St Laurent la Vallée (G9): pretty village with a 13th c. church with 12th c. doorway and 17th c. retable and sculptures; dolmen de Peyrelongue

St Laurent sur Manoire: romanesque church restored in the 16th c.; château, 17th c.

St Lazare: 12th c. church with an 18th c. retable

St Léon sur l'Isle (D6): a small town on the river with a restored romanesque church. Château de Beauséjour, 16th c.

St Léon sur Vèzere (G7): natural troglodytic park 'Le Conquil'; château de Chabans was the property of the Talleyrand family; gisement de Rochette

St Louis en l'Isle: an English bastide created in 1308 well inside French territory

St Mamet, château de: *see* Douville

St Marcory: interesting romanesque church with 17th c. wooden statues

St Martial de l'Albarède: tiny romanesque church; old lime kilns (fours à chaux) now of industrial archaeological interest; former brewery makes food flavourings and was the setting for the film *Plenty* with Meryl Streep

St Martial de Nabirat: 17th c. statues and pictures in the church

St Martial de Valette (E3): a small town on the Bandiat with a fine romanesque church which has a 17th c. porch; château de Montcheuil; château de Puyfaiteau; chapelle de St Martin le Petit, 12th c. capitals

St Martial de Viveyrols: domed fortified romanesque church

St Martial Laborie: *see* Cherveix Cubas

St Martin: *see* Lamonzie St Martin

St Martin, chapel of, Limeuil:

St Martin de Curson: domed romanesque church with a saintongeais façade

St Martin de Freyssingeas: romanesque church; dolmen; château des Merlins

St Martin de Ribérac: domed romanesque church with good windows; château des Gérauds

St Martin du Vieux Castels: *see* Castels

St Martin l'Astier: 12th c. church with curious octagonal choir and a 17th c. retable. Its plan is unique in Périgord

St Martin le Petit, chapelle de: *see* St Martial de Valette

St Martin le Pin: domed romanesque church with a fine 12th c. doorway

St Maurice, château de: *see* St Laurent des Bâtons

St Mayme: *see* Pomport

St Mayme de Pereyrol (E7): romanesque church with a fortified bell tower, reworked in the 16th c.

St Méard de Dronne: 12th c. domed church with romanesque bas reliefs

St Méard de Gurson (B7): rustic church with a 16th c. doorway

St Médard d'Excideuil (G4): romanesque church with a 17th c. retable; château d'Eyssendiéras, where André Maurois lived. The domaine of 250 hectares is now planted as an apple orchard. La Tour des Charreaux, remains of fortified château

St Médard de Mussidan: romanesque church with a good doorway and 17th c. retable

St Mesmin: pretty village on the Auvézère; 12th c. church with 17th c. retable and a 17th c. black Virgin

St Michel d'Auberoche: *see* Change, Le

St Michel de Montaigne: (A8): Papessus; château de Montaigne, tour de la librairie

St Michel de Rivière (A6): romanesque church with gothic additions, interesting façade and 12th c. font

St Michel et Bonnefare: St Michel: 12th and 16th c. church, 17th c. retable and pulpit. Bonnefare: remains of Templar church

St Michel de l'Ecluse et Léparon: St Michel: romanesque church. Léparon: 16th c. church with a 17th c. retable

St Néxans (D8): romanesque church with a saintongeais façade. It was an Hospitaller preceptory

St Pantaly d'Ans: château de Marqueyssac; ruins of 15th c. occupied by the Hautefort family and in the 18th c. by Lagrange-Chancel; château de la Forge d'Ans, remains of house and foundry built by the ironmaster Festugière from Les Eyzies.

St Pantaly d'Excideuil: partially romanesque church with a 17th c. retable; château de la Roche, once Bugeaud's home

St Pardoux de Dronne: 12th c. church enlarged in the 16th c. with a 12th c. font and an 17th c. gilt retable

St Pardoux de Feix: *see* Brantôme

St Pardoux de Mareuil: *see* Mareuil sur Belle

St Pardoux et Viélvic: romanesque churches at St Pardoux and Viélvic; château de Campagnac, 15th c.

St Pardoux la Rivière (E3): a small town on the Dronne with renaissance houses, and modern windows in the church; Musée de la Carte Postale Ancienne du Périgord. There is now a Relais Vert which offers overnight accommodation for hikers in the old presbytère

St Paul Laroche: restored romanesque church with a 15th c. Virgin and Child;

château de Lavalade

St Paul Lizonne (B4): well situated small village with a domed romanesque church, St Pierre and St Paul, with a fine painted 18th c. ceiling by Paradol and a gilded polychrome 18th c. retable; Domaine de la Gauterie, park

St Pierre, château de: *see* St Germain des Près

St Pierre de Chignac (F6): a small town on the Manoire; château de Lardimalie

St Pierre de Côle (F4): a pretty village on the Côle with a restored romanesque church; château de Bruzac, 15th c. ruins; chapelle des Ladres, 17th c.

St Pierre de Frugie: disfigured romanesque church; château de Frugie 16th c.; château de Vieillecour 16th c.; château de Montsigoux

St Pompont (H9): named for St Pomponius a 6th c. evangelist who lived in Naples for eight years and is buried there; charming small town with ruined English fortfications and renaissance houses. The church has been gothicised; château de Castelviel built by Geoffrey de Vivans; château de Mespoulet, 12th c. keep

St Priest de Mareuil: *see* Mareuil sur Belle

St Priest les Fougères: an attractive small town with a romanesque church with three 17th c. retables; château d'Oche

St Privat des Près (B5): Musée de l'Outil et de la Vie au Village, Musée

des Maquettes; château de la Mothe

St Quentin: *see* Marcillac St Quentin

St Quitterie, church of: *see* Château Missier

St Rabier: a restored romanesque church with good capitals

St Raphael (G4): a small village well situated with a romanesque church with good capitals and St Rémy's tomb

St Rémy, chapelle de: *see* Auriac du Périgord

St Rémy, tomb of: *see* St Raphael

St Romain de Monpazier: romanesque church

St Romain et St Clément: St Romain: restored romanesque church with a 17th c. retable

St Saud Lacoussière (F2): restored romanesque church with a 17th c. retable, formerly the Cistercian abbey of Pérouse; château de Beynac; château de Montagnac

St Sauveur: gothic church which contains Maine de Biran's tomb; château de Grateloup, where he lived and died

St Seurin de Prats: château de Prats, 18th c.; château de Pitray, 18th c.; château de Duvigneau, Louis XVI façade

St Sour, grotte de: *see* Terrasson

St Sulpice d'Excideuil: gothic church and pretty 16th c. manoir d'Igonie. Of the château de Prémillac only a 15th c.

tower remains. It was built on the site of the Gallo-Roman villa of Primuliac; château de Labrousse, remains only

St Sulpice de Mareuil (D3): domed romanesque church with a 12th c. doorway; château de la Faye, 16th c. with cross dated 1642 at the entrance; château de la Rivière

St Sulpice de Roumagnac: restored romanesque church with a beautiful 17th c. wooden scupted retable; château de Puid; château de Roumagnac

St Victor: domed romanesque church with a square bell tower

St Vincent de Cosse (G8): château de Monrecour, 18th c.; elegant château de Panassou, 16th c.; château d'Ayguevive

St Vincent Jalmoutiers: domed romanesque church with saintongeais façade and restored romanesque choir; château de St Vincent

St Vincent le Paluel: romanesque church with a 12th c. font and 17th c. retable; château de Paluel, 15th-16th c. in ruins, burnt in 1944 by the Germans; 15th c. manoir in village; gisement de la Silvie

St Vincent sur l'Isle: small romanesque church; château de Bosvieux, modern

St Vivien: *see* Paussac et St Vivien

Ste Alvère (F7): small town on the Louyre; château de Lostanges, 13th c., tower is the only extant remains since Lakanal destroyed the rest; manoir de Pradelle, charming gentleman's country residence

Ste Capraise d'Eymet (D9): romanesque church with fine capitals, a 17th c. pulpit and 18th c. woodwork

Ste Croix, château de: *see* Ste Croix de Mareuil

Ste Croix de Beaumont (F9): a charming village with fine, though restored, 12th c. church which has good capitals; ruins of a priory with 14th-15th c. mullion windows

Ste Croix de Mareuil (C3): heavily restored 12th c. church; château d'Ambelle; château de Ste Croix

Ste Eulalie d'Ans: romanesque church restored in the 16th c.

Ste Eulalie d'Eymet: church with some 16th c. remains; château de Graulet

Ste Foy de Belvès: restored romanesque church with an 18th c. retable; château de Pechmejot

Ste Foy de Longas (E7): restored 12th c. church; château de Longas, 15th-16th c.

Ste Foy la Grande (Gironde) (B8): often thought to be an English creation, was in fact founded by Alphonse de Poitiers in 1255. Ste Foy, founded by act of paréage with the abbot of Conques and so named after its patron saint, led a chequered existence, like so many other bastides between the English and the French crowns, and even after its final reversion to the French it was to continue suffering during the Wars of Religion. Today it still clearly displays its original plan and contains many fine medieval houses

Ste Marie de Chignac (F6): fine 12th c. church with a 17th c. porch; dolmen

Ste Mondane (H8): restored romanesque church and miracle-working fountain; château de Fénelon

Ste Nathalène (H-I7): rustic romanesque church with interesting bell tower; château de La Tour, 16th c.; walnut mill

Ste Orse (G5): romanesque church with crypt and a good porch; château, 16th-17th c.; château de Lafaye, where Bugeaud married Elisabeth Lafaye; dolmen

Ste Trie (H4): romanesque church with fine 14th c. monumental effigy said to be that of Bertrand de Born's sister; ruins of Cistercian abbey of Dalon

Tabaterie, gisement de la: *see* Gonterie Boulouneix, La

Taillepetit, domaine de: *see* Annesse et Beaulieu

Taleyrandie, château de la: *see* St Geyrac

Tamniès: romanesque church

Tarde, manoir de: *see* Roque Gageac, La

Tayac: *see* Eyzies, Les

Temniac: *see* Sarlat

Terrasson (I6): Busy attractive town with slate roofs built in a semi-circle above the Vézère. 19th c. church built on the site of a Benedictine abbey; remains of the 13th c. bridge; restaurant in the former hospice, later gendarmerie until 1966; grotte de St Sour; grotte de Lachaud; abri Mège; Les Jardins de l'Imaginaire

Teyjat (D2): grotte de la Mairie, engravings; romanesque church with gothic additions; château de Brognac; château de Chatelard

Thénac: domed romanesque church; château de Panisseau, 18th c.

Thenon (G6): small town on the edge of the forêt Barade; church destroyed in the 18th c. and rebuilt with some romanesque features

Theulet, château de: *see* Monbazillac

Thiviers (F3): Gallo-Roman site and cross-roads between Brive and Angoulême and Limoges and Périgueux; romanesque church with 17th c. retable, good pictures and statues; numerous manoirs in the vicinity; château de Vaucocour, 15th-16th c.; château de la Filolie; dolmen ; Musée du Fois Gras; Maison de l'Oie et du Canard

Thonac (G-H6): small town on the Vézère with a romanesque church; château de Belcayre, pretty 15th c. château; château de Losse, 15th-16th. Côte de Jor. Centre for Prehistoric Art (Espace Cro Magnon, Musée et Parc Animalier) at Le Thot, 2 km away. A good place for beginners to get their bearings for visits to the region of prehistory

Tinteillac, château de: *see* Bourg des Maisons

Tocane St Apre (D5): small town on the Dronne; château de Fayolle where the Marquis de Fayolle lived; donjon de Vernode, remains of 12th c. château; château de Beauséjour, 17th c. building in which Fénelon's mother was born; dolmen; Musée du Costume; La Mémoire des Greniers

Toulgou, manoir du: *see* Salignac

Tour Blanche, La (C4): Musée de la Ferblanterie; Musée des Records; ruins of a large 12th c. château which belonged to the Bourdeilles family in the 15th and 16th c. and in which Brantôme spent much time; manoir de Nanchapt built 1617; château de Jovelle, ruins; château de Roumeilhac (Roumaillac)

Tour, château de la: *see* Ste Nathalène

Tour de la Vermondie: *see* Vermondie

Tour des Charreaux, La: *see* St Médard d'Excideuil

Tourette, château de La: *see* St Julien de Lampon

Touron, château de: *see* Monbazillac

Tourtoirac (G4): abbey; Musée Archéologique et Lapidaire

Trélissac (E5): town on the Isle, with a modern château; château de Caussade, a small-scale perfect 15th c. building on the edge of the forêt de Lanmary; château de Septfonds, built by the architect Victor Louis, it belonged to the Duc de Choiseul-Praslin; château de Lauterie

Trémolat (F7-8): fine fortified church; cingle de

Tresseyroux, priory of: *see* Lèches, Les

Treyne, La (Lot): an elegant 17th c. château on the banks of the Dordogne

Trigonant, château de: *see* Antonne et Trigonant

Trou de Vent, grotte du: *see* Bouzic

Tursac (G7): small town on the Vézère, with a fortified domed romanesque church; château de Marzac, very fine 15th-16th c. building; pilgrimage site of Notre Dame de Font Peyrine; château de Petit Marzac, ruins of feudal château; fortress of Reignac. Abri Cellier; gisements de Ruth, La Forêt, Liveyre, Roque Barbel and La Madeleine, village and troglodytic site; Préhisto-parc

Urval: château de la Bourlie; château de la Poujade; dolmen

Valadou, château de: *see* Bonneville et St Avit de Fumadières

Valajoulx: romanesque church with 12th c. font; château de Masnegre, 16th-17th c.; gisement de la Combe

Valeuil (D-E4): domed romanesque church with gothic additions; château de Ramefort; 15th c. dolmen de Laprouges; dolmen de Coutoux

Vanxains (B5): fine 12th c. church with good capitals

Varaignes (D2): romanesque church reworked in the 14th c., former seat of the archpriests of the Double; château with 15th c. courtyard housing; Atelier Musée du Tisserand et de la Charentaise

Varennes: domed 12th c. church with 13th c. capitals and 17th c. retable

Vassaldie, château de la: *see* Gouts Rossignol

Vauclaire, chartreuse de: *see* Montpon Ménestérol

Vaucocour, château de: *see* Thiviers

Vaudre, château de: *see* Gabillou

Vaugoubert, château de: *see* Quinsac

Vayssières, château de: *see* Vitrac

Vélines (A8): small town overlooking Ste Foy, with a romanesque church enlarged during the renaissance, having a good retable, pulpit and font; château de la Raye; château de Sardy, with gardens

Vendoire (C3): good romanesque church with fine saintongeais façade and doorway with sculpted capitals; 17th c. château; Musée Sites Les Tourbières de Vendoire (peat bogs)

Verdon (E8): château de Montbrun, elegant single storeyed manor house

Vergt (E6): busy small agricultural town; château de Boiras

Vergt de Biron: village at the foot of the château de Biron; romanesque churches of Sts Cernin and Bertis

Verliac, château de: *see* St Chamassy

Vermondie, tour de la: between Montignac and St Léon sur Vézère, a leaning tower with romantic associations

Vernode, donjon de: *see* Tocane St Apre

Verteillac (C4): pleasant small town; château de la Grénerie; château de la Meyfrénie; château du Breuil

Veyrignac (I8): romanesque church; château, 16th-17th c., heavily restored but with a fine view across the Dordogne; château de Rocanadel, a charming small building beautifully restored.

Veyrines de Domme: reworked romanesque church

Vézac (H8): château de Marqueyssac, 17th c. building with fine garden and magnificent views. The first garden was created towards the end of the 17th c. but the 150,000 box trees were planted by Julien de Cerval who died in 1893. Overhauling the sadly neglected garden is a long task but is being undertaken with skill and imagination. Château de Solvignac; château de Rochecourbe; grotte du Roc

Vieillecour, château de: *see* St Pierre de Frugie

Viélvic: *see* St Pardoux et Viélvic

Vieux Mareuil (D3): romanesque-style church built in 13th c. with 14th c. fortifications; château de Chavaroche; château de Marafy

Vigerie, château de la: *see* St Laurent de Hommes

Villac (H5): a village built of red sandstone and dominated by the ruins of its castle destroyed during the Revolution; romanesque church with 18th c. retable and 16th c. presbytery; château de Pagnac; château du Pont

Villamblard (D6): small town with imposing slate roofed market hall; château Barrière, ruins of 14th-15th c. building; château de Monclar

Villars (E3): 16th c. church with attractive doorway; château de Puyguilhem; abbaye de Boschaud; grotte du Cluzeau with good natural concretions, and engravings

Villefranche de Lonchat (A7): very little evidence remains of this English bastide; château; 14th-15th c. church; Musée d'Histoire Locale

Villefranche du Perigord (G9-10): the market hall and square are the only remains of this bastide. Maison du Chataignier, Marrons et Champignons

Villeréal (Lot et Garonne): French bastide founded by Alphonse de Poitiers in 1269 taken by the English and stayed in their hands until the end of the Hundred Years War

Villetoureix (C5): domed romanesque church dedicated to St Martin de Tours; château de la Rigale, which incorporates the remains of a Gallo-Roman tower similar to the Tour de Vésone at Périgueux

Vitrac (H8): romanesque church; château de Griffoul; château de Mas Robert; château de Rochebois, golf course; château des Vayssières; dolmen; château de Montfort, ramparts and park

Vitrolle, château de la: *see* Limeuil

249

Chronology

80-40,000 **BC** Middle Neolithic Age: Moustrian and Chatelperronian cultures

30-10,000 **BC** Upper Neolithic Age: Aurignacian, Gravettian, Perigordian, Solutrean and Magdalenian cultures

end 3rd century BC First appearance of Celtic coinage

58-51 BC Caesar's Gallic wars; Périgord inhabited by Petrocorii

16 BC Province of Aquitaine created by Augustus: Petrucorian territory becomes *Civitas Petrucoriorum* and *Vesunna* (Périgueux) its capital

2nd-3rd century Construction of the tour de Vésone and the ramparts of Vésone (Périgueux)

313 Edict of Milan by which Christianity became official religion of Roman empire under Constantine

356-36 Diocese of Périgueux created; Paternus first bishop

418 Visigoths conquer Aquitaine

476 Fall of Roman empire

507 Battle of Vouillé; Clovis defeats Visigoths, Franks masters of Aquitaine

581 Gascons in Aquitaine

675 Aquitaine an independent principality

768 Death of Waifre, duke of Aquitaine

732 Charles Martel defeats the Moors at Poitiers

779 Widbod, count of Périgord

800 Charlemagne crowned Holy Roman Emperor

814-817 Foundation of the abbey of Brantôme

849 Devastation of Périgueux by the Normans (Vikings)

866 Wulgrin, count of Périgord

937-938 First mention of the abbey of Sarlat

1096-99 First Crusade

1047 Consecration of St Front at Périgueux

1104-1119; 1123-24 Henry I and Louis VI at war

1120 Foundation of the abbey of Cadouin

1122 Eleanor of Aquitaine born

1137 Eleanor and Louis VII married

1140-1215 Bertrand de Born

1146 St Bérnard preaches Second Crusade (1147-49)

1152 Eleanor and Louis divorced 21 March; Eleanor and Henry Plantagenet married in May

1154 Henry Plantagenet accedes to English throne as Henry II

1155 Henry Courtmantel (The Young King) born

1157 Richard (Cœur de Lion) born

1186 John (Lackland) born

1189 Henry II dies

1190 Third Crusade

1199 Death of Richard I (Cœur de Lion)

1202-1204 Fourth Crusade

1204 Count of Périgord vassal of King of France; death of Eleanor; Philip Augustus acknowledges the bourgeois of Puy-St Front as 'bourgeois du roi'

1209-29 Albigensian Crusade

1218 Simon de Montfort killed at Toulouse

1217-1221 Fifth Crusade

1228-1229 Sixth Crusade

1230 Henry III expedition to recover Aquitaine

1240 Act of Union between Puy St Front and the Cité of Périgueux

1248-1254 Seventh Crusade

251

1251-1295 Archambaud III, Count of Périgord

1255 Commercial privileges granted to Bergerac by Edward II

1259 Treaty of Paris between Henry III and Louis IX who renounces Limousin, Quercy and Périgord

1270 Eighth Crusade

1279 Treaty of Amiens confirms 1259 Treaty of Paris

1281 Foundation of the *bastide* of Domme by the King of France

1285 Foundation of the *bastide* of Monpazier by the King of England

1307 Templars arrested

1317 Creation of the diocese of Sarlat (lasted till 1818)

1326 Edward III does homage to King of France for Aquitaine

1337 Start of the Hundred Years War

1340 Edward III proclaims himself King of France

1346 Battle of Crecy

1348 The Black Death

1355-70 The Black Prince campaigns in Périgord

1356 Battle of Poitiers; King of France taken prisoner

1360 Treaty of Brétigny cedes Aquitaine to English

1362 Périgord attached to the Principality of Aquitaine

1365 The Black Prince's census of the parishes and households in the sénéchaussée of Périgord

1369 Charles V confiscates Aquitaine

1375 Truce of Bruges

1376 Du Guesclin's campaign in Périgord; death of Black Prince

1399 Death of the last Count of Périgord

1413 Henry V claims crown of France

1415 Battle of Agincourt

1453 Battle of Castillon; English finally defeated; death of Sir John Talbot

1460-1490 Improvement in the economy

after the wars leads to resurgence of life in the countryside and towns

1522 Plague in Périgord

1530 Birth of Etienne de La Boëtie (d. 1563)

1533 Birth of Michel de Montaigne (d. 1592)

1544-1545 Revolts against salt tax in Périgueux

1552 Establishment of Présidial at Périgueux

1562 Massacre of Protestants at Vassy starts Wars of Religion

1563 Death of Etienne de La Boëtie; end of first War of Religion

1567 Start of second War of Religion

1569 (October) Massacre at La Chapelle-Faucher

1572 (24 August) Massacre of St Bartholomew (Paris)

1575 Vivant's troops occupy Périgueux

1577 Peace of Bergerac

1580 Peace of Fleix

1580-1588 Montaigne: *Les Essais*

1581 (June) Périgueux retaken by the Catholics

1589 Accession of Henri IV; converts to Catholicism 1593, crowned 1594

1594 Périgueux rallies to Henri IV and Périgord becomes part of royal domain

1594-1595 Revolt of the Croquants

1598 Edict of Nantes permitting Protestants to worship

1610 Assassination of Henri IV

1628-1634 Last appearance of plague in Périgord

1635 Tax revolts in Périgueux

1637-1642 Peasant revolts in Périgord

1648 Parliamentary Fronde

1651 Birth of Fénelon (d. 1715)

1650 Nobility Fronde warfare in Périgord

1685 Revocation of the Edict of Nantes

1698 Famine in Périgord

1707 Revolt of the Tards-Avisés

1709-1710 'Le Grand Hyver' - an exceptionally hard winter

1770-1771 Famine in Périgord

1783 Disastrous flooding of the Dordogne and its affluents

1788-1789 Production of the 'cahiers de doléances'

1789 (March) Election of députés to the States General; July fall of the Bastille

1790 Jan-Feb (26) Formation of the department of the Dordogne

1801-1802 Concordat; Périgueux without a bishop until 1821

1840 Bugeaud governor general of Algeria; died 10 June 1849 and buried in the Invalides

1834-1835 First École normale d'Instituteurs opened in Périgueux

1836 Birth of Eugène Le Roy (d. 1907)

1848 (23 April) First election under universal suffrage

1849 (13 May) Elections to the Législative: 10 deputés from the left

1851 Census figures give 505,789 inhabitants for the department

1852 116 people arrested in the Dordogne after the coup d'Etat of 2 December 1851

1857 (20 July) Opening of the railway from Coutras to Périgueux

1860 Opening of the railway from Bordeaux to Sarlat

1864 Opening of the Ateliers du PO du Toulon at Périgueux

1868 Phylloxera destroys Bergerac vineyards

1885 All Périgordin députés Republicans

1888 (8 April) General Boulanger, elected deputé of the Dordogne

1894-1907 Publication of Eugène Le Roy's novels

1920 Strike by railway workers at Périgueux

1920-1925 Paul Bouthonnier, Communist mayor at Périgueux

1924 Victory of the 'bloc des Gauches' Dordogne radical

1936 Success of the Front populaire in Dordogne

1940 Discovery of Lascaux

1944 (27 March) German reprisals in Périgord

1944 (August) Liberation of Périgueux by the maquisards

1972 Creation of region of Aquitaine

Rulers and Governments of France

987-996 Hugh Capet elected king of the Franks
996-1031 Robert II
1031-1060 Henri I
1060-1108 Philippe I
1108-1137 Louis VI
1137-1180 Louis VII
1180-1223 Philippe II (Auguste)
1223-1226 Louis VIII
1226-1270 Louis IX
1270-1285 Philippe III
1285-1314 Philippe IV
1314-1316 Louis X
1316 Jean I
1316-1322 Philippe V
1322-1328 Charles IV
1328-1350 Philippe V
1350-1364 Jean II
1364-1380 Charles V
1380-1422 Charles VI
1422-1461 Charles VII
1461-1483 Louis XI
1483-1498 Charles VIII
1498-1515 Louis XII
1515-1547 François I
1547-1559 Henri II
1559-1560 François II
1560-1574 Charles IX
1574-1589 Henri III
1589-1610 Henri IV

1610-1643 Louis XIII
1643-1715 Louis XIV
1715-1774 Louis XV
1774-1793 Louis XVI
1789 14 July, fall of the Bastille
1792 10 Aug-20 Sept, Provisional government
1792 21 Sept-2 Dec1804, First Republic
1792-1795 National Convention
1795-1799 Directory
1799-1804 Consulate
1804-1814 First Empire
Napoleon Bonaparte (d. 1821)
1814-1815 First Restoration
1814-1815 Louis XVIII
1815 20 March-22 June, The Hundred Days
1815-1830 Second Restoration
1815-1824 Louis XVIII (d. 1824)
1824-1830 Charles X (d. 1836)
1830-1848 Louis Philippe I – King of the French (d. 1850)
1848-1852 Second Republic
Louis Napoleon President
1852-1870 Second Empire
Napoleon III (d. 1873)
1870-1940 Third Republic
1940-1944 France occupied by Germans
1944-1947 Provisional government
(led by General de Gaulle 1944-1946)
1947-1958 Fourth Republic
1958- Fifth Republic

Périgueux in the seventeenth century

Select Bibliography

There is an immense amount of primary material and secondary literature, as can be seen in Noël Becquart's *Guide des Archives de la Dordogne* (Périgueux, 1970) and Anatole de Roumejoux's *Bibliographie générale du Périgord* (1877-99, reprinted Geneva, Skatkine, 1971), but most of it is in French, out of print or generally inaccessible. For those wishing to pursue their enquiries I have thought it worth including the more important older books, especially as some are available in English libraries.

Today there are any number of beautifully illustrated picture books of the department, such as Jean-Pierre Bouchard's *Périgord, terre de mémoire* (Périgueux, Fanlac 1984). I have not listed them as, beautiful though they are, they are short on facts. Most of them have very little text, captions in French, and are written in what can only be described as 'franglais'. I am constantly appalled by the inability of even quite serious publishers to acquire accurate or literate translations.

The Bremards, at the Librairie du Roc at Bayac, 24150 (tel. 05 53 24 12 32) specialise in departmental history and have a stock of over 800 titles which can be seen at their 'Salons du Livre' held in various towns throughout the department. Apart from the standard works in print, they also have copies of many of the very small local publications, some of which have been submitted to the biennial Clocher d'Or competition for the best monograph on a commune in the department. Not always open, so telephone to make an appointment if you want to visit the Librairie.

General: The single most useful book to have with you when you are out and about is the Green Michelin guide *Dordogne Berry Limousin* (1998), in English and very handy. The Blue Guide *South West France: Dordogne to the Pyrenees* by Francis Woodman (A & C Black, London; W. W. Norton, New York 1994) is altogether slighter.

Other recent works include James Bentley, *Penguin Guide to the Dordogne* (Penguin, Harmondsworth 1996); Arthur E. and Barbara Eperon, *The Dordogne and Lot* (Christopher Helm; A & C Black, London 3rd ed. 1995), *Visitor's Guide: Dordogne* by Barber Mandell, a Moorland Travel Guide (M. P. C. Hunter, 4th ed. 1996); and *The Which? Guide to the Dordogne, the Lot and the Tarn, Discovering the Heart of Rural France* by Andrew Leslie (Which? Books, Consumer Association 1995).

Of the older ones Ian Scargill's *The Dordogne Region of France* (David & Charles, Newton Abbott & London 1974) is reliable and good on geography; as is Helen Martin, *Le Lot* (Columbus, London 1988). Richard Barber's *Companion Guide to South West France* (Collins, London 1977) has been revised and reissued as

Companion Guide to Gascony and the Dordogne (Boydell & Brewer, 1996) but though useful covers too large an area.

Le Guide Dordogne-Périgord (Fanlac, Périgueux 1993) is well illustrated and slightly offbeat; worth having if you can cope with some French. Patrick Ranoux, *Atlas de la Dordogne-Périgord* (Montrem, 1996) is a most excellent work with masses of information presented graphically.

Freda White's *Three Rivers of France* (Faber & Faber, London) was first published in 1953 and has justifiably been in print ever since. It is now available, somewhat revised and with additions, in an illustrated edition with photographs and a commentary by Michael Busselle (Pavilion Books, London 1996).

J. C. Augustus Hare's *South-Western France*, though published in 1890, remains surprisingly accurate and is stylish, and Katharine Woods's *The Other Château Country, the Feudal Lands of the Dordogne* (John Lane; The Bodley Head, London 1931) is a delightful account of a pre-war journey in the region by two enquiring American ladies.

Two others, both valuable, are V. E. Ardouin-Dumazet, *Voyage en France*, volume 20 *Sud-Ouest - Bordelais, Périgord* (Berger Levrault, Paris 1903) and Edward Harrison-Barker, *Two Summers in Guyenne* (Griffith & Sarran, London 1894).

History: Solid and informative general works are *Histoire du Périgord* edited by Arlette Higounet-Nadal (Privat, Toulouse, 1983); R. P. Audierne's *Le Périgord Illustré, guide monumentale, statistique, pittoresque et historique de la Dordogne* (Dupont, Périgueux, 1851); J. J. Escande, *Histoire du Périgord* (Laffitte Reprints, Marseille 1980); Géraud Lavergne, *La Dordogne et ses pays* (USHA, Aurillac, 1931) and Gérard Fayolle, *Histoire du Périgord*, 2 vols (Fanlac, Périgueux 1984).

Eleanor Lodge's *Gascony under English Rule* (Methuen, London 1926) is a useful general work and the more recent *Quand les Anglais vendangaient Aquitaine* (Fayard, Paris 1978) by Jean Marc Soyez provides good background information. Amy Kelly, *Eleanor of Aquitaine and the Four Kings* (Harvard University Press, 1950) is a thorough and detailed work written in lilac rather than purple prose and despite the date of publication worth reading.

The River: The use of the river as an artery of transport, and the economic life it supported on its banks are well covered by Léon Dessalles's *La Dordogne et ses péages* (USHA, Aurillac 1936) and, more recently, in a magisterial work, A-M. Cocula-Vaillières' *Un fleuve et des hommes; les gens de la Dordogne au XVIIIe siècle* (Tallander, Paris 1981). *La Dordogne*, in the series 'Rivières et Vallées de la France', edited by Guy Pustelnik (Privat, Toulouse 1993), consists of a number of wide-ranging and learned accounts on all aspects of the river.

Two seminal articles are Eusèbe Bombal's *La Haute Dordogne et ses gabarriers* (Bulletin de la Société des lettres de la Corrèze 1900/01/02/03), and Jean Gouyon's

Les Maîtres de Bâteau sur la Dordogne in *Bulletin archéologique de la Corrèze* no. 86 (January-December 1964).

There is an informative brochure on the building of the dams by Raymond Dubois, *Les Grands Barrages* (Société de Presse et d'Edition du Limousin, Tulle 1976), and a more recent leaflet put out by EDF, *Aménagement hydroélectrique du bassin de la Dordogne* (1989). Daniel Borzeix, *La Haute Dordogne d'hier et d'aujourd'hui* (Editions Les Monédières, Le Loubanel, Treignac), though slight, is full of fascinating information about the higher reaches of the river.

Christian Signol's novel, *La Rivière Espérance* (Laffont, Paris 1990), is a good story and was made into a successful and colourful film for French television, though the locals complain of innaccuracies. Michael Brown's *Down the Dordogne* (Sinclair Stevenson, London 1991) is the story of the author's brave attempt to walk along the river from its source to the sea.

The Department: *The Generous Earth* by Philip Oyler, first published in 1950, has been mentioned in the text. An earlier and more systematic treatise on conditions in the late eighteenth century is André de Fayolle's *Topographie Agricole du département de la Dordogne* published in Périgueux, 1936 by the Société Historique et Archéologique du Périgord, whose bulletins are full of erudition and fascination. Fernand Dupuy, who made a great point about being a Communist politician, wrote nostalgically of life in his grandmother's day in *L'Albine* (Fayard, Paris 1977). Michel Combat and Anne Sylvia Moretti, *La Dordogne de Cyprien Brard*, 2 vols, (Archives en Dordogne, no. 1, Périgueux, 1995) is a fascinating and detailed analysis of the questionnaire sent out by Brard in 1835 to all the communes in the department.

Caves and Celts: Two old but reliable books on the caves are Glyn Daniel, *The Hungry Archaeologist in France* (Faber & Faber, London 1963) which deals with Dordogne caves in some detail; and Ann Sieveking's *The Cave Artists* (Thames & Hudson, London 1980). See also Henri Breuil, *400 siècles d'art pariétal* (Max Fourny, Montignac new ed. 1974).

Périgueux: Gérard Lavergne's *Histoire de Périgueux* (Fontas, Périgueux 1945) is the standard history of the city and J. L. Galet's *Connaissance de Périgueux* (Syndicat d'Initiative Périgueux 1972) the good small guide to have in the hand while walking round. Alberte Sadouillet-Perrin's *Périgueux A-Z* (Fanlac, Périgueux 1978) traces the history of the street names.

Churches and Castles: *Itineraires romans en Périgord* (Zodiaque, Abbaye Ste Marie de la Pierre qui vire, 1977) by Jean Secret, one of the grand old men of Périgordin history, has beautiful and informative photographs, as does *Périgord* *roman* (Zodiaque 1968) and both include reliable texts, with a short English translation at the end of the former. The most detailed work on castles is Jacques Gardelles's *Les Châteaux du Moyen Age dans la France du Sud-ouest: La Gascogne Anglaise de 1216-1327* (Bibliothèque de la Société Française d'Archéologie, Droz, Geneva, 1972). Guy Penaud, *Dictionnaire des Châteaux de Périgord* (Sud-Ouest, 1966) is a very thorough and useful volume, though by no means all-inclusive.

Bastides are fully covered by Maurice Beresford's *New Towns of the Middle Ages; town plantation in England, Wales and Gascony* (Lutterworth Press, London 1967). For Domme in particular Georges Burgat Degouy's *Domme, cité mediévale en Périgord* (Syndicat d'Initiative, Domme 1977) covers the entire history of the town as does *Ste Foy la Grande* (Groupe Girondin des Etudes locales de l'enseignement public, n.d.) by Jean Corriger for that bastide. For the Templar graffiti in Domme see the articles by P. M. Tonnelier in *Archaeologica* Nos. 32/33/38, 1970-71.

Châteaux and Bourgs: Jean Secret's *Le Périgord: châteaux, manoirs, et gentilhommières* (Tallandier, Paris 1966) is exhaustive and well illustrated.

A. Sadouillet-Perrin in *Sombres Histoires de Périgord Noir* (Fanlac, Périgueux, 1974) recounts some of the darker deeds connected with the châteaux-owning families. J. J. Escande, *Histoire de Sarlat* (Lafitte reprints, Marseilles, 1976) is invaluable and immensely detailed, while *La Renaissance au cœur du Périgord Noir* (Fanlac, Périgueux, 1976) by Jean Maubourguet, the other local sage, is an account of Sarlat's recovery from the Middle Ages.

There has been an explosion in local history over the last ten years or so and there are innumerable on the whole well done small histories of most of the local towns, available in the bookshops there. A recent example of one devoted to châteaux is *Rastignac* published by an erstwhile photographer (Pilote 24, Périgueux).

Classical to Modern Times: Gérard Fayolle's *La Vie Quotidienne en Périgord aux temps de Jacquou le Croquant* (Hachette, Paris 1977) is a serious work covering all aspects of life in the province during the nineteenth century and should be read beside the novels of Eugène le Roy, which are not, alas, translated. Georges Rocal covers social conditions over a wider period in *Croquants du Périgord* (Floury, Paris, n.d. reprint Fanlac, Périgueux, 1970) and his *Les Vieilles Coutumes du Périgord* (Fanlac, Périgueux reissued 1997) is well documented. Folk-tales are seriously related by Marcel Secondat in *Contes et Legendes* (Périgueux, Fanlac 1955) whilst Maguelonne Toussaint-Samat retells old stories for children in her *Contes et Legendes du Périgord et du Quercy* (Nathan, Paris, 1978).

Food and Wine: This is only a selection of the books on regional food. Paul Balard and Georges Rocal, *Gastronomie en Périgord* (Fanlac, Périgueux 1973); Huguette

Castignac, *La Cuisine Occitane* (Solar, Paris 1973); Huguette Couffignal, *La Cuisine Landes-Gironde-Périgord* (Paris 1977); Elizabeth David, *French Provincial Cooking* (Michael Joseph, London 1960); Pierre P. Grassé, *Petit Bréviaire de la Gastronomie Périgordine* (Fanlac, Périgueux 1973); La Mazille, *Bonne Cuisine du Périgord* (Flammarion, Paris 1929 constantly reprinted); Henriette Lasnet de Lanty, *Cuisine Périgordine* (Montsouris, Paris 1971); Raymond Oliver, *The French at Table* (Wine and Food Society, London 1967); Anne Penton, *Customs and Cookery in the Périgord and Quercy* (David and Charles, London and Newton Abbot 1973); Henri Philippon, *Cuisine du Quercy et Périgord* (Denoël, Paris 1979) – one of the best; Robert-Robert, *Guide du Gourmand* (Grasset, Paris 1924); Marcel Rouff and Curnonsky, *France Gastronomique* (Paris 1923); Julian Street, *Where Paris Dines* (Heinemann, London 1929). More recently Michael and Sybil Brown, *Food and Wine in South West France* (Batsford, London 1980); James Bentley, *Life and Food in the Dordogne* (Weidenfeld and Nicolson, London, 1986); Zette Guinadeau-Franc, *Les Secrets de Ferme en Périgueux Noir* (Berger Levrault, Paris, 1986) and immeasurably the best Jeanne Strang's *Goose Fat and Garlic, Country Recipes from South-West France* (Kyle Caithie, London 1991) – really good recipes and plenty of local colour – and its companion volume Paul Strang, *Wines of South-West France* (Kyle Caithie, London 1994).

These can be supplemented, for the historically minded gourmet, by A. Got's *Sa Majesté la Truffe* (La Truffereine, Bordeaux 1966); Jean Rebière's *La Truffe du Périgord* (Fanlac, Périgueux 1974), and Henri Deffarges's *L'Histoire du Foie Gras suivie par la Truffe et son Mystère à travers les Ages* (Virmouneix, Thiviers 1973); Jean-Luc Toussaint, *Les Noix dans tous ses états, 131 recettes gourmandes* (ed. L'Hyère, Castelnaud 1994); J. Y. Catherin, J. J. de Courcelles, R. Mazin, *Le Noyer et les Noix* (Edisud, 1995).

Miscellaneous: R. T. Hill and T. G. Bergin, *Anthology of the Provencal Troubadours* (Yale University Press 1941); *Les Troubadours périgourdins* by l'Ensemble Tre Fontane and Jean Roux (Princi Negri editor, St Médard en Jalas); Jean Secret, *Meubles du Périgord* (Fanlac, Périgueux 1974); Jacques Reix, *Faienceries en Périgord-Aquitaine* (Fanlac, Périgueux 1983).

And finally three oddments which don't fit into the above categories but are well worth having if you share their authors' interests: John Bate, *Lanterns for the Dead* (Lapridge, The Old Rectory, Eardsley, HR3 6NS, 1998); Philip Vickers, *Das Reich: March to Normandy* (Leo Cooper, Pen and Swords Books, Barnsley, 2000); and Jerry H. Simpson Jr, *Cycling France: The Best Bike Tours in All of Gaul* (Motorbooks International, San Francisco 1997).

Picture and text credits

Monochrome illustrations are reproduced by courtesy of:
Alte Pinakothek, Munich, p. 24; L'Atelier du Regard, A. Allemand, pp. 18-19, 26; M. Hervé, p. 25; Bulloz 77733, p. 130; Coutellerie Nontronnaise, Nontron, p. 35; Fred Dubery, p. 137; Maurice Albe *Les Fils emancipés de Jacquou le Croquant* Eugène Le Roy © Editions Fanlac: p. 153, Julien Saraben *Jacquou le Croquant* Eugène Le Roy © Editions Fanlac: p. 154; *La France Gastronomique, Guide des merveilles culinaires et des bonnes auberges françaises; le Périgord*, Curnonsky et Marcel Rouff, pp. 189, 262, 285, 292; Interphototèque, D.F. AQ 337109063 DOCA, p. 31; Jacques Lagrange, Périgueux, pp. 37, 45, 48, 51, 58, 63, 68, 80, 91,93, 96, 98, 104, 111, 112, 114, 115, 121, 122, 124, 129, 147, 170, 177, 191, 192; Joy Law, pp. 17, 140, 256; Richard Law, pp. 39, 60, 82, 101, 105, 159, 161, 169, 183; Loïc-Jahan, p. 13; Musée du Louvre, Paris, p. 130; La Maison de la Truffe, 24420, Sorges, p. 179; Collection Musée du Périgord, Ville de Périgueux, pp. 61, 63, 191; Monsieur Peyronnet, St Céré, p. 22; Guy Rivière, Sarlat, pp. 142, 162; Roger-Viollet BN ND 100 992, p. 118; Roger-Viollet RV 59909, p. 24; Musée du Tabac, Bergerac, p. 51; Sully, Bort les Orgues, p. 14; Zodiaque, pp. 77, 84.

Colour illustrations are reproduced by courtesy of:
Bibliothèque Nationale de France, MSS fr. 12473 f. 50, Frontispiece; French Picture Library, pp. 4, 6, 8, plates 12 and 18; Francis Lasfargue, plates 7, 13 and 16; Hugh Palmer, Front cover, plates 1, 2, 4, 5, 6, 8, 9, 10, 11, 14, 15, 17, 19, 20, 21 and 22; Lucien Roulland, Sarlat, Inside front cover, Inside back cover, back cover.

Maps and plans by Ted Hammond © Pallas Athene 2000.

I have also to acknowledge permission to reproduce quoted material as follows: *The Generous Earth* by Philip Oyler, reproduced by permission of Hodder & Stoughton Limited; *The Colossi of Maroussi* by Henry Miller, reproduced by permission of Heinemann; letters by Kipling sent to *The Kipling Journal* by Mrs George Bambridge and first published in *The Kipling Journal*, Vol. XXXIV, No. 164, December 1967, reproduced by permission of The Kipling Society); *Fénelon Letters* chosen and translated by John McEwan, English translation © The Harvill Press, 1964, reproduced by permission of The Harvill Press, and of Harcourt Inc.; 'Near Perigord' from *A Selection of Poems* by Ezra Pound, reproduced by permission of Faber & Faber; and *Personae* © 1926 by Ezra Pound, reprinted by permission of New Directions Publishing Corp.

Practical Information

Practical Information

GENERAL INFORMATION A most useful brochure called *The Traveller in France* with every kind of practical information is available from the French Tourist Office, 178 Piccadilly, London, W1V 0AL and a leaflet explaining how to deal with medical problems, legal liability, insurance etc, published by COLOC is also available there on receipt of a stamped addressed envelope.

TOURIST OFFICES

Comité Départementale du Tourisme de la Dordogne, 25 rue Wilson, Périgueux, 24000. Tel. 05 03 35 50 24.

BT: Borne Télématique
OT: Office de Tourisme
PI: Points d'Information
SI: Syndicat d'Initiative

Prefix all telephone numbers with 05 53 in France. Ringing from outside France omit the 0.

Angoisse 24440	PI summer	52 69 62
Beaumont 24440	OT	22 39 12
Belvès 24170	SI	29 10 20
Bergerac 24100	OT	57 03 11
Beynac 24220	OT	29 43 08
Bourdeilles 24310	SI	03 42 96
Brantôme 24310	SI	05 80 52
Bugue, Le, 24260	OT/PI/BT	07 20 48
Buisson, Le, 24480	OT	22 00 41
Carlux 24370	SI	59 10 70
Coquille, La, 24450	PI summer	52 80 56
Creysse 24100	SI	23 20 45
Domme 24250	OT	31 71 00
Excideuil 24160	SI	62 95 56
Eymet 24500	OT	23 74 95
Eyzies, Les, 24620	OT/PI	06 97 05
Hautefort 24390	SI	50 40 27
Issigeac 24560	SI	58 79 62
Javerlhac 24300	SI	56 34 68
Jumilhac le Grand 24630	SI	52 55 43
Lalinde 24150	OT	61 08 55
Lanouaille 24270	SI	52 60 21
Limeuil 24510	SI	63 38 90
Mareuil 24340	SI	60 99 85
Monbazillac 24240	PI	58 22 76
Monpazier 24540	OT	22 68 59
Montignac 24290	OT/BT	51 82 60

Montpon-Ménesterol 24700	OT	82 23 77
Mouleydier 24520	SI	23 20 41
Moulin Neuf, Montaigne et Gurçon RN89	PI	81 51 42
Mussidan 24400	BT	81 73 87
Neuvic 24190	SI	81 52 11
Nontron 24300	OT	56 25 50
Périgueux 24200	OT	53 10 63
Périgueux 24200	BT/PI	35 50 24
Piégut-Pluviers 24360	OT	60 74 75
Ribérac 24600	OT	90 03 10
Roche Chalais, La 24490	SI	90 18 95
Rouffignac 24580	SI	05 39 03
Salignac-Eyvigues 24590	SI	28 81 93
Sarlat 24200	OT	31 45 45
Saussignac 24420	SI	29 49 11
Sigoulès 24240	SI	58 48 16
Siorac en Périgord 24170	SI	31 63 51
Sorges 24420	SI	05 04 85
St Astier 24110	SI	54 13 85
St Aulaye 24410	SI	90 63 74
St Cyprien 24220	SI	30 36 09
St Jean de Côle 24800	SI	62 30 21
St Pardoux la Rivière 24470	SI	56 79 30
Ste Alvère 24510	SI	27 59 99
Terrasson 24120	OT	50 37 56
Terrasson RN89	PI	50 68 58
Thenon 24210	SI	06 35 10
Thiviers 24800	SI	55 12 50
Tocane St Apre 24350	SI	90 44 94
Trémolat 24510	SI	22 89 33
Varaignes 24360	SI	56 23 66
Vergt 24380	SI	03 45 10
Verteillac/Vendoire 24320	SI	90 37 78
Villamblard 24140	SI	82 26 28
Villefranche de Lonchat 24610	SI	58 63 13
Villefranche du Périgord 24550	SI	29 98 37

Getting there and getting around

By air from England:
Air France. Tel. 020 8742 6600
Bluebird Express. Tel. 0990 320022
Brit Air c/o Air France
British Airways. Tel. 0345 222111
British Midland. Tel. 0345 554554
Easy Jet. Tel. 0990 292929

Airports (France)
Bordeaux-Meyrignac. Tel. 05 56 34 50 50
Toulouse-Blagnac. Tel. 05 61 42 44 00
Périgueux-Bassillac. Tel. 05 53 02 79 70
Bergerac-Roumazière. Tel. 05 53 57 00 09
Brive Aerodrome. Tel. 05 55 86 88 36

Bicycle hire Some railway stations can produce bicycles and they are available locally; the relevant Tourist Office will have a list of suppliers.

Car hire in France A list of companies who will supply a car on arrival is held by the French Government Tourist Offices in London. A variety of companies will organize fly-drive hire cars at airports.

Coach services Enquiries to Eurolines 01582 404511. There are very few long distance coaches though some locally.

Information from Gare Routière Internationale 00 33 1 49 72 51 51 or local tourist offices and coach stations.

Cross Channel By ferry, hovercraft or seacat:
Brittany Ferries, Portsmouth.
  Tel. 0990 360360
Holyman Sally Ferries, Ramsgate.
  Tel. 0990 595522

Hoverspeed Fast Ferries, Dover/ Folkestone. Tel. 0990 240241
P&O European Ferries, Portsmouth. Tel. 0870 600 3300
P&O Stena Line, Dover. Tel. 0870 600 0612
SeaFrance, Dover. Tel. 01304 212696

Motorail Book via French Travel Centre, 179 Piccadilly, London, W1V 0BA. Tel. 020 7203 7000 (you can hang on a long time to get hold of them; try going in early in the morning or if you can't manage to do that, try a travel agency and let it have the hassle).

Calais-Brive: only goes for a week or two at Easter and in the summer and early autumn.

Paris-Brive: runs most of the year but the car goes overnight while passengers can go at any other time. Useful if you have a friend or a cheap hotel in Paris.

Motorway tolls These can amount to a considerable sum so if you are going to use the *autoroutes* be prepared with cash or a valid credit card.

By train Eurostar from Waterloo or Ashford to Paris; Le Shuttle from Folkestone.

SNCF Rail: Paris to Brive, Souillac, Gourdon; Bordeaux; Bergerac; Périgueux; Ribérac.

Bordeaux-Bergerac-Sarlat.

Périgueux, Bergerac, Sarlat, Nontron. Tel. 08 26 35 35 35.

Taxis These are generally available at main line stations but can easily be found locally.

What to do

COURSES (*stages*) A wide choice of subjects can be studied. The following list shows those courses available in 1998:
Bookbinding: Villefranche de Périgord
Crafts (*artisanat*): Echournac
Cycling (*VTT*): Montagrier
Dance: Brantôme
Fishing: Excideuil and St Julien de Lampon
Geology: Varaignes
Glass-making: Sarlat
Gold panning (*orpaillage*): Jumilhac le Grand
Golf: Rochebois
Helicopter: St Geniès
Judo: Sarlat
Karate: Thiviers
Languages (English, French and Spanish): Bourdeilles
Mime: Périgueux
Mineralogy: Varaignes
Mosaics: Montpon Ménesterol
Music: Jumilhac le Grand, Périgueux, St Amand de Coly and Tocane St Apre
Painting: Cénac, Lanquais, Lisle, Sarlat and St Avit Senieur
Patchwork: Villefranche de Périgord
Piano: Lanquais
Piloting and gliding: Bassillac
Piloting: Ribérac
Singing: Brantôme
Stained glass: Ribérac
Theatre: Villefranche de Périgord
Weaving: Trémolat

EXCURSIONS There are a large number of different types of excursions available. Detailed information is available from the Comité Départementale in Périgueux or local Tourist Offices.

Autorail Espérance: In high summer small trains creep along the valleys of the Dordogne and the Vézère with their entrancing views from Sarlat to Bergerac or from Sarlat to Périgueux (and vice versa). Gastronomic treats - and a commentary – are provided on the outward journeys. Tel. 05 53 31 53 46

Canoe trips (*canoës*): Information and reservations. Tel. 05 53 35 50 24. Canoe trips, with accommodation in camp sites or hotels are available from April to November 'Sur les traces des gabarriers' and 'Dordogne – rivière d'enchantement' on the Dordogne and from Montignac to Le Bugue on the Vézère.

Carriage rides (*promenades en calèche*): Full or half day trips can be made by horse-drawn carriages from:

Boisse	05 53 58 72 87
Brantôme	05 53 05 80 52
Excideuil	05 53 62 95 56
Festalemps	05 53 90 09 42
Lisle	05 53 03 58 35
St Rémy sur Lidoire	05 53 46 62 57
Mazeyrolles	05 53 29 98 99

Horse-drawn caravans (*roulotte à cheval*): Details from Comité Départementale de Tourisme service Loisirs Acceuil. Tel. 05 53 35 50 05. Fully equipped horse-drawn caravans with accommodation for 4 people are available from the Base de Minjou at Faurilles near Issigeac and the Base de Beauvignière at Quinsac. The suggested itineraries cover about 15 kilometres a day, and meals can be taken in local hotels or farms. Full provision is made for the horse. *Le Périgord en roulotte de cheval* – 15 km a day, Issigeac and Quinsac.

Minibus from Sarlat: Tours designed round a theme to suit you can be arranged via the Tourist Office in Sarlat. Tel. 05 53 31 45 45.

Plane trips (*promenades aeriennes*): Flights by small low-flying aircraft are another attractive way to see the local countryside. They are operated from:

Belvès	05 53 29 01 50
Bergerac	05 53 57 31 36
La Roque Gageac	05 53 28 89 32
Périgueux	05 53 54 41 19
Ribérac	05 53 90 24 99
or by Paramoteurs	05 53 59 45 99

River trips (*promenades en bateau*): These operate from:

Bergerac	05 53 24 58 80
Beynac	05 53 28 51 15
Brantôme	05 53 05 80 52
Creysse	05 53 23 20 45
La Roque Gageac	05 53 29 40 41/
	” ” ” ” 95
Mauzac	05 53 23 90 36

Taxi minibus: These are available for privately organised trips at:

Périgueux	05 53 09 09 09
Sarlat	05 53 28 10 04
Le Buisson	05 53 06 93 06
Lalinde	05 53 27 88 52

Visits to farms (*circuits bienvenue à la ferme*): These are planned circuits to visit farms to see methods of farming and to taste the local produce. Nearby sights and craft workshops are often included in the tours, which are run from:

Brantôme	05 53 05 80 52
Jumilhac	05 53 60 52 07

Hautefort	05 53 50 40 27
Ribérac	05 53 90 03 10
Sarlat	05 53 28 60 80
Trémolat	05 53 22 77 38
St Astier	05 53 54 13 85
Beaumont	05 53 22 39 12
Molières	05 53 63 65 20
Villefranche du Périgord	05 53 29 98 37

SPORTS AND OUTDOOR ACTIVITIES
Sporting and leisure facilities in the Dordogne are excellent. Water sports and riding are particularly popular, but there is a wide range of activities to choose from.

Abseiling (*parcours à cordes*)
St Jory de Chalais 24800: *Association Arc en soi*. Tel. 05 53 55 07 55

Ballooning (*Montgolfière*)
Arranged on demand:
Compagnie des Passagers du Vent.
   Tel. 05 53 54 59 57
La Roque Gageac 24250: *Montgolfières de Périgord*. Tel. 05 53 28 18 58

Canoeing (*canoë*)
River Dordogne: Le Buisson 24480: *Canoë river*. Tel. 05 53 22 95 88
Carlux 24370: *Animation Dordogne BEES*.
   Tel. 05 53 29 83 43
Carsac Aillac 24200: *Aqua Viva*.
   Tel. 05 53 59 21 09
Castelnaud La Chapelle 24250: *Kayak Club BEES*. Tel. 05 53 29 40 07
Cénac et St Julien 24250: *Randonnée Dordogne*. Tel. 05 53 28 22 01 or 285300?
Cénac Périgord Loisirs. Tel. 05 53 29 99 69
Canoë Sioux. Tel. 05 53 28 30 81
Domme 24350: *Espace Canoë*.
   Tel. 05 53 59 42 21
Grolejac 24250: *Explorando*.
   Tel. 05 53 28 57 13
Grolejac Canoës. Tel. 05 53 28 93 70
Association Rando Veyrignac. Tel. 05 53 30 23 55

Lalinde 24150: *Moulin de la Guillou BEES*.
Tel. 05 53 61 00 44

Limeuil 24510: *Jean Rivière Loisirs*.
Tel. 05 53 63 38 73

Canoës Perdigat. Tel. 05 53 61 83 36

Mauzac et Grand Castang 24210: *Base de Voile*. Tel. 05 53 22 52 14

Porte Ste Foy 33220: *Base Nautique*.
Tel. 05 53 58 32 49

La Roque Gageac 24250: *Canoë Dordogne BEES*. Tel. 05 53 29 58 50

Canoës Vacances. Tel. 05 53 28 17 07

St Laurent des Vignes 24100: *Juniorland*.
Tel. 05 53 58 33 00

St Vincent de Cosse 24220: *Les Canoës du Port d'Anveaux*. Tel. 05 53 29 54 20

Siorac en Périgord 24170: *Canoë Raid*.
Tel. 05 53 31 64 11

Vézac 24220: *Espace Canoës*.
Tel. 05 53 59 42 21

Couleur Périgord. Tel. 05 53 30 37 61

Vitrac 24200: *Canoës Loisirs BEES*.
Tel. 05 53 28 23 43

Soleil Plage. Tel. 05 53 28 33 33

River Vézère: Le Bugue 24260: *Les Courrèges*. Tel. 05 53 08 75 37

Condat sur Vézère 24570: *Randonnée Vézère*. Tel. 05 53 51 38 35

Les Eyzies 24620: *Base des 3 Drapeaux*.
Tel. 05 53 06 91 89

Animation Vézère BEES. Tel. 05 53 06 92 92

Limeuil 24510: *Jean Rivière Loisirs*.
Tel. 05 53 63 38 73

Canoës Perdigat. Tel. 05 53 61 83 36

Montignac 24290: *Animation Vézère*.
Tel. 05 53 51 91 14

Les 7 Rives. Tel. 05 53 50 19 26

St Léon sur Vézère 24290: *Aventure Plein Air BEES*. Tel. 05 53 50 67 71

River Dronne: Bourdeilles 24310: *Canoës Bourdeilles*. Tel. 05 53 04 56 94

Brantôme 24310: *Brantôme Canoë*.
Tel. 05 53 05 77 24

Allo Canoë BEES. Tel. 05 53 06 31 85

Ribérac 24600: *Cap Nature Randonnée*.

Tel. 05 53 90 12 73

River Isle: Périgueux 24000: *Animation Isle Canoë Kayak BEES*. Tel. 05 53 53 06 72

Trélissac 24750: *L.A.S.T. BEES*.
Tel. 05 53 08 63 95

River Auvézère: Angoisse 24270: *Base de Loisirs BEES*. Tel. 05 53 52 32 25

St Mémin 24270: *Relais Nature*.
Tel. 05 53 52 78 02

sur lac: Hautefort 24390: *Le Moulin des Loisirs*. Tel. 05 53 50 46 55

Cycling

Good maps are available showing circular tours.

Mountain bikes (*Centres VTT Vélos Tous Terrains*)

Lalinde 24150: *Centre régional VTT BEES*.
Tel. 05 53 24 12 31

Montagrier 24350: *Mairie*. Tel. 05 53 90 71 03

Cycling tours (*randonnées cyclo*)

For information about these three circular tours, ring 05 53 35 50 05:

1) *Chemins verts du Périgord*
2) *Découverte de la vallée de la Dordogne et de ses châteaux*
3) *Deux vallées en Périgord Noir*

Maps and leaflets such as '*Les sentiers du Périgord*' and a list of suppliers and repair shops can be had from the Comité Départementale du Tourisme at Périgueux

Diving (*plongée*)

Périgueux 24000: *Sub Périgord Plongée BEES*. Tel. 05 53 09 66 81

Fishing (*pêche*)

A fishing permit (*vignette halieutique*) is obligatory and obtainable locally; ask at the mairie or tabac. (Amateur fishermen are forbidden to sell any of their catch.)

Le Club halieutique interdépartementale, Bt C1, Route des Calanques, Perpignan 6000.

Fishing is possible in all the rivers and

their tributaries and there are four lakes in the department administered by the Fédération de Pêche:

Retenue de Miallet: carp, roach (*carpes, gardons*).

Plan d'eau de Farganaud, St Laurent des Hommes: pike, roach, carp, tench, black bass (*brochets, gardons, carpes, tanches, bass noirs*).

Plan d'eau de Fongrand, Thonac: roach, carp, trout (*gardons, carpes, truites*).

Plan d'eau de Valajoulx, Montaigne: pike, carp, roach, perch (*brochets, carpes, gardons, perches*).

Golf

Marsac sur L'Isle 24430: *Golf public de Périgueux*. Tel. 05 53 53 65 90

Monestier 24240: *Château de Vigiers*, near Bergerac, 18 holes. Tel. 05 53 61 50 33

Mouleydier 24520: *Golf Club Château Les Merles*, near Lalinde, 9 holes. Tel. 05 53 63 13 42

Périgueux: *Périgueux Golf de Saltgourde*, 18 holes. Tel. 05 53 53 02 35

Sadillac 24500: *Château Sadillac*. Tel. 05 53 58 46 09

St Félix de Reilhac et Mortemart, near Le Bugue: *Golf de la Croix de Mortemart*, 18 holes. Tel. 05 53 03 27 55

St Geniès 24590: *Golf Swin La Peyrière*, 18 holes. Tel. 05 53 31 57 00

St Germain de Belvès 24170: *Golf de Lolivarie*, 9 holes. Tel. 05 53 30 22 69

Vitrac 24200: *Golf Domaine de Rochebois*, near Sarlat, 9 holes. Tel. 05 53 31 52 80

Hang gliding (*vol libre de parapente et deltaplane*)

Terrasson 24120: *Association 'Espace de Voleurs'*. Tel. 05 53 51 53 64

Microlite (*ULM*)

St Pardoux et Vielvic 24170: *Montblanc Air Concept*. Tel. 05 53 59 44 99

Domme 24250: *Ulm Evasion*. Tel. 05 53 28 18 08

Motor sports (*sport motorisé*)

Vallereuil 24190: *Cross Car 'Les Brandes de Guibert'*. Tel.05 53 81 60 64

La Douze 24330: *Garden Karting 'Les Martinies Est'*. Tel. 05 53 38 28 55

Teyjat 24300: *Circuit du Périgord*. Tel. 05 53 56 36 11

Parachuting (*parachutisme*)

Bergerac 24100: *Centre Ecole Régional*. Tel. 05 53 57 98 09

Riding stables (*centre équestre*)

Allès sur Dordogne 24480: *Ferme équestre Haute Yerle ATE*. Tel. 05 53 63 35 85

Antonne et Trigonnat 24420: *Cercle Hippique d'Antonne BEES*. Tel. 05 53 35 22 14

Archignac 24590: *Ferme équestre Mayac ATE*. Tel. 05 53 28 91 10

Bourdeilles 24310: *Ferme équestre Le Naudonnet ATE*. Tel. 05 53 08 66 74

Bourrou 24110: *Les Ecuries de Monciaux BEES*. Tel. 05 53 81 17 58

Brantôme 24310: *Les Ecuries de Puynadal*. Tel. 05 53 06 19 66

Campagne 24260: *Arc en Ciel Poney Club BEES*. Tel. 05 53 07 23 66

Castelnaud La Chapelle 24250: *La Vallée des Châteaux BEES*. Tel. 05 53 29 51 86

Cause de Clérans 24150: *Liberté Passion Périgord*. Tel. 05 53 58 51 15

Champcevinel 24750: *Etrier Périgordin BEES*. Tel. 05 53 04 62 54

Péri-cheval-Foncroze BEES. Tel. 05 53 09 51 69

Champs Romain 24470: *Ferme Equestre La Bruyère ATE*. Tel. 05 53 56 95 03

Cornille 24750: *Haras de la Forêt BEES*. Tel. 05 53 04 64 03

Coubjours 24390: *Les Attelages du Haut Repaire*. Tel. 05 53 50 32 79

Creysse 24100: *Club hippique bergeracois*

BEES. Tel. 05 53 57 77 16

Eygurandes 24700: *Centre equestre d'Eygurandes BEES*. Tel. 05 53 80 39 90

Faux 24560: *Equitation et Roulottes du Périgord ATE*. Tel. 05 53 24 32 57

Fleurac 24580: *Les écuries de Fleurac ATE*. Tel. 05 53 05 49 19

Hautefort 24390: *Ecole Elémentaire d'Equitation BEES*. Tel. 05 53 50 53 56

Jumilhac le Grand 24630: *Les Ecuries de Jumilhac ATE*. Tel. 05 53 52 52 89

La Roche Chalais 24490: *Poney Club de la Borde BEES*. Tel. 05 53 91 30 91

Leguillac de l'Auch 24110: *Centre Equestre BEES*. Tel. 05 53 54 53 94

Faucherie Les Cavaliers du Vern. Tel. 05 53 04 95 78

Les Bardys 24130, Bosset: *Ensel Périgord*. Tel. 05 53 81 01 00

Marsalès 24540: *Cassang, Jean Claude BEES*. Tel. 05 53 22 63 14

Maurens 24140: *Ecuries de Baillard ATE*. Tel. 05 53 24 59 48

Mazeyrolles 24550: *Périgord en Calèche*. Tel. 05 53 29 98 99

Milhac de Nontron 24470: *Domaine de La Grelière BEES*. Tel. 05 53 56 55 95

Monbazillac 24240: *Promenade en voiture à cheval ATE*. Tel. 05 53 58 33 63

Monpazier 24540: *Centre équestre de Marsalès*. Tel. 05 53 22 63 14

Périgueux-Atar 24750: *Association des Cavaliers du Haras de Bagnec*. Tel. 05 53 53 28 73

Rouffignac de Sigoulès 24240: *La Jumenterie BEES*. Tel. 05 53 58 42 98

Sagelat 24170: *La Ferme de Bugou ATE*. Tel. 05 53 31 68 69

St Antoine d'Auberoche 24330: *Centre Cheval Poney*. Tel. 05 53 04 46 48

St Antoine de Breuilh 24230: *Eperon Laurentais BEES*. Tel. 05 53 24 80 36

St Barthelèmie de Bellegarde 24700: *Auberge de Jeunesse ATE*. Tel. 05 53 81 64 40

St Estèphe 24360: *Centre équestre de Mérigaud BEES*. Tel. 05 53 56 86 96

St Félix de Reilhac 24260: *Ferme Equestre La Franval ATE*. Tel. 05 53 03 23 98

St Germain des Près 24520: *Ecurie de la Cavale BEES*. Tel. 05 53 24 30 91

St Germain et Mons 24250: *Centre équestre La Caval*. Tel. 05 53 24 30 91

St Julien de Crempse 24140: *Centre équestre Loisirs Le Grand Vignoble BEES*. Tel. 05 53 24 20 98

St Laurent des Hommes 24400: *Centre équestre de BEES*. Tel. 05 53 81 70 43

St Méard de Gurçon 24610: *Les Ecuries St Méaroises BEES*. Tel. 05 53 81 31 95

St Médard de Mussidan 24440: *Ecuries Pas de Loup*. Tel. 05 53 80 60 02

St Paul de Serre 24380: *Ecuries du Rosier ATE*. Tel. 05 53 03 93 18

St Pierre d'Eyraud 24130: *Centre équestre Poney Club BEES*. Tel. 05 53 22 55 31

St Sauveur 24520: *Centre équestre Poney Club BEES*. Tel. 05 53 27 50 56

Sarlat 24200: *Centre Hippique Fournier Sarlovèze BEES*. Tel. 05 53 59 15 83

Tamniès 24620: *Le Gîte de Favard BEES*. Tel. 05 53 29 68 62

Tourtoirac 24390: *Les Tourterelles ATE*. Tel. 05 53 51 11 17

Trélissac 24750: *Centre équestre La Cravache de Trélissac BEES*. Tel. 05 53 08 14 58

Tursac 24620: *Viseur, Michel*. Tel. 05 53 06 93 83

Vergt 24380: *La Poussiere Poney's Ballade BEES*. Tel. 05 53 46 70 27

Ferme équestre de Boutazac. Tel. 05 53 54 92 00

Vergt de Biron 24540: *La Bride du Cazal ATE*. Tel. 05 53 63 16 41

Verteillac 24320: *Centre équestre Poney Club BEES*. Tel. 05 53 91 69 38

Vitrac 24200: *L'Etrier de Vitrac BEES*. Tel. 05 53 59 34 31

Riding tours (*randonnées équestres*)

One tour, accompanied, for 6 days, starts at Monpazier as does another for a weekend.

The Ferme équestre de Hauteyerle near Le Buisson also organises unaccompanied tours.

Rock climbing (*escalade*)

Bergerac 24100: *Comité Départementale d'Escalade BEES*. Tel. 05 53 63 61 73

Veyrines de Domme 24250: *Vialès, Frédérick*. Tel. 05 53 29 41 56

St Martial de Nabirat 24250: *Keller, Mathieu*. Tel. 05 53 28 51 15

Rowing (*aviron*)

Bergerac 24100: *Sport nautique de Bergerac*. Tel. 05 53 57 85 02

Sailing (*voile*)

Mauzac et Grand Castang 24160: *Club Nautique Mauzacois*. Tel. 05 53 22 52 14

Speleology/Potholing/Caving (*spéléologie*)

Grolejac 24250: *Comité Départementale de Spéléologie BEES*. Tel. 05 53 31 27 30

Veyrines de Domme 24250: *Viales, Frédérick BEES*. Tel. 05 53 29 41 56

Vezac 24220: *Lignac, Laurent BEES*. Tel. 05 53 30 37 61

Swimming (*natation*)

The best is in the many rivers and streams though there are now a number of good municipal pools.

Tennis

There are plenty of courts; ask at the mairie in the vicinity.

Walking (*randonnée pédestre*) There are detailed guide books and maps for the Grandes Randonnées: Topo-Guides FFRP; Ref. 321 GR36 *Angoumois-Périgord-Quercy;* Ref. 605 GR6 *Quercy et Périgord, Figeac, Les Eyzies*; GR64 *Domme, Gourdon, Rocamadour*, and a number of leaflets obtainable from Comité Départementale de la Randonnée pédestre, 30 rue Chanzy, Périgueux 24200. Tel. 05 03 29 99 94.

Organised walks with a specific theme and accommodation in hotels or bed and breakfast:

Balade au pays de l'homme: (Apr-Nov, 7 days hotel)

Pays de la Truffe, Sorges: all year (weekend hotel)

Pays de Lascaux: (5 days hotel)

Balades romanes, accompanied: (6 days bed and breakfast)

Unaccompanied: (Apr-Nov, 7 days hotel)

There are also two other accompanied theme walks on prehistory and archaeology and *balades romans* and three unaccompanied: *une terre d'enchantement, au pays de la Truffe* and *pays de Lascaux*.

Walking tours arranged at:

Le Coux et Bigaroque 24220: *Pas à Pas*. Tel. 05 53 30 34 26

Cadouin 24480: *Au Fil de Temps*. Tel. 05 53 22 06 09

Périgueux 24000: *Dryade*. Tel. 05 53 54 18 56

Water skiing (*ski nautique*)

Trémolat 24510: *Base nautique*. Tel. 05 53 08 59 94

Places to visit

This is a quick check-list of sights normally open to the public under categories which I hope may be of use to people looking for a specific kind of sight to see. Look at it in conjunction with the map which will show what there is to see within any one area. Many châteaux, churches and abbeys do not necessarily figure on the map under their own name but under that of the nearest town or village. Details of opening hours and telephone numbers are given on the following pages.

Prehistoric sites These fall quite neatly into four categories: caves with man-made decorations, those with astonishing natural concretions – stalagtites and stalagmites (if you can't remember which is which, a helpful mnemonic is tite = *tombe*, fall; mite = *monte*, rise); rock shelters (*gisements*) and troglodytic sites. Sometimes two or more will be found in the same place. See also **Caves and Rock Shelters**, p. 282.

1) Decorated caves
Bugue, Le
Cabrerets (Lot)
Eyzies, Les
Gourdon (Lot)
L'Hospitalet (Lot)
Lascaux II (tickets must be bought
   at Montignac)
Marquay
Meyrals
Rouffignac
St Cirq du Bugue
Teyjat
Thonac
Villars

2) Caves with concretions
Audrix-Le Bugue
La Cave (Lot)
Domme
Les Eyzies
Gramat (Lot)
Manaurie

3) *Gisements*
Stratified accumulations of debris, no exact equivalent in English:
Les Eyzies
Montignac
Peyzac Le Moustier
Savignac de Miremont
Sergeac

4) Troglodytic sites
Belvès
Les Eyzies
Peyzac Le Moustier
Roque Gageac, La
St Léon sur Vézère
Tursac

Châteaux

Dordogne has almost as many châteaux as small romanesque churches. Most of them are modest in size and vary in style from the renaissance to (a few) eighteenth-century. However, most of the outstanding ones, which merit a special journey, are – with the exception of Hautefort – medieval fortresses, marked with an *

Ajat
Antonne
Beaumont du Périgord
Beauregard de Terrasson
Bergerac
Beynac*
Biron*
Bonaguil (Lot et Garonne)*
Bourdeilles
Brantôme
Castelnaud La Chapelle*
Champagne et Fontaine
Champeaux
Château l'Evêque
Creysse
Fleurac
Hautefort*
Issac
Jumilhac le Grand*
La Cave (Lot)
La Chapelle Faucher
Lalinde

Lanquais
Lussas et Nontronneau
Mareuil sur Belle
Marquay (Puymartin)
Miallet
Milandes, Les
Monbazillac
Montignac
Neuvic sur l'Isle
Rouffignac (L'Herm)
Salignac-Eyvigues
Sarlat
Sorges
St Jean de Côle
St Michel de Montaigne
St Pierre de Côle
Ste Mondane (Fénelon)
Thonac
Villamblard
Villars
Vitrac

Churches and abbeys

As virtually every hamlet and village has a church, however small, it would be impossible to list them all, though those of general interest are included in the Gazetteer, and those of special interest in the text. As the abbeys are treated more like museums with opening hours, here is a list of them.

Agonac (Ligueux)
Brantôme
Cadouin
Carennac (Lot)
Chancelade
La Chapelle Gonaguet (Merlande)
Limeuil

Paunat
St Amand de Coly
St Avit Sénieur
Souillac (Lot)
Tourtoirac

Museums

None of the departmental museums is on a grand scale save only that of prehistory at Les Eyzies. Many are quite small and specialised but nonetheless worth seeing if you are in the neighbourhood.

Auriac du Périgord	Nojals et Clottes
Belvès	Nontron
Bergerac	Périgueux
Beynac	Petit Bersac
Brantôme	Peyzac Le Moustier
Bugue, Le	Pomport
Cadouin	Port Ste Foy
Carennac (Lot)	Salignac-Eyvigues
Cassagne, La	Sarlat
Castelnaud La Chapelle	Siorac en Périgord
Chourgnac d'Ans	Sorges
Couze St Front	Souillac (Lot)
Creysse	St Aulaye
Daglan	St Avit Sénieur
Domme	St Just
Echourgnac	St Pardoux la Rivière
Eymet	St Privat des Près
Eyzies, Les	Thiviers
Hautefort	Thonac
Jumilhac le Grand	Tocane St Apre
Limeuil	Tour Blanche, La
Mareuil sur Belle	Tourtoirac
Milandes, Les	Tursac
Molières	Varaignes
Montcaret	Vendoire
Montignac	Villefranche de Lonchat
Mussidan	Villefranche du Perigord

Gardens

Most of these are formal French gardens.

Bergerac	Neuvic sur l'Isle
Campagne: mushrooms	Roche Chalais, La
Carlux	Salignac-Eyvigues (Eyrignac)
Castelnaud La Chapelle: Lacoste	Terrasson
Cherval	Vélines
Creysse	Vézac
Hautefort	Vitrac
Limeuil	

PLACES TO VISIT BY LOCATION

This is not a completely detailed list but gives general indications as to when the sites are open (hours are not specified). Some sites close at lunch time; others remain open all day.

'All year' indicates only that the site is open throughout the year but it may be closed one or two days a week. 'Otherwise by arrangement' means that you can arrange to see the site out of season by telephoning.

It is always advisable to check with local information when you are on the spot.

Town or commune	Telephone	Open
Agonac		
Ligueux: abbey	05 53 05 03 01	July-Aug
Ajat		
Sauveboeuf, château de	05 53 05 25 07	July-Aug
Antonne		
Bories, château des	05 53 06 00 01	telephone
Audrix-Le Bugue		
Gouffre de Proumeyssac: caves with concretions	05 53 07 27 47	Feb-Nov
Auriac du Périgord		
Abeilles du Périgord, miellerie et élévage	05 53 51 01 91	Apr-Oct
Beaumont du Périgord		
Bannes, château de	05 53 61 19 54	June-Sept
Beauregard de Terrasson		
Mellet, château de	05 53 51 24 94	mid July-Aug; otherwise by arrangement
Belvès		
Musée Organistrumet Vielles à roue du Périgord Noir	05 53 29 10 93	by arrangement
Troglodytic site	05 53 29 61 17	all year
Filature (spinning mill); museum	05 53 59 66 08	by arrangement
Bergerac		
Mounet Sully, château de	05 53 57 04 21	closed at present
Institut du Tabac; garden	05 53 63 66 00	July-Aug
Musée d'Intérêt National du Tabac, Musée Peyrarède	05 53 63 04 13	all year
Musée d'Art Sacré (private)	05 53 63 40 22	pm, not Mon
Maison des Vins; Cloître des Récollets: museum	05 53 63 57 57	Apr-Oct; otherwise by arrangement
Musée Ethnographique du Vin, de la Tonnellerie et de la Batellerie	05 53 57 80 92	all year

Town or commune	Telephone	Open
Beynac		
Beynac, château de	05 53 29 50 40	all year
Musée Parc Archéologique	05 53 29 51 28	Mar-Dec
Biron		
Biron, château de	05 53 63 13 39	Feb-Dec
Bonaguil (Lot et Garonne)		
Bonaguil, château de	05 53 71 90 33	Feb-Nov
Bourdeilles		
Bourdeilles, château de	05 53 03 73 36	Feb-Dec
Brantôme		
Hierce, château de la	05 53 05 87 17	May-Oct
Abbey and troglodytic site	05 53 05 80 63	Feb-Dec
Richemont, château de	05 53 05 72 81	July-Aug
Musée Rêve et Miniatures	05 53 35 29 00	Apr-Oct
Musée Fernand Desmoulins	05 53 05 80 63	Apr-Sept
Bugue, Le		
Bara Bahau: cave, engravings	05 53 07 27 47	May-Sept
Aquarium du Périgord Noir	05 53 07 16 38	Feb-Nov
Village de Bournat	05 53 08 41 99	Apr Aug
Maison de la Vie Sauvage: museum	05 53 08 28 10	Apr-Dec
Les Jardins d'Arborie: museum	05 53 08 42 74	Easter-Nov
Cabrerets (Lot)		
Pech-Merle: cave	05 65 31 27 05	all year
Cadouin		
Abbey; cloister, Musée du Suaire	05 53 63 36 28	Feb-Dec
Musée de la Vélocipède	05 53 63 46 60	all year
Campagne		
Champignonnerie Le Solleilal: garden	05 53 07 01 04	Easter-16 Oct
Carennac (Lot)		
Prieuré	05 65 10 07 07	Apr-Oct
Maison de la Dordogne Quercynoise	05 65 32 59 19	Apr-Oct
Musée des Alambics et Aromathèque	05 65 10 91 16	all year
Carlux		
Cadiot, Jardin de: garden	05 53 29 81 05	May-Sept
Cassagne, La		
La Grange Dimière - Musée SEM	05 53 51 66 43	July-Aug pm; otherwise by arrangement
Castelnaud La Chapelle		
Castelnaud, château de	05 53 31 30 00	all year
Ecomusée de la Noix du Périgord	05 53 59 69 63	Apr-Sept

Town or commune	Telephone	Open
Castelnaud La Chapelle contd.		
Castelnaud: Musée de la Guerre du Moyen-Age	05 53 31 30 00	all year
Lacoste, château de; park and garden	05 53 29 99 94	July-Aug; w/e June & Sept
Champagne et Fontaine		
Clauzuroux, château de	05 53 91 03 73	by arrangement
Champeaux		
Bernardières, château des	05 53 60 38 59	June-mid Sept; otherwise by arrangement
Chancelade		
Abbey	05 53 04 86 87	Easter-Ascension; July-Aug
Chapelle Faucher, La		
Chapelle Faucher, La, château de	05 53 51 84 48	June-July
Chapelle Gonaguet, La		
Merlande: Priory chapel		all year
Château l'Evêque		
l'Evêque, château de	05 53 04 66 84	June-Sept
Cherval		
Limodore; gardens	05 53 90 86 83	Apr-June pm; otherwise by arrangement
Chourgnac d'Ans		
Musée des Rois d'Araucanie	05 53 50 53 46	all year
Couze St Front		
Moulin La Rouzique, Ecomusée du Papier	05 53 24 36 16	Apr-Oct; otherwise by arrangement
Creysse		
Tiregand, château de; terrace	05 53 23 21 08	by arrangement
Tiregand, château de; park	05 53 23 21 08	all year
Préhistoire, Vin de Pécharmant	05 53 23 20 45	June-Sept; w/e Apr-May, Oct
Musée Aquarium de la Rivière Dordogne	05 53 23 40 45	June-Sept; w/e Apr-May, Oct
Daglan		
Musée de la Pierre Sèche	05 53 29 88 84	July-Aug; otherwise by arrangement
Domme		
Grotte de la Halle: caves with concretions	05 53 28 37 09	
Musée des Arts et Traditions Populaires	05 53 28 37 09	Apr-Oct
Porte des Tours		
Prison des Templiers: museum	05 53 28 37 09	by arrangement

Town or commune	Telephone	Open
Echourgnac		
Ferme du Parcot; Habitat de la Double: museum	05 53 81 99 28	Jul-Sept pm; May-June, Sun pm
Eymet		
Musée Archéologique et Historique	05 53 23 74 95	enquire at SI
Eyzies, Les		
Abri Pataud: Musée du Site, rock shelter sculptures	05 53 06 92 46 05 53 06 92 46	Feb-Dec Feb-Dec
Combarelles: cave, engravings	05 53 35 26 18	all year
Font de Gaume: cave, paintings	05 53 35 26 18	all year
Grotte du Grand Roc: caves with concretions	05 53 06 92 70	Feb-Dec
Laugerie Basse: *gisements*, prehistoric dwellings	05 53 06 92 70	Feb-Dec
Laugerie Haute: *gisement*, *abri*	05 53 06 90 80	by arrangement
Micoque, La: *gisement*	05 53 06 90 80	by arrangement
Poisson, Le: rock shelter	05 53 06 90 80	by arrangement
Roc de Cazelle: prehistoric park, troglodytic fort	05 53 59 46 11	all year
Musée National de Préhistoire	05 53 06 45 45	all year
Musée de la Spéléologie	05 53 35 43 77	July-Aug
Jardin botanique	05 53 06 92 81	closed
Fleurac		
Fleurac, château de	05 53 05 95 01	May-Aug; otherwise by arrangement
Gourdon (Lot)		
Cougnac, grottes de: caves	05 65 41 47 54	all year
Gramat (Lot)		
Padirac, gouffre de: caves with concretions	05 65 33 64 56	July-Aug
Hautefort		
Hautefort, château de; park and gardens	05 53 50 51 23	Feb-Nov Apr-Sept; some other times
Charreaux, Châteaux des; jardin anglais	05 53 50 40 81	May-June some Sun pms
Musée de la Medicine (former hospice)	05 53 51 62 98	Apr-Sept
L'Hospitalet (Lot)		
Merveilles, grotte des: cave	05 65 33 67 92	July-Aug

Town or commune	Telephone	Open
Issac		
Montréal, château de;	05 53 81 11 03	July-Sept
chapelle de la Ste Epine		Jan-Jun, Oct-Nov
		by arrangement
Jumilhac le Grand		
Jumilhac le Grand, château de	05 53 52 42 97	June-Sept
		w/e Mar-Apr, Oct;
		otherwise by arrangement
Musée de l'Or	05 53 52 55 43	June-Sept;
		Apr-June, Sept-Oct
		Sun pm
La Cave (Lot)		
La Treyne, château de;		
gardens and exterior	05 65 27 60 60	July-Aug
Grotte; cave with	05 65 37 87 03	July-Aug
concretions		
Lalinde		
Baneuil, château de	05 53 57 48 80	Aug
Lanquais		
Lanquais, château de	05 53 61 24 24	Mar-Nov
Limeuil		
Chapelle St Martin	05 53 63 38 90 SI	by arrangement
Jardin Musée;	05 53 63 32 06	July-Sept,
La Maisonette		June and Oct
		by arrangement
Lussas et Nontronneau,		
near Nontron		
Beauvais, château de	05 53 56 07 51	July-Aug;
		Jan-June/Sept-Dec
		by arrangement
Manaurie		
Grotte de Carpe Diem: caves		
with concretions	05 53 06 91 07	Apr-Oct
Mareuil sur Belle		
Mareuil, château de	05 53 60 74 13	all year
Musée de la Pierre Taillée	05 53 60 99 85	May-Sept
Marquay		
Cap Blanc: rock shelter,	05 53 59 21 74	Apr-Oct
engravings		
Puymartin, château de	05 53 59 29 97	Apr-Oct
Meyrals		
Bernifal: cave, paintings,		
engravings	05 53 29 66 39	June-Sept

Town or commune	Telephone	Open
Milandes, Les		
Milandes, château des	05 53 59 31 21	all year
Musée de la Fauconnerie	05 53 59 31 21	all year
Musée Josephine Baker	05 53 59 31 21	all year
Molières		
Maison de la Noix	05 53 63 19 23	July-Aug;
en Pays des Bastides: museum		otherwise by arrangement
Monbazillac		
Monbazillac, château de;		
and Musée	05 53 63 65 00	Jan; Mar-Dec
Montcaret		
Villa et Thermes Gallo-Romains,		
Musée Tauziac	05 53 58 50 18	all year
Montignac		
Aubas, château de	05 53 51 89 46	15 Sept-15 Oct
Musée Eugène Le Roy	05 53 51 82 60	Feb-Dec
Regourdou, Le: *gisements*	05 53 51 81 23	all year
Musée Ours Vivants	05 53 51 81 23	all year
Montignac (tickets): Lascaux II		
cave, paintings (facsimile)	05 53 51 95 03	Feb-Dec
Mussidan		
Musée des Arts	05 53 81 23 55	June-mid Sept;
et Traditions Populaires		w/e Mar-May,
		Oct, Nov
Neuvic sur l'Isle		
Mellet, château de; botanical	05 53 53 50 37	Apr-Oct pm
gardens		otherwise by arrangement
Fratteau, château de	05 53 81 11 02	July-Aug
Nojals et Clottes		
Rucher école	05 53 22 40 35	by arrangement
	05 53 22 39 12	via OT Beaumont
Nontron		
Musée des Poupées et		
Jouets d'Antan	05 53 56 20 80	Mar-Oct
Paunat		
Abbey church of Notre Dame	05 53 63 00 73	all year
Périgueux		
Musée du Périgord	05 53 06 40 70	all year
Musée Militaire	05 53 53 47 36	Jan-Mar, Wed, Sat pms
		Apr-Sept, Mon-Sat
		Oct-Dec, Mon-Sat pms
Petit Bersac		
Musée Gallo-Romain	05 53 90 08 61	July-Aug pm

Town or commune	Telephone	Open
Peyzac Le Moustier		
Le Moustier: *gisement abri*	05 53 06 90 80	closed
Expo Musée 'Fossiles Préhistoire'	05 53 50 81 02	July-Aug
Le Ruth: *gisement*, Collection Pagès	05 53 50 74 02	all year
La Roque St Christophe: troglodytic fort	05 53 50 70 45	all year
Pomport		
Musée de Voitures Anciennes, château de Sanxet	05 53 58 37 46	all year
Port Ste Foy		
La Maison du Fleuve, Musée de la Batellerie	05 53 61 30 50	May-Sept pm
Roche Chalais, La		
Valouze, La; gardens	05 53 91 31 12	Jan-May Fri pm; Sat am; by arrangement
Roque Gageac, La		
Village and troglodytic site	05 53 31 61 94	Apr-Nov
Rouffignac		
Grotte aux Cent Mammouths; cave, engravings	05 53 05 41 71	Apr-Oct
L'Herm, château de; chimney and Renaissance doorway	05 53 05 46 61	Apr-mid Sept; otherwise by arrangement
Salignac-Eyvigues		
Salignac, château de	05 53 28 80 06	July-Aug
Musée Vivant de Plein Air Arts et Traditions Populaires	05 53 59 44 52	by arrangement
Eyrignac, manoir de; garden	05 53 28 99 71	all year
Savignac de Miremont		
La Ferrassie: *gisement abri*	05 53 06 90 80	by arrangement
Sarlat		
Temniac, ruins of bishop's palace	05 53 30 25 26	May-Oct
Musée Automobile	05 53 31 62 81	July-Aug; Apr-June, Sept pm
Sergeac		
Castelmerle: *gisements abris*	05 53 50 79 70	Easter-Sept
Siorac du Périgord		
Musée du Château: objets de cuisine, poterie du terre et du feu	05 53 31 63 69	Apr-Oct
Sorges		
Jaillac, château de	05 53 05 03 16	mid July-mid Sept; otherwise by arrangement
Ecomusée de la Truffe	05 53 05 90 11	closed Mondays

Town or commune	Telephone	Open
Souillac (Lot)		
Musée de l'Automate	05 65 37 07 07	Apr-Oct daily; rest of year not Mon/Tues
Musée d'Attelages de la Belle Epoque	05 65 37 05 75	July-Aug all day; Apr-Oct pm
St Amand de Coly		
Abbey church	05 53 51 83 49	Apr-Dec
St Aulaye		
Musée du Cognac, du Vin et du Pineau	05 53 90 81 33	July-Aug pm; Jan, Mar-June, Sept-Dec, Sat pm
St Avit Sénieur		
Abbey church	05 53 22 32 27	July-Sept
Musée Géologique, Salle Archéologique	05 53 22 32 27	telephone
St Cirq du Bugue		
Grotte du Sorcier: cave, engravings	05 53 07 14 37	Mar-Dec
St Jean de Côle		
La Marthonie, château de	05 53 62 30 25	July-Aug
St Just		
Musée du Ver de Soie: Magnanerie de Gourmondie	05 53 60 76 10	Apr-Sept
St Léon sur Vézère		
Natural troglodytic park: 'Le Conquil'	05 53 51 29 03	Mar-Oct
St Michel de Montaigne		
château de, et tour de la librairie	05 53 58 63 93	Mar-Dec
St Pardoux la Rivière		
Musée de la Carte Postale Ancienne du Périgord	05 53 60 76 10	Apr-Oct
St Pierre de Côle		
Bruzac, château de	05 53 67 05 54	Aug
St Privat des Près		
Musée de l'Outil et de la Vie au Village	05 53 91 22 87	July-Sept pm
Musée des Maquettes	05 53 91 22 87	Jan-Mar, Oct-Dec by arrangement
Ste Mondane		
Fénelon, château de	05 53 29 81 45	all year
Terrasson		
Jardins de l'Imaginaire	05 53 50 27 56	Apr-Oct

Town or commune	Telephone	Open
Teyjat		
Grotte de la Mairie: cave, engravings	05 53 53 30 29	July Sat otherwise by arrangement
Thiviers		
Musée du Fois Gras, Maison de l'Oie et du Canard	05 53 55 12 50	all year, not Sat/Sun
Thonac		
Losse, château de	05 53 50 80 08	Apr-Oct
Thot, Le: Espace Cro Magnon: cave	05 53 50 70 44	Feb-Dec
Musée et Parc Animalier	05 53 50 70 44	
Tocane St Apre		
Musée du Costume La Mémoire des Greniers	05 53 90 44 40	June-Sept, not Mon pm or Tues
Tour Blanche, La		
Musée de la Ferblanterie	05 53 91 10 62	mid June-Aug; otherwise by arrangement
Musée des Records	05 53 91 10 62	mid June-Aug; otherwise by arrangement
Tourtoirac		
Abbey and Musée Archéologique et Lapidaire	05 53 51 12 17	July-Aug; otherwise by arrangement
Tursac		
La Madeleine: village and troglodytic site	05 53 06 92 49	Feb-Oct
Préhisto-parc	05 53 50 73 19	Mar-Nov
Varaignes		
Atelier Musée du Tisserand et de la Charentaise	05 53 56 35 76	all year
Vélines		
Sardy, gardens	05 53 27 51 45	July-Sept, Apr, May, Oct w/e or by arrangement
Vendoire		
Musée Site Les Tourbières (peat bogs) de Vendoire	05 53 90 79 56	mid Apr-Sept; Feb-Apr by arrangement
Vézac		
Marqueyssac, château de; park	05 53 31 36 36	all year
Villamblard		
Monclar, château de	05 53 82 41 31	Easter to Nov by arrangement

Town or commune	Telephone	Open
Villars		
Puyguilhem, château de	05 53 54 82 18	Feb-Dec
Grotte du Cluzeau: cave,		
paintings, engravings, geology	05 53 54 82 36	Apr-Oct
Villefranche de Lonchat		
Musée d'Histoire Locale	05 53 80 77 25	Apr-Sept;
		otherwise by arrangement
Villefranche du Perigord		
Maison du Chataîgnier,	05 53 29 98 37	June-Sept
Marrons et Champignons		Oct-May, Tues-Sat
Vitrac		
Montfort, château de;		
ramparts and park	05 53 28 57 80	Apr-Oct

Caves and rock shelters

Archaeological and speleological sites

Audrix-Le Bugue
The **gouffre de Proumeyssac**: a remarkable natural site whose underground pool is reached by a long passage way. The natural concretions, which are still being formed, are particularly impressive. Open Feb-Nov. Tel. 05 53 07 27 47

Belvès
Troglodytic *abri*. Open May-Oct. Tel. 05 53 29 10 20 or 05 53 31 44 00

Bugue, Le
Grotte de Bara-Bahau: The engravings in the cavern at the end of a 100-metre passage here are important because some of them are believed to date from the Aurignacian period – that is, very early. The drawings, made by a silex tool, show bears, bison and other large animals. Open end Mar-mid Nov. Tel. 05 53 07 27 47

Domme
The **grotte de la Halle** has extensive natural concretions. Open all year, out of season by arrangement. Tel. 05 53 28 37 09

Eyzies, Les
Grotte des Combarelles: This cave displays some of the best and most important examples of the engravings of pre-historic man and a visit is to be recommended. It was discovered in 1901 and consists of two galleries (containing in all over 600 configurations) of which the one open to the public is more than 240 metres long. The last 105 are covered with nearly 300 engravings of a wide range of animals – bison, horses, reindeer, mammoths, lions, and also a number of shapes which have not been fully identified. Dating from the Magdalenian period they display great virtuosity and skill. Open all year. Tel 05 53 06 90 80

Abri de Cro Magnon: There is now only a plaque commemorating its discovery in 1868.

Grotte de Font de Gaume: This was discovered in 1901 at the same time as Les Combarelles, and consists of a corridor 120 metres long with three lateral galleries. Here you may see fine coloured paintings second only to those at Lascaux with a large row of mammoths, deer, oxen and some tectiforms all painted on to the natural contours of the rock with ineffable skill and delicacy. There are over 200 configurations and signs. A visit is recommended. Open all year. Tel. 05 53 06 90 80

Grotte du Grand Roc: This consists of a number of small chambers within a tunnel of 45 metres long with astonishing natural concretions. Within it the abri de Marseilles has furnished evidence of occupation from Magdalenian times to the Gallo-Roman period. Open Feb-Dec. Tel. 05 53 06 92 70

Abri de Laugerie Basse: (discovered in 1863). This also affords a remarkable number of animal engravings, dating from the Magdalenian period. Some of the 600 tools and implements – awls, harpoons and needles, lamps, bones and pottery – and the 'Venus impudique' may be seen in the display cabinets in the cave itself which also show finds from the abri de Marseilles from the Grotte du Grand Roc. Open Feb-Dec. Tel. 05 53 06 92 70

Abri de Laugerie Haute: consists of a

long passage some 200 metres long, on the walls of which animal engravings can be deciphered, and cabinets display some of the objects found in the cave during the excavations. The cave is particularly important for having enabled archaeologists, Lartet, Hauser, Peyrony and Bordes in particular, to identify a variety of periods, for the stratification shows succeeding levels of Solutrean, Magdalenian, Aurignacian, Protomagdalenian and Perigordin, one on top of another. Many of the objects found here are now in the Musée at Les Eyzies though some have been dispersed to museums outside France but the cave itself, one of the largest in the region, is worth visiting. Can be visited all year but only by arrangement. Tel. 05 53 06 90 80

Gisement de la Micoque (discovered in 1895): Important stratifications. Not normally open to the public but can be visited by special arrangement. Tel. 05 53 06 90 80

The **Musée National de Préhistoire** contains the most important collection of palaeolithic objects in France. Open all year. Tel. 05 53 06 45 45

Abri Pataud: This consists of a series of stratifications showing it to have been occupied continuously between 33,000 and 18,000 BC and there is a small museum devoted to objects found therein. Open end Jan-Dec. Tel. 05 53 06 92 46

The **Gorge d'Enfer** is a stretch of valley in which several small caves are found; the **Abri du Poisson** (discovered in 1892) has an engraving of a magnificent fish a metre long – probably a salmon – on its rocky roof and dates from about 25,000 BC. The area surrounding the cave has been turned into an animal preserve and covers about 12 hectares. There you may walk along a forest trail seeing in the flesh those animals depicted on the walls by our forebears, amongst them wild boar, red deer, mountain goats, bison, wild asses, horses

including the Prejalski, ducks and many species of wild bird. All year by arrangement. Tel. 05 53 06 90 80

Roc de Cazelle: prehistoric park, troglodytic fort. Open all year. Tel. 05 53 50 70 45

Manaurie

Grotte de Carpe Diem: This consists of a long passage way (200 metres) in which there are a wonderful series of variously coloured stalactites and stalagmites. Open Apr-Oct. Tel. 05 53 06 91 07

Marquay

Abri du Cap Blanc: This is a small Magdalenian gisement with very impressive sculptures of horses and bison, some of which are over 2 metres long. Open Apr-Oct. Tel 05 53 59 21 74.

Meyrals

Grotte de Bernifal:. Three rooms show paintings and engravings of animals including mammoths and tectiforms including human hands, which, while of relatively modest skill, are interesting and important in assessing Magdalenian art. Open June-Sept. Tel. 05 53 29 66 39

Montignac

Gisement du Regourdou: The most spectacular object found in this gisement, otherwise of interest mainly to specialists, is the well preserved Neanderthal jaw bone excavated in 1954. Open all year. Tel. 05 53 51 81 23

Grotte de Lascaux: Lascaux II, a brilliant facsimile of two galleries, is open end Jan-Dec. Tel 85 53 51 95 03. Tickets for the grotte must be obtained in advance in Montignac.

Peyzac Le Moustier

Abri du Moustier: (discovered in 1863).

Important stratifications. Closed.

Le Ruth gisement, Collection Pagès. Open all year. Tel. 05 53 50 74 02

La Roque St Christophe: troglodytic fort. Open all year. Tel. 05 53 50 70 45

Roque Gageac, La: troglodytic fort. Open Apr-Nov. Tel. 05 53 31 61 94

Rouffignac

The **grotte de Rouffignac** (sometimes known as grotte de Granville): A little distance from the village, this is the largest of all and contains over eight kilometres of galleries. A small electric train has been installed to make an extensive visit possible. Also called the 'Grotte de Cent Mammouths' there are 123 mammoths, 23 bison, 13 horses, 13 deer, 11 rhinoceros, 9 other animal depictions and 8 anthropomorphs. The cave was re-discovered in 1956 (there were textual references to it as early as 1575) and it dates from the Magdalenian period. It attracts huge crowds of visitors, so the early morning or immediately after lunch are the best times to see it, at any rate in the high season. Open Apr-Oct. Tel. 05 53 05 41 71

The village is worth a detour, for though it was burned by the Germans in 1941, the church was spared and has an imposing renaissance portal.

Savignac de Miremont

Gisement de la Ferrassie: occupied from the end of the Mousterian to the Perigordin periods; it contains tombs of the Neanderthal period and a fine set of engravings on blocks of stone discovered in the Aurignacian layer. Important stratifications. Open all year by arrangement. Tel. 05 53 06 90 80

Sergeac

Several abris form the **Abri de Castel Merle** (Reverdit, Roc d'Acier, Labattut and de la Souquette) and the objects found in them range from the palaeolithic period right through to the stone age. Several thousand objects are arranged in the small museum. Open Apr-Sept. Tel. 05 53 50 79 70

St Cirq du Bugue

Grotte du Sorcier: a small cave discovered in 1951 distinguished for its engravings of horses and other animals, and an anthropomorphic figure known as the '*sorcier*'. Open Mar-Dec. Tel. 05 53 07 14 37

Teyjat (near Javerlhac)

The **grotte de la Mairie** has a series of fine line engravings perhaps of more interest to the specialist than the average tourist. Open July Sat, otherwise by arrangement. Tel. 05 53 53 30 29

Thonac

The **Espace Cro Magnon, Le Thot**: a visit to this centre would make a good start to a day's archaeological sight-seeing as it expounds palaeolithic art in a pleasant and painless manner. It is set in a park with live animals such as those painted in the caves, replicas of extinct species and prehistoric huts furnished to give a taste of life then. Open Feb-Dec. Tel. 05 53 50 70 44

Tursac

Gisement de la Madeleine: a troglodytic village and site. Open Feb-Oct. Tel. 05 53 06 92 49

Villars: cave, paintings, engravings, geology. Open Apr-Oct. Tel. 05 53 54 82 36

It would be chauvinistic not to mention some of the other caves to be found in the neighbouring department of the Lot.

The **grotte de Cougnac** (near Gourdon) was discovered in 1949 and consists of two distinct chambers. There are paintings of animals including mammoths and a rare depiction of a man pierced by assegais, all combined with the natural contours of the rock. Of considerable interest. Open July and August. Tel. 05 65 41 47 54

The **grotte de Pech-Merle** (near Cabrerets) is a vast cavern with seven chambers covering 1200 metres containing five polychrome paintings of animals and tectiforms, once again using the natural formation of the rock to best advantage. A visit is to be particularly recommended because this cave combines both natural and man-made works of outstanding beauty. Open all year. Tel. 05 65 31 27 05

If you find yourself going to see the pilgrimage town of **Rocamadour** you will want to know about the caves in its vicinity:
The **grotte des Merveilles** at L'Hospitalet outside Rocamadour, consists of a small cave of one room; with a few paintings. Open July and August. Tel. 05 65 33 67 92

The **gouffre du Padirac** (Gramat) is a stupendous underground cavern reached by lift. Visitors travel across the underground lake and streams by boat and the concretions are lit to give a magical effect. The gouffre and its river lie over 110 metres below the causse de Gramat. Open July and August. Tel. 05 65 33 64 56
The **grotte de La Cave**, reached by a small electric train, is full of interesting natural concretions. Open July and August. Tel. 05 65 37 87 03

Prehistoric theme parks

Parc archéologiqe at **Beynac**: Open 1 July-15 Sept. Tel. 05 53 28 51 28
Le Bugue: Village de Bournat. Open Apr-Aug. Tel. 05 53 08 41 99
Les Eyzies: Tursac Prehisto parc. Open 1 Mar-11 Nov. Tel. 05 53 50 73 19
St Léon sur Vézère: Natural troglodytic park, 'Le Conquil'. Open Mar-Oct. Tel. 05 53 51 29 03

Accommodation and food

ACCOMMODATION There is an enormous choice of accommodation in the department though the greatest selection is in Périgord Noir as it is the most frequently visited. A personal selection is given overleaf.

Hotels: these vary from the simple to the comfortable, with a few which might be considered luxurious. Those run by the Logis de France are well worth seeking out.

While you may be spoiled for choice, it is advisable to book ahead at weekends and between 14 July and the end of August. Be warned that some hotels get filled by old age pensioners on trips after the school holidays end. School holidays are staggered throughout France but the red Michelin guide gives a list of them each year on publication round about Easter.

Apart from making your own choice from such reliable guides as the red Michelin and Gault-Millau, you can get informative leaflets from the French Government Tourist Office, 178 Piccadilly, London , W1V 0AL (sae).

Bookings in Dordogne can be arranged by the Loisirs Accueil Service de Réservation of the Comité Départementale du Tourisme: 25 rue Wilson, Périgueux, 24000. Tel. 05 53 35 50 24 and 05 53 35 50 00.

A list of hotels with facilities for the disabled is also available from the FGTO.

You can also rent *gîtes*, stay in bed and breakfast accommodation, holiday villages, residential leisure parks, tourist residences, or you can camp or live in your own or a hired caravan.

Chambres d'hôtes (bed and breakfasts): lists are available from the Comité Départementale du Tourisme: 25 rue Wilson, Périgueux, 24000 Tel. 05 53 35 50 24.

Gîtes: these are privately owned self-catering accomodation (though some will provide meals). Check whether you have to take your own linen. *Gîtes de France Dordogne-Périgord* lists over 300 and is available for 55 FF from the Comité Départementale du Tourisme as above. Lists are also available from local tourist offices. *Clévacances Dordogne-Périgord*, a list of lettings and bed and breakfast accommodation is also available, at 20FF, from the Comité Départementale du Tourisme.

Some accommodation can also be booked in UK via Brittany Ferries 0990 360 360 and there are of course innumerable agencies who can provide help.

Camp sites: lists are available from the Comité Départementale du Tourisme.

Caravan sites: lists are available from the Comité Départementale du Tourisme . There are also caravan sites where you can hire a caravan at St André d'Allas, Biron, Badefols, Prats de Carlux and Atur.

FOOD Périgordin cooking is discussed in detail in Chapter 7, 'Sans Beurre et Sans Reproche', and some favourite local restaurants are listed here. To explore regional cooking in greater depth, there are organized cookery classes and tastings of regional food. For detailed information about dates, prices and reservations, tel. 05 53 35 50 24. Most of these courses take place in winter.

Eyliac: *Cuisine du Canard* (duck)
Meyrals: *Cuisine de l'Oie* (goose)
Monbazillac: wine (*œnologie*) all year
Sorges: *Cuisine périgordine*

Découverte du Monde de la Truffe
St Crépin Carlucet: *Saveurs de la Truffe*
  Les Mystères du diamant noir
Vézac: *Cuisine périgordine*
Villefranche du Périgord: mushrooms
  (*champignons*), spring-autumn
The owners of the *gîtes* at La Ferme de Laupilière in Sarrazac and La Ferme de l'Embellie in Le Buisson will prepare and serve local dishes. There are also three gastronomic tours organised in hotels: *à la découverte des châteaux et de la préhistoire*, *à la découverte des parcs et jardins du Périgord* and one in the chain of the Logis de France.

Buying food Although supermarkets now proliferate there are still good village shops – butchers, bakers and grocers. While it makes sense to buy dry goods from the supermarkets the only way to keep the village shops alive is to patronise them. Fresh fruit and veg can easily be bought in all the markets – most of them *are* fresh – and locally produced. The producer will choose say, a melon for you if you tell him whether you want it for today or in three days' time. You can usually also pick out the items you want – no trouble about 'do not touch me till I'm yours'.

There are now literally hundreds of shops (not all open in the winter) selling pâté and conserves. Obviously the quality varies but sometimes you can taste them before buying. You can also buy direct from many farms.

Buying wine Local grocers and supermarkets alike sell a wide range of local wines but the most exciting and often rewarding way to buy wine is to taste what is on offer from the producers on market days or visit the château where it is produced. If you are a bit doubtful but have enjoyed one you have had in a restaurant, make a note of its producer and see where you can obtain it.

Fêtes, fairs and markets Nearly every village has one or more fêtes a year. They are usually simple and rather charming celebrations accompanied by a few or more stalls selling food, and *buvettes* dispensing drink. There are amusements for children, sometimes full-blown mechanical roundabouts and dodgems, and frequently lucky dips. For adults there are shooting ranges, skittles and so on. Sometimes an al fresco meal is served and the evening almost always ends with a 'bal', rising to a grand finale with fireworks about midnight.

Dates can be obtained from the local Tourist Office, leaflets are often scattered about the town or village and they are listed under *fêtes foraines, fêtes votives* in a useful booklet, *L'Officiel des Foires, Marchés et Brocantes de Dordogne*, which lists every fair and market selling goods under the following headings: *animations, braderies, foires expositions, animaux, art, artisanat, vieux métiers, antiquités, brocantes, troc, collections, vide-greniers, autos, motos, comices et matériels agricoles, fêtes foraines, fêtes votives, gastronomie, produits régionaux, livres, monnaies, musique, vieux papiers* and *vegetaux*.

Special markets There are also markets that specialize in particular products.

For **foie gras**: Périgueux, mid Nov-end Mar, Wed and Sat am; Ribérac, 16 Nov-15 Mar, Fri am; Thiviers, Nov-Mar, Sat am.

For **truffles** (from the beginning of December to mid February): Ste Alvère, Mon; Excideuil, Thurs; Brantôme, Fri; Vergt, Fri; Périgueux, Sat; Bergerac, Sat.

For **bread**: Terrasson, May; Brantôme and La Coquille, August.

For **garlic**: Terrasson, May; St Martial de Nabirat, August.

Market days: mornings only

	Mon	Tues	Wed	Thurs	Fri	Sat	Sun
Abjat		Tues					
Beaumont du Périgord		Tues				Sat	
Belvès (June-Sept*)			Wed			Sat	
Bergerac			Wed		Fri	Sat	Sun
Bourdeilles (May-Sept)							Sun
Brantôme (July-Aug)		Tues			Fri		
Bugue, Le		Tues				Sat	
Buisson, Le					Fri		
Cadouin			Wed				
Cénac St Julien		Tues					
Coquille, La				Thurs			
Coulounieix		Tues			Fri	Sat	
Couze et St Front							Sun
Creysse							Sun
Daglan							Sun
Domme				Thurs			
Douze, La							Sun
Excideuil				Thurs			
Eymet (July-Aug*)				Thurs			Sun*
Eyzies, Les (Mar-Oct)	Mon						
Fleix, Le	Mon						
Force, La				Thurs			
Gardonne			Wed				Sun
Hautefort (July-Aug*)	Mon		Wed			Sat*	
Issigeac							Sun
Jumilhac le Grand (July-Aug*)			Wed				Sun
Lalinde				Thurs			
Lanouaille		Tues					
Lardin, Le					Fri		
Limeuil							Sun
Mareuil		Tues					
Molières (June-Sept)							Sun
Montignac			Wed			Sat	
Montpon-Ménesterol			Wed				
Mouleydier				Thurs			
Mussidan						Sat	
Neuvic sur l'Isle		Tues				Sat	
Nontron						Sat	

	Mon	Tues	Wed	Thurs	Fri	Sat	Sun
Payzac		Tues					
Périgueux			Wed			Sat	
Piégut Pluviers			Wed				
Port Ste Foy		Tues					
Préssignac Vicq (July-Aug)							Sun
Prigonnieux		Tues					
Razac			Wed			Sat	
Ribérac (May-Sept*)		Tues*			Fri		
Roche Chalais, La						Sat	
Rouffignac St Sernin							Sun
Salignac-Eyvigues (July-Aug*)		Tues			Fri*		
Salignac les Eglises		Tues					
Sarlat			Wed			Sat	
Sigoulès					Fri		
Siorac du Périgord			Wed				
Sorges (July-Aug)					Fri		
St Antoine de Breuil							Sun
St Astier				Thurs			
St Aulaye		Tues					
St Cyprien							Sun
St Front de Pradoux (July-Aug)							Sun
St Geniès							Sun
St Jean de Côle (July-Aug)							Sun
St Léon sur Vézère (June-Sept)							Sun
St Pardoux la Rivière		Tues		Thurs			
St Pierre de Chignac						Sat	
St Saud Lacoussière				Thurs			
Ste Alvère	Mon						
Ste Nathalène (July-Aug)							Sun
Terrasson				Thurs			
Thenon		Tues					
Thiviers						Sat	
Tocane St Apre	Mon					Sat	
Tourtoirac	Mon						
Trélissac					Fri		
Trémolat		Tues					
Vélines			Wed				
Verteillac						Sat	
Villamblard	Mon						
Villefranche de Lonchat	Mon						
Villefranche du Périgord						Sat	

There are also some evening markets in July and August at Le Bugue, Montpon Ménesterol, Ste Alvère, St Georges de Montclar and St Pardoux.

HOTELS AND RESTAURANTS

This is a selection of the many good hostelries in the department. If you are writing to make a reservation, you only need give the name, town and postcode.

H = Hotel, R = Restaurant

Antonne et Trigonnant 24420
Les Chandelles (closed Jan and Feb). R. Regional, innovative. Tel. 05 53 06 05 10
Hostellerie L'Ecluse, H. Tel. 05 53 06 00 04

Bergerac 24100
L'Imparfait, interesting menu and wine list. R. Tel. 05 53 57 47 92
Le Terroir (closed 15 Dec-15 Jan), pricey but correct. R. Tel. 05 53 57 12 83
Hôtel de Bordeaux (closed 15 Dec-15 Jan), adequate. H. Tel. 05 53 52 12 83
Cyrano (closed 20-29 Dec). R. Good value. Tel. 05 53 57 02 76
St Julien de Crempse: Manoir Grand Vignoble (closed 16 Nov-1 Mar), quiet. H. Tel. 05 53 24 23 18
Moulin de Malfourat: La Tour des Vents (closed Jan), generous helpings; good value. R. Tel. 05 53 58 30 10

Beynac 24220
Taverne des Remparts (closed Nov-Mar), classic *terroir*, good value for money. R. Tel. 05 53 29 57 76

Brantôme 24310
Moulin de l'Abbaye (closed 2 Nov-25 Apr), H elegant; food delicious. R+H. Tel. 05 53 05 80 22

Les Frères Charbonnel, delicate food, pricey. R. Tel. 05 53 05 70 15
Hôtel Chabrol. H. Tel. 05 53 05 70 15
Au Fil de l'Eau. H. Tel. 05 53 05 73 65

Bugue, Le 24260
Domaine de la Barde (closed 2 Nov-10 Apr). H. Tel. 05 53 07 16 64
Les Trois As (closed Feb), trying hard. R. Tel. 05 53 08 41 57

Buisson, Le 24480
Manoir de Bellerive (closed 15 Dec-1 Mar), R+H. R adequate; H quiet and pricey. Tel. 05 53 27 16 19

Champagnac de Belair 24530
Moulin du Roc (closed 1 Jan-7 Mar); charming, good value. R. Tel. 05 53 02 86 00

Chancelade 24650
Château des Reynats (closed Feb-9 Mar), R+H. R first class ingredients; H comfortable. Tel. 05 53 03 53 59

Domme 24250
Esplanade (closed 2 Nov-14 Feb), R+H. R lavish, pricey; H charming, grand. Tel. 05 53 28 31 41

Les Eyzies 24620
Le Centenaire (closed Nov-Apr). R +H. R calm, agreeable; H elegant, expensive. Tel. 05 53 06 68 68
Cro Magnon (closed 8 Oct-8 May). H. Tel. 05 53 06 97 06
Moulin de la Beune (closed Nov-Apr). H. Tel. 05 53 06 94 33
Au Vieux Moulin (closed Nov-Apr). R. Tel. 05 53 06 93 39

Glycines (closed mid Apr-mid Oct). H. Tel. 05 53 06 97 07

Le Centre (closed Nov-Feb). R+H. Agreeable. Tel. 05 53 09 97 13

Lalinde 24150
Hôtel du Château (closed Jan & mid Sept). R+H. R expensive, variable; H quiet. Tel. 05 53 61 01 82

St Capraise de Lalinde 24150
Relais St Jacques (closed Feb). R+H. Classic, good value. Tel. 05 53 63 47 5

Limeuil 24510
Les Terrasses de Beauregard (closed Oct-May). R. Quiet. Tel. 05 53 63 30 85

Marquay 24620
Bories (closed 2 Nov-1 Apr). H. Quiet. Tel. 05 53 29 67 02

Condamine (closed 2 Nov-1 Apr). H. Quiet. Tel. 05 53 29 64 08

Monbazillac 24240
Château de Monbazillac. R. Beautiful situation, good value. Tel. 05 53 58 38 93

Monestier 24240
Château des Vigiers (closed Jan, Feb). H. Tel. 05 53 61 50 00

Montignac 24290
Château de Puy Robert (closed 15 Oct-1 Mar). R+H. R elegant, quiet; H pricey. Tel. 05 53 51 92 13

Roseraie (closed 1 Nov-Easter). H. Tel. 05 53 50 53 92

Le Relais du Soleil d'Or (closed 19 Jan-15 Feb). R+H. R good value; H nice. Tel. 05 53 51 80 22

Montpon-Ménesterol 24700
Auberge de l'Eclade (closed 1-15 Mar & Oct). R. Adventurous. Tel. 05 53 80 28 64

Château des Grillauds. H. peaceful. Tel. 05 53 80 49 71

Mussidan 24400
Relais de Gabillou (closed Jan). H. Tel. 05 53 81 01 42

at Sourzac: Chaufourg (closed out of season). H. Magnificent garden, expensive. Tel. 05 53 81 01 56

at Beaupouyet: Le Clos Joli (closed Feb). R. Regional food, good value. Tel. 05 53 81 10 01

Nontron 24300
Chez Pélisson. R. regional food. Tel. 05 53 56 11 22

Grand Hôtel Pélisson. H. rustic, family hotel. Tel. 05 53 56 11 22

Périgueux 24200
Bristol. H. No R. Tel. 05 53 08 75 90

Perigord. H. Tel. 05 53 53 33 63

Ibis. H. Tel. 05 53 53 33 63

L'Univers. R+H. Decent food. Tel. 05 53 53 34 79

Les 8 (closed July). R. Regional. Tel. 05 53 35 15 15

Le Roi Bleu. R. Classic. Tel. 05 53 09 43 77

Les Berges de l'Isle (closed 16-31 Aug). R. Small, regional. Tel. 05 53 09 51 50

Le Rocher de l'Arsault. R. Good value. Tel. 05 53 53 54 06

Razac sur l'Isle 24430
Château de Lalande (closed 15 Nov-15 Mar). H. Quiet, large park. Tel. 05 53 54 52 30

Ribérac 24600
Hôtel de France. R+H. Good value. Tel. 05 53 90 00 61

Roque Gageac, La 24250
Belle Etoile (closed 25 Oct-1 Apr) regional. Tel. 05 53 29 51 44

Gardette (closed 1 Nov-5 Apr). Tel. 05 53 29 51 58

La Plume d'Oie. R+H. (R closed 20 Nov-12 Dec; H closed mid Jan-Mar) Tel. 05 53 28 94 93 (R). Tel. 05 53 28 94 93 (H)

St Cyprien 24220
L'Abbaye (closed 18 Oct-5 Apr). H. Quiet, no restaurant. Tel. 05 53 29 20 48

Terrasse (closed 15 Dec-8 Feb). H. Tel. 05 53 29 21 69

St Laurent sur Manoir 24330
St Laurent. H. Quiet. Tel. 05 53 04 99 99

St Martial Viveyrol 24320
Hostellerie Les Aiguillons (closed Jan, Feb). R+H. Adequate. Tel. 05 53 91 07 55

St Saud Lacoussière 24470
Hostellerie St Jacques (closed Nov to Easter). R+H. R welcoming; H good value. Tel. 05 53 56 97 21

Salignac-Eyvigues 24590
Meynardie (closed 1 Dec-8 Feb). R. Careful, good value. Tel. 05 53 28 85 98

Sarlat 24200
La Madeleine (closed 1 Jan-9 Feb). R+H. R traditional; H large rooms. Tel. 05 53 59 10 41

de Selves (closed 4 Jan-5 Feb). H. No restaurant. Tel. 05 53 31 50 00

St Albert and Montaigne. R+H. R standard; H comfortable. Tel. 05 53 59 19 99

Rossignol. R. Good value. Tel. 05 53 31 02 30

La Hoirie, La Caneda. R+H. Calm.

Tel. 05 53 59 05 62

3 km SW, Relais de Moussidière (closed 15 Nov-1 Apr). H. Quiet. Tel. 05 53 28 28 74

3 km NW, Hostellerie Meysset (closed 10 Oct-5 Apr). H. Quiet. Tel. 05 53 59 08 29

Sorges 24420
Auberge de la Truffe. R+H. Truffles, truffles. Tel. 05 53 05 02 05

Hôtel de la Mairie, H. Small. Tel. 05 53 05 02 11

Tamniès 24620
La Borderie (closed 1 Nov-4 Apr), quiet. Tel. 05 53 29 68 59

Terrasson 24120
L'Imaginaire (closed 21 Dec-18 Jan). R. Good; no rooms. Tel. 05 53 51 37 37

Trémolat 24510
Le Vieux Logis. R+H. R expensive, but slipping? H elegant, charming. Tel. 05 53 22 80 06

Vézac 24220
Relais des Cinq Châteaux (closed 4-15 Jan). R+H. R good value, enterprising; H simple. Tel. 05 53 30 30 72

Vieux Mareuil 24340
Château de Vieux Mareuil (closed 2 Jan-2 Mar). R+H. R careful cooking; H large park, elegant. Tel. 05 53 60 77 15

Vitrac 24200
Domaine de Rochebois (closed Nov-mid Apr). R+H. Pricey, golf course. Tel. 05 53 31 52 52

Index

Numbers in **bold** refer to items mentioned in the Gazetteer
Numbers in *italic* refer to illustrations
Dates are given for selected artists, writers and historical figures

A Spoon with Every Course (Miriam Osler) 186
Abadie, architect 67, 119
Abeilles Bergeracois 176
Abjat 62, **207**
Aboukir, the battle of (1801) 71
abri 55
Abrillac **207**
Abrissel, Robert d' 75
Abzac family of La Douze, the 63, 69, 126; Charles d', **127**; Gabriel III d', **127**; Jean II d', **127**; Marie d', **127**; Pierre d', **127**; Pierre d', archbishop of Narbonne, 126
Abzac, grotte d' (Les Eyzies de Tayac) **221**
'Acropolis of Périgord', the [Domme] 99
Adalbert, Count of Périgord 85
Adalbert III, Count of Périgord 87
Adana, Cilicia 27
Adhémar de Monteuil, Bishop of Le Puy 76
Adhémar de Neuville, Bishop of Périgueux (1581-1660) **216**
Adjustants, the Route des 16
Agenais 33
Ages, château des (Monsec) **230**
Agincourt, the battle of (1415) 57, 108, **221**
Agnelas, grotte de las (Sourzac) **239**
Agonac **207**
Agriculture, Société d'Algérie, the 49; the Société d', Paris 46
Aguesseau, d' family **225**

Aigle, barrage, de l' 14, 16
Aillac 28
Ajat **207**
alambic (still) *169*
Albigensians, the 92, 94, 99
Albret family, the d' 108; Albret, Jeanne d' **211**, **220**
Aldoin, Count of Périgord 85
Alexander VI (Rodrigo Borgia, 1431-1503, Pope from 1492) 93
Algais, Martin d' (d. 1214) 92
Allas l'Evêque (St André d'Allas) **239**
Allas les Mines **207**
Allemans **207**
Allès sur Dordogne **207**
Alphonse de Poitiers 95, 97, **245**, **249**
Altamira, Spain 56
Ambelle, château d' (Ste Croix de Mareuil) **245**
Ambès, Bec d' 32
Anglard, Saut d' 15
Angle, rocher de l' (Les Eyzies de Tayac) **221**
Angoisse **207**
Angoumois 33
Anjou 86
Anjou, Philip, Duc d' (1683-1746), later Philip V of Spain 152
Anne of Austria (1601-66), Queen of France from 1615-61 144
Anne of Brittany (1477-1514), Queen of France 77
Annesse et Beaulieu **207**
Antoniac, château d' (Razac sur l'Isle) **235**
Antonne et Trigonant **207**
Aquilanus, Abbot of Moissac 82
Aquitaine, feudatory 85; principality 107; region 33
Aquitania and the Aquitanii 61
Arborie, Jardins d' **207**; (Le Bugue) **213**

Archambaud I, Count of Périgord 87
Archignac **207**
Ardagh, John (*France in the new century: Portrait of a Changing Society*) 166
Argentat (Corrèze) 17, 20
Argentat, Quai d' (Libourne) 17
argentats 20
Argentine **236**
Argentonnesse, château d' (Castels) **214**
Armandie, château de l' (Limeuil) **227**
Arnaut *see* Daniel, Arnaut
Arpajon, the Duc d' 156
Artigeas, château d' (Châtres) **217**
Artois, Comte d' **225**
Atelier Musée du Tisserand et de la Charentaise (Varaignes) **248**
Atur **208**
Aubas **208**
Aubazine, Cistercian abbey at 77
Auberoche, château d' (Fanlac) **221**
Auberoche, château-fort and Chapelle St Michel d' 69, (Le Change) **216**
Auberoche, Guillaume d', Bishop of Périgueux 83
Aubespin, château de l' (Monsaguel) **230**
Aucors, château d' (Beaussac) **210**
Audi, abri d' (Les Eyzies de Tayac) **221**
Audrix-Le Bugue **208**
Augereau, General 131
Augignac **208**
Augustinian Canons 74, 83
Augustus (63 BC-AD 14) 61
Auracania 155
Auriac du Périgord **208**
Ausone, Château 31

PALLAS ATHENE

Pallas Guides
Pallas for Pleasure Guides
Pallas Editions

Pallas Athene publish fine books related to
travel and the fine arts.

Details of some of our publications are given on the
following pages.

For more information, please write to us at
59 Linden Gardens, London W2 4HJ
or visit our website
www.pallasathene.net

PALLAS GUIDES

Pallas Guides to Europe

From our launch title *Czechoslovakia*, which was the first detailed guide-book published to the country since the war, Pallas Guides have earned the reputation of being the best on the market. Detailed, scholarly, intelligent and approachable, they are equally attractive on the road and in the armchair.

CZECH REPUBLIC
by Erhard Gorys
Highly informative and quite admirable *The Art Newspaper*
Rich and rewarding *Traveller Magazine*

POLAND
edited by Sebastian Wormell
No one interested in Polish culture, landscape, its people and life in Poland should be without this book *Polamerica*
This hefty book is a cultural treasure *Polish American Journal*

ANDALUCIA
by Michael Jacobs
The best one volume guide to Andalucía *Rough Guide*
No other book can compare *Cosmopolitan*

FORTHCOMING
THE MIDI by Joy Law
PROVENCE by Michael Jacobs
ROMANIA edited by John Villiers
BAROQUE ROME by Anthony Blunt

PALLAS GUIDES

Pallas Guides to Britain

The Pallas Guides to Britain are written by Peter Sager, who lives and works in Hamburg. A highly distinguished journalist (the winner of the prestigious Egon-Erwin-Kisch prize, the German equivalent of the Pulitzer), he has the sharp yet generous eye of the outsider, and his guidebooks are lyrical, witty, offbeat and wise. They have been rapturously received:

WALES

Certainly the best book on the country *New York Times*
A passionate and fabulously detailed book *The Rough Guide*
A wonderful thing *Jan Morris*
A brilliant book ... I love it. Peter Sager has opened my eyes to my own country *Mavis Nicholson, South Wales Echo*
Peter Sager's splendid book *Eric Griffiths, Evening Standard*
A thumping good read *New Welsh Review*
Splendidly illustrated, lively and highly readable *Bulletin of the Welsh Academy*

EAST ANGLIA

An unsung genius *Val Hennessy, Daily Mail*
A breadth of knowledge few natives could rival *The Times*
A stunningly good guide – literate, amusing, colourful, informative and lavishly illustrated *Mail on Sunday*
As superior to the average guidebook as Jan Morris's *Venice Independent*
One of the most detailed accounts of the region ever published – his knowledge and enthusiasm are awe-inspiring *East Anglian Daily Times*
Thorough and thoroughly readable *Griff Rhys-Jones, BBC1 Bookworm*

FORTHCOMING
WEST COUNTRY
SOUTH-EAST ENGLAND

PALLAS GUIDES

Pallas for Pleasure

Based on the legendary *Venice for Pleasure*, these walking guides to some of the most beautiful and historic cities in Europe are personal, idiosyncratic and always enlightening. Illustrations are carefully chosen old paintings, photographs and engravings, showing the traveller how the city became what it is rather than just what can be seen today.

VENICE FOR PLEASURE
by J. G. Links
Not only the best guide-book to that city ever written,
but the best guide-book to *any* city ever written
Bernard Levin in The Times
One of those miraculous books that gets passed by hand,
pressed urgently on friends
Sean French in the New Statesman
The world's best guide book
William Boyd in the Spectator

FLEMISH CITIES EXPLORED
by Derek Blyth
No one should travel to Bruges without a copy
Val Hennessy, Daily Mail

AMSTERDAM EXPLORED
by Derek Blyth
Ideally you would take Derek Blyth with you to Amsterdam, but
Amsterdam Explored is almost as good
The Times

MADRID OBSERVED
by Michael Jacobs
He has a gift for finding exotic corners in a familiar city and of
resuscitating the forgotten with colourful intensity
Paul Preston in the TLS

PALLAS ATHENE

Pallas Editions

Pallas Editions, produced in conjunction with Ostara
Publishing, aim to bring back forgotten or neglected classics
unified by the general theme of abroad. The list will be
eclectic, ranging from scholarly collections of letters to
books that are simply fun.

Suggestions from readers for new titles in this series
are most welcome. Please write to us at
59 Linden Gardens, London W2 4HJ,
or contact us via our website,
www.pallasathene.net.

In addition to being published on paper, Pallas Editions
will also be available in Rocket editions, which can be
read on the portable Rocket reader.
Travellers will thereby be able to have all the fun of reading
without the hassle of carrying heavy books.

PALLAS EDITIONS

Effie in Venice

Mrs. John Ruskin's letters home, 1849-52
Edited by
Mary Lutyens

Even if these letters had not the special interest of being from John Ruskin's wife, they would be absorbing in their picture of the social life that dominated Venice at this particular period
Marghanita Laski in the Observer

A lively picture of the *ancien régime* re-establishing itself for its last fling. Mary Lutyens has put so much into the narrative linking these hitherto unpublished letters and is so at home with the vast cast of characters, that the book is as much hers as Effie's. It is perhaps the most radiant episode in Ruskin's life
The Times

An admirable book, completely engrossing, with footnotes that are really fascinating and show us not only the social history of the time but facts about Venice and foreign travel
Evening Standard

Superbly edited by Mary Lutyens from the original letters discovered by her untouched in the archives, Effie Ruskin's letters home from Venice give an unparalleled view of Victorian travel and society through the eyes of a highly intelligent and lively young woman. John Ruskin took his wife to Venice for the first time in 1849, and while he worked on books that would define the Victorian aesthetic ideal, Effie explored Venice with growing freedom and independence of thought.

Rightly considered a classic both of travel literature and of writing about Victorian art and the milieu where much of it was made and appreciated, *Effie in Venice* makes a welcome return to print in time for Ruskin's centenary in 2000.

PALLAS EDITIONS

The Light Garden of the Angel King
Travels in Afghanistan
with Bruce Chatwin
Peter Levi

This is a beautiful book, a poetic evocation and worthy of a place on the
shelf beside Kinglake's *Eothen* and Robert Byron's *Road to Oxiana*
John Morris in the Sunday Times

Rich in anecdote and general speculation
Simon Raven in the Observer

From time immemorial Afghanistan has been a mountainous crossroads.
Through it have come merchants with indigo and Chinese silk, Alexander
the Great, nomads from the steppes, colonies of Buddhist monks, great
Moghul conquerors and the ill-fated armies of the British Raj.

In 1970 Peter Levi, classical scholar, archaeologist and later Professor of
Poetry at Oxford, set off with Bruce Chatwin to seek the clue which each
migration left. It is this quest that gives his fascinating book its theme.
How far east did Alexander really establish himself? Who built the great
upland castle that exists on no map? Could the sculptors of Athens really
have influenced the early Buddhist artists? In drawing back the curtain on
Afghanistan, Levi reveals not a rocky wilderness ranged over by plunder-
ers, but, in the words above Babur's tomb, 'a highway for archangels'.

First published in 1973, this account of Afghanistan is an acknowledged
classic of travel writing. It is now reissued with fresh photographs from
the Chatwin archives and a new introduction in which Peter Levi looks
back on a lost Afghanistan, 'an island in time, a ruined paradise', and on
his friendship with the young Chatwin.

PALLAS EDITIONS

In the Glow of the Phantom Palace
From Granada
to Timbuktu
Michael Jacobs

Jacobs is an engaging, wonderfully informative and ever-surprising
companion *Jan Morris*

Funny, learned and beautifully written *New Statesman*

He is the ideal companion we all dream of but rarely find: patient, lively
and endlessly generous with his encyclopaedic, cultivated mind
Irish Independent

The George Borrow of the High-Speed Train Era *ABC Madrid*

In this new book, Michael Jacobs follows the trail of the Moors of Spain,
exiled from their last kingdom of Granada in 1492. This extraordinary
journey takes in ruins and discos in Andalucía, masseurs and literary lions
in Morocco, before finishing in the mud mosques of Timbuktu, where
families still keep the key to the house in Granada that they fled five hundred years ago.

On the way Jacobs conjures up a cast of irrepressibly alluring adulterers,
louche fixers, kings, professors, poets, cobblers and voyagers, in a kaleido-
scope of fiction, history, journey and imagination. How, Jacobs asks as he
journeys southwards, can we be sure who, where, or when we are?

Michael Jacobs is widely regarded as the leading Hispanist of his generation, and his books have been acclaimed both here and in Spain. *Andalucía*
and *Madrid Observed* have been published by Pallas Athene. He is cur-
rently Fellow in Hispanic Studies at the University of Glasgow.

PALLAS EDITIONS

Gatherings from Spain
Richard Ford
in a new edition by
Ian Robertson

The splendid result of the toil, travel, genius and learning of one man,
and that man an Englishman
George Borrow

You may live fifty years without turning out any more delightful
thing than the *Gatherings*
J. G. Lockhart, writing to Ford

Ford transferred to his glowing and accurate pages that vivid appreciation
which he so singularly possesses of all that is characteristic of Spain.
Spain lives in his book, clad in her peculiar and intimate colouring
Lord Carnarvon

As soon as it appeared, Richard Ford's *Handbook to Spain* was hailed as a
major work of literature. How far Ford had burst out of the guidebook
genre was amply proved the next year when Murray's produced a com-
pendium of the material they had forced Ford to discard from the
Handbook. Characteristically, Ford also added much that was new, all of it
treated with energy, diamond wit and irresistible charm. Much of what he
describes of the Spanish character remains valid today; much of romantic
Spain was already fast disappearing: 'Many a trait of nationality in manners
and costume is already effaced; monks are gone, and mantillas are going,
alas! going.'

For many readers, Ford remains the greatest travel writer of all. 'Time
has not dimmed the scintillating perspicacity of Ford's observation, nor
weakened the verve of his engaging style,' writes Ian Robertson in this
new edition – the first for a generation – of *Gatherings from Spain,* which
is illustrated with drawings by Ford himself, and enriched by a fully anno-
tated index, the fruit of many years' research by Robertson, the leading
scholar in the field.

Front cover: La Chapelle Saint Robert, by Hugh Palmer
Inside front cover: Farm in Périgord, Lucien Roulland
Back cover: Selling truffles, Lucien Roulland
Inside back cover: The cingle at Trémolat, Lucien Roulland

This book is part of the Pallas Guides series, published by Pallas Athene.
If you would like further information about the series, please write to:
Pallas Athene, 59 Linden Gardens, London W2 4HJ
or visit our website,
www.pallasathene.net

Series editor: Alexander Fyjis-Walker
Series assistant: Barbara Fyjis-Walker
Publishing editor: Jenny Wilson
Series designer: James Sutton
Maps editor: Ted Hammond

A CIP record for this book is available from the British Library

First published by Macdonald Futura Publishers, London, 1981
This fully revised, updated, enlarged and illustrated edition
first published by Pallas Athene London, 2000

ISBN 1 873429 28 2

Printed in Belgium